CRYSTAL WOMAN

CRYSTAL WOMAN
THE SISTERS OF THE DREAMTIME
LYNN V. ANDREWS

WARNER BOOKS

A Warner Communications Company

Book Design by Nick Mazzella

Printed in the United States of America

First Printing: September 1987

10 9 8 7 6 5 4 3 2 1

Library of Congress Cataloging-in-Publication Data

Andrews, Lynn V.
  Crystal woman.
  1. Cree Indians—Religion and mythology.   2. Indians of North
America—Religion and mythology.   3. Andrews, Lynn V.
4. Shamanism.   I. Title.
E99.C88A523 1987   299'.7'0924   [B]   87-40162
ISBN 0-446-51391-1

For Ginevee and the Koori women of High Degree.
And for Guboo Ted Thomas and his family for
showing me Mumballa Mountain.

Special acknowledgment to Al Lowman and
Claire Zion for their kind perseverance and
guidance.

This is a true story.
Some of the names and the places in this book
have been changed to protect the privacy of those involved.

CONTENTS

❖❖❖❖❖❖❖❖❖

CONTENTS

KOORI PASSAGE

Blue Australian waters,
My gestated story now tears itself free,
Organic molecule,
Painted aboriginal circles,
Each piece will fall to its place.
Together they reveal
Black Swan Woman
Primeval womanness.
Dismember me through flesh consuming fire,
Reorder me with embedded quartz,
And reconstruct me for our secret purpose . . .

Her artistry
A gift and challenge in a stone.

Blue waters,
The terror of voyaging beyond fear,
The wonder of those precious moments,
The burden of that insurmountable task . . .

I struggle to comprehend
Sounds of traffic and barking dogs,
The faces of those I love . . .

Too easily I switch to that parallel dream:
From red dirted austerity
I've touched a fecund and compelling vastness . . .

Australian waters,
Your tranquility comforts and belies
That when I embrace myself
I find I'm not the same . . .

Paul Talmage

INTRODUCTION
❖ ❖ ❖ ❖ ❖ ❖

I am a shamaness. I have been apprenticed for twelve years to a woman of knowledge whose name is Agnes Whistling Elk. She is an American Indian from Manitoba, Canada.

Many years ago I was initiated into the Sisterhood of the Shields. The Sisterhood is comprised of forty-four women, each representing a different indigenous culture from somewhere in the world. When a woman of the Sisterhood passes on to other rounds, a new member is initiated. Our purpose is to memorize and preserve the different laws of magic and the various codes and traditions of shamanism from around the world. We believe that because these traditions are rooted in the essence of female understanding and wisdom, it is particularly important at this time of patrilineal imbalance to recognize that these ancient ways are needed to alchemize our mother earth back into a state of wholeness.

I am not Indian and for that reason I did not at first fully understand why I was initiated by a secret society of native women. But my purpose within the Sisterhood of the Shields has since become apparent. According to Agnes and Ruby Plenty Chiefs, my mentors, I have walked the moccasin path as a shamaness in previous lifetimes. Perhaps this is why a white woman from Los Angeles is so committed to learning and recording in written form the ancient wisdom as it relates to the needs of mother earth in the twentieth century. I have never been sure of this explanation, but I do know that I have dedicated my life to this endeavor. I am not an anthropologist and have not approached my work as an academic, but as a woman who is committed to the sacredness in life.

On occasion, the Sisterhood meets somewhere in the wilderness to display in a great circle our shields which represent our symbols and our position within shaman reality. Each shield is magnificently crafted and rich with the colors and designs that represent each woman's lifetime of training and acquired wisdom. At one such meeting about a year and a half ago a woman named Ginevee, an aboriginal woman from the red center of Australia, picked up the talking stick, which allows the holder to speak as long as she likes. She walked across the circle and presented herself to me. Before this I had only seen Ginevee in ceremonies, after which she had always disappeared, mysteriously drifting off into the shadows. Now, I was confronted by her ancient black face and the weathered furrows of her skin. Her hair hung loosely in gray ropes that framed her kind face. She looked through me with electric eyes, then smiled at me.

"Stories are like spirits," she said, speaking English mixed with a few words of her Australian aboriginal language, Koori. "They look around for a good storyteller, someone like you, to inhabit. Stories are good sorcerers. When a story lives inside of you it makes you think that the story is your idea. There is a story lurking around you. It will make its home within you very soon, yea. I will see you in Australia maybe, hmm? You will join the women of high degree in the Outback and become a clever woman."

Since that meeting it has become clear to me that somehow I probably am to spend the rest of my life becoming immersed in the various shaman cultures represented by the different extraordinary women in the Sisterhood of the Shields.

To write adequately about shamanism, one has to become a shaman. You cannot write about shamanism like an engineer writes down mathematical theories. Shamanism is a subtle and alchemical process designed to transform and elevate the spirit beyond the constructs of the known limits of reality. It is the space program of the soul and launches you out into the unchartered territory of the stars. It teaches you to experience the wisdom of the Pleiades and the universe, not just the physical properties of the planets.

We are capable of so much simply as human beings. We have extraordinary abilities yet to be explored. I'm sure a quantum physicist would agree that we are just beginning to conceive of the possibilities that this reality has to offer.

The ancient shamans have always understood energy and how to transform it and use it to heal and enlighten. Out of the bones of lizards, the crystal of the Rainbow Serpent, and the sound of the Bull Roarer came a call from the sacred ghosts of the Dreamtime. A story did inhabit me. It was born from the Koori people of Australia. Through their process of teaching me their traditions of shamanism, a strange and wonderful story was born.

After that first meeing with Ginevee, Agnes, Ruby, July (Ruby's apprentice), and I followed her to the Outback of Australia. Over the past year I have tried to write down faithfully the extraordinary events that took place. This book is that story.

I have changed names and locales to protect the privacy of those involved. The Koori languages were very new to me. I have tried to be true to what I learned and to record the legends, words, and phrases as clearly as they came to me. The tasks that confronted me were from different traditions, because the power of the women I met came from various tribes. Please do not assume that what I have written is traditional Koori training. I am not Koori, so what I learned and the way the ancestral figures presented themselves to me was not necessarily traditional; what I experienced was initiation for a white apprentice. This is the story of a woman unraveling the mysteries of selfhood. It is a personal journey and not an exposé of traditional aboriginal belief systems.

We learn to love . . .

to know the desert
as our own

even to long for it
like a blade that
yearns for the sharpening
stone

      —Elizabeth Herron

CHAPTER ONE
❖❖❖❖❖❖
GOOD TUCKER

The sun rose slowly over the sere landscape of Central Australia. The grass-trees trembled in the early morning wind like tribal dancers wearing tall, spiked headdresses. Ginevee, an aboriginal woman of high degree, picked some of their starry blossoms. These she rubbed together with crushed leaves and grass in her hands, and then she sucked them for their honey. She handed some grass to me, her dark fingers dripping with nectar. I sucked on the sweet grass and smiled at her.

Ginevee was said to be from Central Australia, where I had come to learn from her the meaning of a mysterious dream that had haunted me. This woman of knowledge held the key that would open the gateway to my new circle of learning.

Her elderly dark face was creased and withered like the crusty earth from which she was born. The cool wind lifted the hem of her yellow cotton print dress and gently blew her thick gray ropes of hair.

Her glittering saurian eyes were fringed by soft wisps of gray, like angels' hair silhouetted against the pink dawn. The vast landscape all around us was flat with only low clumps of brush called mulga and spinifex grasses and an occasional ghost gum or eucalyptus tree standing against the red horizon.

Agnes Whistling Elk, a medicine woman and my teacher from Manitoba, Canada, had been traveling with Ginevee and me for several days. We had driven a Land-Rover down the Gunbarrel Highway across the Gibson Desert of Western Australia. We were headed for an area, 150 miles from Ayers Rock, which was known as the ancient ceremonial center and sacred heart and lifespring of aboriginal Australia. Our destination was a little-known village where many aboriginal women of high degree or healers were gathered to share their ancient knowledge with apprentices and each other. This meeting was held in secret, Agnes had told me, because there were many male warrior societies who were against such a gathering of female power.

As we journeyed on, I was settling into a feeling of wonder and awe in this new, surreal landscape. I was vividly aware of the fact that Central and Western Australia were only new to me and were, in fact, part of the oldest continent on earth. The rest of the world had gone on bursting with volcanic eruptions long after Australia had settled her weathered integument into a peaceful, if primeval, rest. The land of the red center is austere, intractable, and sprinkled with a carefully disguised primitive life. She is old, bald, and hard on the surface, as if she has rejected the life of man. Her moisture recedes from her billabongs so that the sacred waterholes often appear stagnant and dark. Yet below the red sandy crust, I felt a movement, an urgency for the expression of a new sort of growing; it was a spiritual stirring tingling on the soles of my feet and up into my calves.

I pulled my eyes away from the spectacular rising sun as Ginevee winked at Agnes. She pulled three small eggs out of her dilly bag, a small basket she carried that was plaited with what appeared to be twisted reeds or rushes. She held the eggs up to the golden light; their shells looked thin, almost transparent.

"These are good tucker," she said. Her face was so dark it became one with the shadows. "A gift from the mallee hens in the bush." Saying that, she pointed to a thorny cluster of low trees, then took my hand. Her fingers felt like dried bark.

"If these eggs were your spirit totem, yea, your warrigan, then we would not eat them. If you asked me, 'What is your meat?' I would say kangaroo and I would be telling you my clan totem. I would never eat or injure a kangaroo. It is also said that if you eat the warrigan of your sister it would be like stealing her spirit. Then day would be like night for you, because you would lose your ability to see; everything would be darkness for you, yea. Is it not that way in your society?" She peered into my face, her head slightly tilted back, looking down her nose.

After a moment, I answered her. "Yes, we call a totem spirit our medicine. In our way, our medicine spirit is of the four-leggeds or winged ones. They represent our spiritual counterpart. I am black wolf; the spirit of the wolf is my spirit. I am a teacher and I go down all the trails of the earth to learn truth. Wolf is my warrigan."

Pursing her lips, Ginevee cocked her head sideways for a moment. The dawn light bounced off her wide, round cheeks.

"The nature of your warrigan is very sacred," she said. "I am honored that you share this knowledge with me. It is safe with me. I am swan spirit. She lives inside of me, here." She pressed her lower abdomen. "We have respect for each other." Ginevee smiled widely.

I looked at her trying to understand fully her broken English, which was interspersed with lyrical aboriginal words. Her voice was strong and held a quiet force like her eyes. Her tone was kind and playful, yet she seemed never to say anything to me that didn't have special meaning. I must have looked very intense, for Agnes Whistling Elk started to make a clucking sound with her tongue and flapped her wing-like arms in imitation of a mallee hen.

"You could have chicken medicine," she said. "Cluck, cluck." Agnes laughed good-naturedly at me.

I have been traveling and studying with Agnes, an American Indian woman of power and knowledge, for twelve years. I am her apprentice. When she wants me to learn something that is outside her expertise, she introduces me to the world of other shaman women who are members of the ancient Sisterhood of the Shields. There are forty-four in this Sisterhood. Except for me, each woman represents a different indigenous culture from around the world. I was initiated into the Sisterhood several years ago. I remembered Ginevee from many ceremonies in the past, but I had never been closely acquainted with her until these last few days.

Ginevee started to giggle like a delighted child, flapping her arms and joining Agnes in a flurry of dust. Then she stopped, swept hair out of her face, cracked an egg on a stone, and plopped the yolk into her mouth, smacking her lips. Grinning, revealing startlingly white teeth, she indicated for me to do the same. I took a deep breath, cracked the egg, and swallowed the entire insides.

"That was quite delicious," I said, also smacking my lips as I watched Agnes, too, eat her breakfast.

"In danger there is great power," Agnes stated flatly, wiping her mouth.

"What?" I asked, surprised by her quick change of mood.

"Can't you feel the fear in these eggs? They knew they were going to be eaten and that creates a tension that can be used."

I stared at her. "I don't like what you're saying, Agnes."

"Why?" A lizard had crawled onto her hand. It had a frill of skin around its neck.

"Because it makes me uncomfortable."

"All living things eat other living things to survive. That is life, that is the nature of our dream, yea," Ginevee said.

"That doesn't mean I have to like it."

"Oh good, Lynn. Those eggs were full of life-force ready to be born; instead their power will now be born in you. You have transformed them and helped them along their way. And you sit there righteously saying, no, you don't want that kind of power. Just let me shut my eyes and live off you without honoring you." Agnes raised her eyebrows.

"That's not it at all. I just don't want to kill things. It's wrong."

"My wolf sister, it is not right or wrong, it is what is," Ginevee said. "When you take the life spirit of an animal or a plant and respect the power of that spirit, it is warrigan; it is eating of the deities that makes you part of them. It is good tucker. You have given that unborn chick a rite of passage; you have marked its trail and changed its destiny, hmm. How many eggs in Australia meet with such good luck? You are a mother goddess for that unborn spirit." Ginevee watched me.

Agnes added, "You remember, Lynn: never throw sand in the eyes of the buffalo before you kill it. In Australia a shaman woman is made just like you are made of other life-forms. You take spirit power from those life-forms and you are made into an extraordinary being that is comprised of parts of all living things. You experience all life and then you can heal all life as it heals you." By now Agnes was petting the tiny head of the lizard.

"See that extending place on the lizard's neck?" Ginevee asked, gently pointing at the small creature. "We have an old myth about Tannar, the frill lizard—a lizard like this one, yea. It is also about Wombri, the black snake. In the Dreamtime they were neighbors, but they fought and Wombri ordered Tannar to stay away. Tannar persisted in sticking his head into Wombri's nest hole and his head got stuck in a shell. He ran away with the shell still around his neck, and to this day he still wears it. See, that's what's around his neck. It became a part of his living body, yea. He cut the legs off Wombri with his shell. So now he shows the shell to all who pass by so they will leave him alone. He has the power to grow back his own leg and he has the power to transform himself into the Rainbow Serpent. You will learn about the Rainbow Serpent after many days: the Rainbow Serpent is one of our ancestral beings. The shell reminds us of that. He is my little brother."

"Everything is made of power, Lynn," Agnes added. "But if you ignore that possibility, that knowledge is wasted and is of no use to you." Agnes turned to hand Ginevee the lizard, and he leapt into her palm.

"But you are a woman of power," Ginevee said. "You have no choice, yea." Ginevee gave the lizard to a flat rock and stood up. She picked up her dilly bag and we all moved toward the Land-Rover. I was intrigued by the conversation, but I could see that it was over for now.

"How old are you, Ginevee?" I asked, watching her sling a very heavy pack into the jeep with little effort. She slowly turned to me. I hoped I hadn't offended her.

"I am close-up dead," she answered very seriously. We three stood in long silence. Then Agnes giggled. We all started to laugh.

"That's what they say and they've been saying it for many long time. Sometimes the people see me as black swan. In the beginning they saw me as white swan. Long ago, there was a sacred land far away; it was the land of women, yea. It was beyond the mountain where Baiame, the sky god, had his home in the clouds. Only us women lived there and we made hunting tools—spears, shields, boomerangs. The best anywhere. If men were brave and could cross the great desert without water they would come to our sacred lake. The lake represented the Dreamtime of all women. Men could not swim there in those days because they would drown. But we taught them how to swim and in return they stole our weapons and sacred hunting tools. They even stole the sacred symbols, the ranga, from our rolled-up bark mats. They even sent white swans to trick us. We tried to capture the white swans while the men secretly built canoes and crossed our dream waters. A great hawk descended from the sky world and picked all the white feathers from the swans. My little brother Wahn, the crow, was horrified, yea. He came down and gave his own black feathers to the naked swans. That's why there are now black swans. When you see me in the Dreamtime, you see me as Black Swan. Swans have great power. They did not mean to, but they helped trick woman and the earth has lost her balance. When you see Ginevee in the Dreamtime as a white swan you will know that my work has been completed on earth and that man and woman swim equally in the billabongs, the sacred waters, and balance has been restored among all living things."

I fumbled with my knapsack, my eyes riveted to Ginevee's face. As she spoke, her eyes had turned silver in the rose light. She moved quietly and for a second she appeared almost transparent, as if she were the morning fog. I watched the mist lifting slowly from the scraggly brush in the field, revealing the reality of trees and dirt and life to me only for a moment. Then it shifted, settling down again, a soft cloud cover obscuring everything from my view. The way the fog impaired and then seemingly heightened my vision reminded me of how I felt when Ginevee told me a story.

I was blinking and rubbing my eyes when she said, "Well, are you going to drive us or not?"

Agnes and Ginevee sat waiting in the jeep. I mumbled something and got into the driver's seat.

I turned the ignition key. At first nothing happened; then the engine gulped and coughed and finally turned over. Agnes and I breathed a deep sigh of relief. For a second we had both imagined starving to death in this barren land, which had briefly lost its primeval beauty and appeared to us as only desolate, forlorn, and void of any human convenience, like a gas station. All the while, though, Ginevee appeared unconcerned; she looked down the rutted red road with eager intensity. She was like a child, full of wisdom and yet innocent.

The driving was slow going. We had left the paved road a few days back and I had begun to worry about what it would be like if it started to rain.

"Does it rain this time of year?" I asked Ginevee, although I wasn't sure I wanted to hear the answer.

"On and off." Agnes and Ginevee giggled at my expression of dismay.

"It looks like this road could get very muddy," I said.

"Lynn doesn't like to get stuck in the mud," Agnes said. I remembered my experience in the Yucatán with the medicine woman named Zoila. She had taught me about my addictive nature as I had stood hip-deep in jungle quicksand. Although I had learned a lot, the experience had been terrifying. Agnes was right; after that, I had a healthy respect for mud.

We lapsed into silence as I navigated a particularly rough section of the road. There were huge potholes, big enough to consume the whole front section of the car. The jeep lurched and groaned its way slowly over the nearly impossible terrain.

After several hours, we all needed a rest. We bounded to a stop at the side of the road under a ghost gum tree that offered a snowflake pattern of shade on the maroon and orange earth. Grateful for the stillness, we spread a mat and sat down with our water canteens and some cheese and fruit that we had brought.

Exhausted, I sat with my back against the tree. Looking up into the branches I watched the sunlight bouncing off the white bark. Gusts of warm wind swayed the branches in a rhythmic dance. The tiny green leaves shimmered and then were perfectly still. Watching them, I thought back to a few months before, when Agnes and I had been in California together.

I turned then to the memory of the event and the dream that had brought Agnes Whistling Elk and me to the Outback of Australia.

No matter how far we travel towards a
    hill,
paying attention to surrounding terrain,
    stone and
flower, we are unprepared
for whatever lives waiting

on the other side.
No one will tell you this:
our bodies understand
the dreams that are truly our own.

              —Jack Crimmins

CHAPTER TWO
❖❖❖❖❖❖
DOLPHINS DREAMING

Agnes and I had camped out for the night on a low cliff over the ocean. We were on the coast north of Santa Barbara. There had been a warm Santa Ana condition. The tall oat grass had turned golden in the fall heat, and the unusually temperate wind had been blowing in from the desert in hot, sweet-smelling gusts. The wind had caressed us for hours like a hungry lover, relentless and soft.

Agnes woke me before dawn. We gathered stones for a medicine wheel and sat together within it as the sun blazed over the horizon. We sang to the rising sun, to the new dawn of woman; we praised the Great Spirit, mother earth, the powers of the four directions, and our ancestors; then we dedicated our ceremony to the dolphins. We held a vigil all that day, praying for our sister spirits on this mother earth. We prayed for the balance of the male and female within us all and we prayed for the animals and winged ones.

As the sun progressed on its journey through the heavens, we turned accordingly within the wheel. Near sunset we were looking out to sea, facing the great orange ball of the sun as it sank into turquoise blue water. We began to drum and chant sacred sounds. The waves below us were curling in from a southerly swell.

Without warning a single shard of lightning crackled in front of us. It split the sky only for a moment and then was gone. Shortly afterwards thunder rolled far out over the ocean. Just as surprising was a family of dolphins that suddenly appeared in the frothy curve of the incoming waves. There were seven of them swimming in side by side. As suddenly as they had appeared, they disappeared, then reappeared in calmer waters farther out. They swam in a large and perfect circle, moving round and round clockwise.

We watched them till the sun went down. Every once in a while they would blow jets of water above them and we could hear them calling.

As soon as the sun set, Agnes hurried me over to a tall eucalyptus tree. I lay down on my back and she told me to rest my head so that it touched the trunk of the tree. Agnes placed her hands on either side of my head, cupping her palms over my ears. She spoke to me in a language that I recognized later as being Koori. Without warning, I felt like the ground was gone from under me: my head became riveted to the eucalyptus tree as if my blood had turned to slow-moving sap and my life source were the tree trunk itself. I floated on the wind like a low-hanging branch, perceiving the world from an inert wisdom and a more ponderous dignity than I could remember ever having experienced before. I was rooted out of time and place. Slowly I began to hear an ever-increasing whirring sound, as if someone were twirling something in the air very, very fast. It gave me an eerie feeling. It was then that I realized I was unable to move, except at the mercy of the wind.

"Don't be frightened. Roll your eyes back, Lynn, and look up the tree," I could hear Agnes' voice saying to me.

At that moment I became electrified by some unseen current. It coursed through me at will; all I could do was look up and listen. I could still hear that strange sound, like the buzzing of a giant bug. It was louder now. I became aware of a dark mass at the top of the tree. It was a cloud-like formation that obscured the branches and seemed to be burning them. I could feel the fire inside of me, as if I were connected somehow.

Out of the dark cloud an aborigine warrior leaped into view. He was chanting a war song and holding a spear. His black body was painted with luminous white and he wore a red loincloth. He was standing in the mouth of a cave. At his feet was a woman holding an infant and screaming. First he speared the child, then the woman; he killed them both.

On the other side of the tree, a huge patch of something that looked like mistletoe was growing, rapidly enveloping the branches. Long vines were curling out and grasping from one limb to another. I wanted to scream but couldn't. I could see and feel that two equally horrible but different entities were consuming the tree and sucking the life-force out of its branches, my branches.

A giant warrior, adorned with mistletoe and wearing a mask of my own face and a huge black snake, appeared from within the branches. He also sang a war song but had painted himself in a snake-like design. The eerie sound became louder as he picked up a flat object tied to a long string and twirled it over his head. Lightning began to crackle between the black mass and the mistletoe connecting the two warriors. I closed my eyes in pain.

The next thing I knew I was back by the cliff laying by a campfire with Agnes.

I started to speak as I opened my eyes, but Agnes held her finger to her lips.

"Just listen," she said. "The dolphins have given you a vision. I am glad. They have come to you and given you a sign. It is good."

The fire spit sparks into the inky blackness. Stars and a half-moon were now and again obscured by the large strings of clouds trailing on the high wind currents. The smell of the oak-burning fire and the sound of Agnes' deep voice relaxed my churning fears. The bloody vision was in front of me as if it had just happened.

"It was so horrible," I said.

Agnes shushed me. "You see, eucalyptus trees are from Australia. They were brought here to America because they grow so fast. What people didn't realize is that the wood is hard and heavy, making it useless as lumber. But the trees are very dense in quality giving them very unusual abilities."

"What do you mean 'abilities'?"

"All plants have talents. Some can be used to heal bruises, some can lower a temperature, some can intoxicate you, and so forth. That is their ability and their purpose on earth. We are different than plants. A plant knows what its life is about from the moment it sprouts as a seedling. We humans, on the other hand, are only a possibility when we are born. We must discover our purpose and meaning and then we must find the courage to follow that purpose. Some plants have the ability to give signs; they can mark our path. As a woman of power, you need only learn how to follow the trail. Do you understand?"

Agnes stoked the fire with a long, forked stick. Sparks flew into the air in a spiral as she did so.

"You mean . . . I should interpret the vision I saw?"

"Yes, but first, how do you think the vision came to you?"

"I don't know. From the dolphins?"

"Yes, but dolphins cannot speak our language, so they sent you pictures. The pictures had to be received by an antenna. Do you know what that was?" Agnes' face was completely in shadow. Only her hair was lit by the reflections of the red-orange flames of our campfire.

"The antenna must have been the eucalyptus tree. Is that right?"

"Yes. There are shamans, called doowans or initiated men and women in Australia, who know the talents of the eucalyptus trees. They use the eucalyptus as antennas to connect with other shamans in different parts of the world."

"But what I saw was killing. It was dark and evil-feeling to me."

"Were there two warriors who were connected by lightning?"

"Yes. Did you see them, too?"

"I have seen them before. The lightning is a juraveel, a totemic spirit-helper for the dolphins. They wanted you to see into the Dreamtime of Australia, where there are two evil sorcerers who are destroying the women's ceremonies and the women's dreaming. They work together. They have stolen the lightning from the sky world. They use the song of the trees for power and have turned man against woman and filled the people's hearts with fear. Many of our sisters have been murdered or beaten. The dolphins have knowledge of this because of their 'juraveel,' the lightning. It is their helper and tells them things in ways we don't understand. As we have often said, this earth walk is a teaching about the dance of energies. All energies speak to one another in some way. Energy follows thought. We feel energy shifts in other parts of the world as surely as you feel the warm wind on your face now. You must learn to use your own body to read energy."

"I felt tremendous energy from the tree tonight."

"Yes, my daughter, you became a branch of that tree. Like a chameleon who changes her colors to become invisible, you are learning to alter your luminosity to fit your environment."

"You said something, Agnes, about the song of the trees."

"Yes, didn't you hear it?"

"Well, I heard an eerie sound—like whirrings."

"That is the song of the eucalyptus tree. She is an enchantress and she carries thought waves perfectly, even thought waves of evil sorcerers like those you saw."

"What can we do?" I asked, starting to cry. "Why did the one sorcerer wear a mask of my face?"

"Your vision was a plea for help, from the dolphins." Agnes' eyes were eclipsed by the shadows as she squatted down next to the fire. She was in deep thought. She said, "If that sorcerer was wearing a mask of your face, it means either that he wants to kill you or he wants your help in some way. This worries me. We must go and find our sister Ginevee."

Agnes stretched out our sleeping bags and pointed a long brown finger at me. "Sleep, my Black Wolf. Your eyes have disappeared."

"Yes, *ma'am*," I said, smiling. Gratefully, I curled up in my dark green bag.

Agnes knelt down beside me. She took a sprig of silver sage and lit one end in the fire. The sage blazed with pungent smoke. Agnes took her beaded eagle-feather fan out of her bundle and patted the smoke all over me with the feathers, smudging me and cleansing my energy field. The smoke coiled and spread in the darkness like the ghost of a cobra.

"Tonight dream well, Lynn. Follow your dreams as you have always done." Agnes placed her sleeping bag behind me and lay down so that her head was touching mine. In the faraway voice of one almost asleep, she said, "Come with me dreaming. We will join the Sisterhood of the Shields in Canada. They are expecting us."

Before I could answer, I fell into a deep sleep in which I was nonetheless fully aware of sleeping. I smelled the glowing embers of the fire and I was aware of the wind still drifting in from the northeast.

The pressure of Agnes' head on mine was intense. I have no idea how long I floated in this strange trance-like state, but soon I began to see a violet light around me. Slowly my body began to vibrate, a sensation that started at my feet and moved upward. I felt as if a runaway freight train was moving through me. A cracking sound startled me—it had come from my back. I felt no pain, but I had the sensation that my whole body was being immersed within an extraordinary pressure. My physical body seemed to become a separate, leaden thing below my spirit. I was looking down on my own and Agnes' bodies from somewhere over by the eucalyptus tree. Agnes' spirit was next to me, holding my hand. We both looked down at ourselves sleeping contentedly.

For a moment I was scared and very cold; then I was ecstatic with my newfound freedom. Agnes directed me and we began to fly with no effort except the outward vision of our intent. Before I knew what was happening we were in the Far North. I recognized the high pine trees and vast rolling tundra of Canada. I had forgotten about Santa Barbara, the dolphins, and dreaming.

I had no idea the elf owl
Crept into you in the secret
Of night.

—James Wright

CHAPTER THREE
❖❖❖❖❖❖
THE SISTERHOOD
OF THE SHIELDS

A cold wind swept across the plains of Manitoba, carrying with it the first hint of fall. The poplar leaves danced above us, reflecting the crimson light of the setting sun. Forty-three native women and myself sat around a crackling fire. Zoila Guitterez from the Yucatán and my dear friend Twin Dreamers, the shapeshifter who had taught me about the stars, sat near to me. Twin Dreamers showed me a tiny star sapphire that twinkled in the palm of her wrinkled hand. A large black kettle of vension stew bubbled at one end of the fire, supported by hand-hewn poles. My mouth watered every time a whiff of steam passed my way. I wondered how a spirit could be hungry and if the women I saw were also in spirit form. Great round medicine shields with vividly colored symbols painted on their stretched hides glowed proudly in the failing light. The shields were displayed on wooden tripods behind each woman. Rows of feathers hung from each and fluttered in the breeze as if the shields were preparing for flight and were tethered only for a moment.

This is my circle, the Sisterhood of the Shields. Each woman is a shaman and represents a system of knowing from a different tribal nation in the world. Each shield is different and represents the essence of its maker. Each is startling in its originality and design.

My shield carries the wolf imprint, and I was proud to be sitting before it. From across the circle an aboriginal shaman woman from Australia was watching me. Like all the women, she seemed very young and yet very old.

"Your moods make rabbits today," Agnes, who sat next to me, whispered in my ear.

"What do you mean?" She had startled me.

"You think little thoughts and they multiply like jackrabbits."

I laughed. The old aboriginal woman went to the center of the circle and picked up the talking stick. It was carved and painted in a mockingbird design with feathers hanging from one end. When the stick was passed, she who held it could speak as long as she liked. But to hold it also meant that she must speak from her medicine place, her own personal truth.

"My name is Ginevee," the old, aboriginal woman said, looking at me. "Sometimes your moods make owls. When your moods make owls, it means that a story is lurking nearby." She came toward me. Ginevee was wearing a red wool shawl over a long jean skirt, with boots and a sweater. Her face was dark like the approaching shadows of night. Her eyes were intensely black with a silvery quality. She handed me the talking stick and everyone murmured.

As one, all the women said, "Ho." They were then silent and listened.

"I don't understand," I said.

The woman Ginevee sat down across from me on my blanket, her hand on the talking stick. "Owls can be storytellers. Owls can frighten people who don't know about the power of stories." Ginevee chewed on a twig with her large white teeth.

"Tell me more, Ginevee." My interest seemed to delight her. Everyone moved closer to listen, their faces—marked with power and etched by time—all as different and mysterious as the ancient cultures they represented. Just then an owl hooted in a tree off to our left. We all turned to look and I offered a pinch of tobacco to the spirit of the owl. A prickle went up my spine.

"That owl, she is telling you that a story is coming to visit you."

"How can a story come to visit me?"

"There are many stories that live in the woods and around the sacred places of the world. Every once in a while they find someone that they like and they come to them, yea. Sometimes they even live in you for a while."

"Inside of you?" I was incredulous.

"Yes. You see, you have a story that has come to live in you. Now you must tell that story."

"But why? I mean why me?"

"Stories need a voice. This story can see that you are a storyteller and it likes you. When I say your moods make owls or eagles, I mean for you to listen. A story has moved into your hut and wants to be heard."

"A story?"

"It is as true as you are, yea."

"Do I know the story?"

Ginevee started to smile. "You will soon. This story is a part of your future life. People think that stories are outside of them, like truth and power. But they inhabit you like your own life-force and they animate your being. You are about to go on a long journey. It is a journey of life and death. You will learn to heal the evil forces of darkness. You are a warrioress in the fight against ignorance. The sorcerers in life are created within each of us. You will learn a new way to fight the two sorcerers you saw in your dream. They are evil and are killing our sisters."

"But how did you know about that dream?"

Ginevee smiled at me and began to back away. The wind howled around us and we were all lost in darkness. Everything faded away but the stars and then it was dawn.

I awoke with a start. Agnes was sitting on her red trade blanket by the fire sipping tea out of a yellow enameled cup. She was watching the silvery glimmer of a new day reflect in the placid ground swells of the ocean below.

"Agnes, I had the most extraordinary dream."

I looked around very disoriented. Suddenly I realized it was not the ocean rolling in below us, but the great wasteland of Central Australia floating on scintillating heat waves. My vision blurred, and for a moment I thought I saw several kangaroos headed straight for us. They ran and hopped, but never seemed to get close. They were lost in the mirage of heat waves. In desperation I leaped to my feet and the hallucination faded away.

"Do you want some billy tea?" Agnes asked, smiling at my turmoil. I swirled around, almost losing my balance. Agnes held out the yellow enameled cup of steaming liquid.

"Too hot for me," I managed to say.

"Me three," Ginevee said.

I sat back down against the tree. I touched its bark with my fingers and then placed my palms on the warm red earth. For a while I didn't know if I was still in my sleeping bag in Santa Barbara, dreaming. I stared at the two old women and they stared back. I realized I was in Central Australia, resting with my teachers beneath a ghost gum tree.

"Owls," Ginevee said. "Your moods still make owls."

I started to ask a question, but Agnes and Ginevee rolled up our mats, stowed the food, and seemed too busy to talk.

❖

Our images multiply and the earth turns
        into a midget
as arrows are shot into my eyes at dawn

—Philip Lamantia

❖

CHAPTER FOUR
❖❖❖❖❖❖
THE BUGEEN

T he rest of the day we drove down the Gunbarrel Highway in relative silence. Each time we drove through a small grove of eucalyptus trees and then out again onto the open terrain, I was taken anew by the ancient barrenness of the land. The orange mother earth appeared to have lost her hair. In places, there was a low golden stubble and then the land would roll on to the horizon bald and empty. My thoughts pulled back again and again to my dream of the two sorcerers. Why had the one been putting on a mask of my face? I felt lost in timelessness. The land around us seemed forgotten by time. And what is time, that it has such power to change all that exists back into powder, an unseen force like the wind that can shape the land and our lives? But just as I became lost in these thoughts, the jeep lurched and bounced over a deep rut. Several bundles in the back fell onto the floor.

"I-ee-," Ginevee yelled. "Too much thinking, I think," she said, poking my shoulder.

"Time holds form together. It is part of our universal dream lodge," Agnes said, staring straight ahead as she always did in a car.

"How do you always know what I'm thinking, Agnes?" I was continually astonished when she did that and it made me nervous. She glanced at me, then rolled her eyes to the roof of the jeep.

"Sorry, sorry." I patted her knee, the wheel almost jerking out of my grasp as I did so.

"Ginevee, is there no other road to Ayers Rock? I thought a lot of tourists went there these days."

"Many do. The government gave the sacred area back to us and we in turn have leased it back to them, so tourists can visit. I do not believe this should have been done. It is our great sacred land, and many have forgotten the old ways and are only interested in money. That doesn't matter now. We have to arrive safely at our ceremonial grounds. The two sorcerers you saw in your vision are aware of you. In a way you are in a war, and I must protect you as my guest and my sister."

I must have turned sheet-white, because for a second I thought I would faint.

"What war, what do you mean a war?" I was past wondering how the two women maneuvered their way into my every thought. They stared at each other a moment before Agnes grabbed the wheel and helped me miss a low-hanging ghost gum tree that grew close to the road. Its branches loudly scratched the side of the jeep, and I slowed to the edge of the rut and stopped in order to regain my balance. Ginevee rubbed my shoulders and talked to me, almost crooning in a soft voice.

"You are beginning a new circle of learning. It is not easy to walk the earth as a power woman, a healer, yea. You are bursting through the last of the old crust on your previous layer of existence. You must fight for what you need to learn. You are in a new land, in the heart of you and with your feet. Listen with great care and watch where you step. Your very life depends on it. Now we must drive quickly until sundown. I feel the bugeen . . . around us . . . there is a darkness. It is not good."

I threw the jeep into low gear and concentrated on the road.

My heart was pounding with fright. What have I gotten myself into now, I wondered. Ginevee was sitting in the back rigidly upright, with eyes closed. She had taken out her singing sticks and began clapping them together and chanting. She did not stop the strange, primitive music until dusk, when we ground to a dusty halt near a scraggly eucalyptus tree. I was so exhausted I wasn't even scared anymore. I peed behind a bush, ate a crust of bread, and was asleep on my mat, covered by a trade blanket, before Agnes and Ginevee had even started a fire.

❖

You give yourself no time
for God
relying on shining metal suitcases
that lead nowhere
and you can't make decisions
because you've lost your point of view
and the solitary demons come in to haunt
    you

—Jack Crimmins

❖

CHAPTER FIVE
❖❖❖❖❖❖
MUNI-MUNI

Early in the morning I awoke to a scurrying sound like dried leaves swept crablike across pavement in the wind. I warily opened a bloodshot eye. In the center of a cleared area of puce-colored sand sat Ginevee, the angles of her face dark and jutting in the early light. She was pouring sand onto a large, dried, flat leaf and rubbing her hands together like a child happily playing a game. Agnes sat across from her and was moving two other leaves across the sand like little boats up a river. She wore two turquoise necklaces, turquoise earrings, and a white dress. I raised myself up on an elbow, instantly curious and wide awake.

"What are you doing?" I asked.

"Snooze you lose," Agnes retorted without even looking up. I scrambled over next to them, knowing she was right.

"Shush," Ginevee said. "You'll disturb the family."

"What family? You mean the leaves?"

"We're playing muni-muni. There might be something of interest here even for a sleepyhead like you."

I watched, wiping the sleep from my eyes. The dawn was golden and edged the two medicine women with a fringe of radiant light. Both women, from opposite ends of the world, now blended easily like sisters who had grown up in same family, because theirs were ancestors both born of the same inimitable power and speaking the same unspeakable language of the shaman spirit. I watched with fascination as these two women moved the big reddened leaves back and forth at separate areas of the circle, never touching each other. Their eyes were intent on the game as if they were playing a million-dollar chess match.

"Look," cried Ginevee as the leaf with the sand in it began to tip over. It was situated between the two bigger leaves.

"That's you, Lynn. Can't you see?" Ginevee asked.

She reached a long arm over and grabbed me by the scruff of the neck and shook me like a bitch shaking her pup. I yelled, then I saw the sand particles in the leaf begin to shimmer like tiny seed crystals, similar to the kind I have gathered from anthills all over New Mexico. Their reflection danced in the yellow light and started playing tricks on my eyes. The leaf was suddenly floating on a vast sparkling sea. It was listing to windward like a boat about to capsize. I was totally compelled into the circle, as if I were the boat.

I felt a great wind coming out of the east blowing in my face. East is the direction of the sacred clown on the medicine wheel; the east wind meant to destroy my power and sink me. I could see a dark force being born from the leaf and then I recognized the sorcerer from my vision in Santa Barbara. He was wearing my face like a mask and his giant black body was painted with red-ochre dots and designs.

Then another wind blew from the west. It was powerful. On the medicine wheel it is a wind of transformation and death. There again was the other sorcerer, smaller in stature and born of a distorted sacred dream. I could see his tormented genius. He could not bear to see the power of a woman because his own femaleness was in bondage. He reached out through the black west winds and tried to empty the sand crystals out of my leaf. I was a spirit boat about to sink and drown.

Again Ginevee grabbed me by the scruff of the neck and shook me. I yelled at her and then screamed from some wounded place deep within me that I hadn't even known existed. I stopped screaming and stared into Ginevee's dark eyes. At that moment she was a hated demon. Somehow she or her leaf game had reached down inside of me and touched my deepest vulnerability, vulnerability I couldn't even define. I didn't want to look into that emptiness.

"This is muni-muni, our children's game. It teaches you about food."

"Some children's game!" I was gasping for breath. "What do you mean, 'food'?"

"You are starving—inside of you, yea. You are starving." After many minutes of looking into Ginevee's piercing and predatory eyes, I nodded.

"Yes, I understand." The place we had touched was throbbing. It felt like a sore that needed salve, ached like a desperately hungry stomach. I wanted to double over in the sand, but I watched Ginevee, afraid to move.

"That is the place where the sorcerers will find you." She poked me.

"The sorcerers?" I said weakly, still absolutely terrified.

"Sorcerers are like disease. They serve only one good purpose."

"What's that?"

"They force you to learn your lessons or you die. It is simple. The leaves never lie."

"What is this, some kind of fortune-telling?" I was yelling and was angry and sacred. Ginevee threw up her hands and looked at Agnes.

"See, I told you. Instead of thanking me she's mad. I knew she had a temper. It's part of her fear."

"Lynn can get very angry. She doesn't see the truth."

Agnes and Ginevee started breaking camp.

"Dammit, what do you mean I don't see the truth? I'm here, aren't I? I'm trying, aren't I? What other red-blooded, sane woman would be out here in the middle of nowhere, starving with kangaroos and playing with goddamn leaves that make sorcerers out of nothing, and I haven't even had time to wake up!" They both ignored me, so I calmed a little. I grabbed both the old women. "Okay, I'm sorry. Please wait. Let me have some tea, please. I'm just scared. Let's talk."

They looked at each other and finally sat back down. Ginevee stacked the leaves one on top of the other. Now they just looked like leaves. Agnes started to heat water for tea. Ginevee slowly and deliberately picked up one leaf and placed it before me.

"This was your spirit boat."

"What does it mean, Ginevee?"

"You tell me."

I looked at it, then I closed my eyes. I felt the pain in my body where she had poked me and instantly knew.

"Trust," I said as Ginevee retrieved the leaf.

"It's more. You don't believe that a real relationship is even possible."

"Between who or what?"

"Between you and a man."

"Oh." I thought about that. "But what does that have to do with sorcery?"

"When you choose not to trust, you invite those who are untrustworthy into your hut. This time you've really done it. You've called in a real challenge."

"But I didn't call anyone!"

"No? Then what are they doing here? You know your power, but you're not yet at ease with it. Your food is trust. Eat it or you will starve to death," Ginevee said.

"How do I eat trust?"

"The sacred Dreamtime, your initiations will teach you. Then there will be no doubt. Then no one can hurt you. It is good that Black Swan and Black Wolf meet at this time. You will learn many new things."

Silently we watched the rising sun, its radiant light broken only by the branches of the eucalyptus tree. We sipped pungent billy tea. My whole system was beginning to transform in this new land. I felt like a drop of water on a leaf about to evaporate in the intense sunlight.

❖

Begin, my friend,
        for you cannot,
                you may be sure,
takes your song,
        which drives all things out of mind,
                with you to the other world.

                        —William Carlos Williams

❖

CHAPTER SIX
❖❖❖❖❖❖
THE GUARDIAN
OF SOLITUDE

That afternoon, Ginevee left our camp. Usually, she ate very little for lunch, but this day she ate nothing. Taking one of her medicine bundles with her wrapped in a bark mat, she got up quite abruptly. Turning without a word, she walked over a hill and vanished. I looked to Agnes for some explanation, but she kept nibbling on some cheese and only shrugged.

"Was it something I said?" I asked.

Agnes shook her head. I decided to relax and lay back on the grass mat. A soft melancholy had come over me, like a blanket of fog. I looked over at Agnes who sat, back against a tree, mending a moccasin. She caught the thread between her teeth and knotted it, as I'd seen her do many times before. Twelve years apprenticeship, I thought, and I've still not gotten the best of sadness.

"It's not as bad as it used to be," Agnes said, using her bone awl on the leather sole.

"What isn't?"

"Your sadness."

"Oh, Agnes, get out of my head!"

"Sadness is still your big addiction. Every time you do that to yourself you die a little."

"Why die a little?"

"Because it's your personal way of throwing power away. That kind of energy loss is a small death. Some energy you can thrust out into the sacred rounds of life and it will return to you like a boomerang."

"What kind of energy is that, Agnes?"

"The energy of creativity."

I watched her brown face and the afternoon light reflecting silver and tan from her round cheekbones.

"What kind of creativity?"

Agnes stuck the end of her awl into the pinkish sand and drew a circle.

"You remember the medicine wheel?" She winked at me. "Energy always returns to its source when it is born of creativity." She pointed the bone awl to the north position on the wheel. "In the north, your spirit is inspired with the wisdom of an idea. You take it to the south, to trust and innocence and you dress that inspiration with a physical presence—you manifest your spirit, say, into a book. Then you travel north again for recognition and the fullness of your spirit becomes an exchange of energy with the world. There's a circle there and new energy is born. In throwing out a negative mood or thought, the movement is straight like this stick. You start at one end and drop off the other. There is no returning." She tossed the dry stick away and it splintered on a rock.

"You're right, Agnes. So where is Ginevee?"

"She's with her guardians."

"You mean she wants to be alone?" A great black bird flew over us, heading toward the west.

"You might say that. Now rest while you can. Never disturb Ginevee." Agnes closed her eyes and dropped off into a deep sleep. I rolled around on the mat, swatting flies, and watched the sun for a long while until it became a giant red ball on the horizon, finally sliding slowly beneath the hills. The air became instantly cooler and I put a scarf over my shoulders. Agnes never moved. I wondered where Ginevee possibly could have gone. I was impatient. We had lost a whole afternoon of driving.

Finally, Ginevee came back over the hill. Puffs of dust billowed around her feet with every step she took. I looked up sleepily from my nap and watched her enter camp full of exhilaration. She said nothing.

I must have dozed off again. I awoke with a start as

Ginevee snapped several dried branches over her knee. She was stacking them for the fire. Agnes was gently blowing on a tiny flame. She bent over it gracefully, like a mother tending her child. The fire caught with an orange flare and we were suddenly sitting in a magically glowing sphere of firelight. The tree branches curved like a canopy above us; a slice of silvery moon was visible through the leaves that shimmered in the intermittent breeze. The darkness was densely black, surrounding us as if all the world had dropped away. We could have been moving through space, a star unto ourselves. We three sat around the fire on our mats, passing the water canteen and our assortment of nuts, dried fruit, cheese and crackers. Ginevee appeared to be much more at ease. Her shoulders had lost their tension. She knew I was bursting with curiosity and kept avoiding my gaze with a smile.

Finally I broke the silence, unable to contain myself any longer.

"Ginevee, where have you been? We . . . I've been worried." I caught Agnes' forceful glance out of the corner of my eye. Ginevee still did not answer.

Instead she took a short grass broom and began sweeping the earth in a flat place. After preparing the area with smoke from burning sage that we had given her, she chanted several long songs and began drawing ranga—sacred symbols—in the brushed dirt. The symbols were spirals with lines stretching out on each side. Then she took a special long digging stick and tunneled under the sand to make ridges. It looked like a learned mole had invaded the place. It was beautiful, the light softly shading the symbols with purple colors.

Next, she made mounds of cornmeal taken from a special sack that had been rolled up in her mat. Carefully and with great tenderness, Ginevee placed a configuration of crystals in the form of a cross with some crystals at random around it.

I had been so fascinated watching the expert precision of Ginevee's movements that I hadn't even realized that the moon was behind clouds and I was struggling to see in the shadows. A flash of sheet lightning revealed the intensity on Ginevee's face. The eucalyptus trees stood like ghostly sentinels around us. I could smell the rain in the distance. Again there were bursts of light in the night sky lending an exquisite silvery glitter to the crystals and making Agnes' and Ginevee's dark skin glow.

"These crystals are a juraveel. They are part of my dreaming. A long time ago when I was young, a gilarrmavell, a fairy woman, told me that Ginevee was the name of the Southern Cross." She pointed up to the great cross of stars in the sky. I had never seen it before coming to Australia, because you cannot see it in the northern hemisphere.

"See." Ginevee pointed to the arrangement of crystals. "That is the black swan flying there and those two male crystals are the tip and tail of a spear thrown by some clever fella to kill Ginevee. But he failed. You see, when the white man came to Australia he brought the Southern Cross. Ginevee is juraveel, a sacred totem. You won't see her anywhere else."

"I don't really understand," I said.

"Put it in your stomach, my daughter. It may take you a long time but you will understand one day." I looked at the crystals and saw how they corresponded perfectly with the position of the stars.

"Sit there, Lynn, at the center of the cross. Hold that middle crystal in your lap." I did so, feeling an instant clamor of power needling my body. The crystal was large, weighing about two pounds, and had many smooth facets.

"Look at me," Ginevee said, handing one crystal to Agnes and taking another crystal from the end of the cross for herself.

"These crystals are juraveel. They are sacred beings from the Dreamtime. They have been brought from the sacred billabongs, our sacred lagoons by Nagalyod, a being who was transformed into the Rainbow Serpent. They come from Nyimbun, the sacred one in the mountains, and from the eternal beings in the sky. You could say that each crystal is a chip off the throne of the Great Spirit. Each crystal is part of the solitude necessary for the act of creation and we are but a dream in the life of a crystal. That's why I am the keeper of the crystals. I am the guardian of solitude."

"Is that why you left today, to be alone?"

"Yes, to be with my solitude and to talk to it. Solitude is my great ally. I think you understand that, Black Wolf. We are both of the west, the direction of inner life."

"Yes, and I feel extraordinary power sitting here." Tears were rolling down my cheeks. I closed my eyes and let the explosion of energy settle itself in my solar plexus. I could understand sitting for hours alone with these crystal beings. They filled me with an ecstasy I had never known before.

I must have passed out because I awoke just before daybreak curled up by the smoldering fire. I got up and looked around. The crystals had been put away, the ground swept, and Agnes and Ginevee were asleep on their mats. I lit a small fire and heated some tea water, or billy tea as Ginevee called it. By the time it boiled Ginevee and Agnes were up too and busy around the camp.

❖

Sometimes I have the strange sensation
of things separating
I can actually feel
the universe expand . . .

    I wonder
if I haven't found the secret
to disappearances

                —Elizabeth Herron

❖

CHAPTER SEVEN
✦✦✦✦✦✦
SHE WHO WALKS
WITH THE WIND

Not long after, the first light of dawn threaded its way through the top branches of the trees. I watched a delicate web of shadows creep slowly toward me. Something shiny caught my eye to the left. I turned and gasped in surprise. Standing tall and slender, silhouetted against the dim lavender glow, was a mysterious figure. At first I thought it was a man because the person held a spear pointed toward the sky. Then the wind picked up from the south and I realized I was seeing legs through a thin skirt. It was a woman standing alone on a low hill above us. I grabbed Ginevee's arm without taking my eyes off the woman.

"Ginevee—look!" I hissed through my teeth.

"Don't be nervous," she answered as Agnes came up and held my elbow. The figure did not move.

"She Who Walks With The Wind," Ginevee whispered.

"What?" I asked.

"That's her name."

"Oh."

"She comes when the south winds blow. I have known her for many years. No one seems to know where she comes from or what her blood is."

"What dialect does she speak?" I asked.

"Her version of whatever is spoken."

Whatever I had seen that was shiny glittered again in the hazy sunlight. This time I could see that She Who Walks with the Wind was holding an object, turning a reflection of rainbow beams toward us. Suddenly the area between us was filled with a blast of white light. For a moment I was blinded by its sudden intensity and then the reflections were gone. There was an afterglow of countless shadows. I looked up, following Ginevee's pointed fingers.

"See, she is gone."

"Perhaps she just walked away over the hill," I offered, looking around. Agnes smiled at me.

"Go see for yourself." Ginevee indicated the small rise where the woman had stood.

"Okay." I ran to the top of the hill. On the other side was rolling desert, flat and with hardly a tree or scrub of brush. There were no rock outcroppings and there certainly was no woman with a spear.

"Humph." As I walked back to camp, I had an eerie feeling crawling up my spine.

"See anything?" Agnes asked.

"Nope."

"Imagine that," Agnes said.

"Well, where . . . what happened?"

"Guess she doesn't like white people much," Ginevee said. "She must have heard my crystal people talking. She likes them." Ginevee went over to my pack and rummaged around. She found my compact and brought it over to me. She handed it to me, her black fingers looking rough and cracked against the shiny green plastic.

"Open it."

I did as I was told.

"Look into the mirror so that you see your face and the sun at the same time."

I moved it around, catching a sliver of sunlight that flashed in my eye.

"This hurts my eyes," I complained.

"Keep looking, Lynn. The sun is right." Ginevee held my hands and the mirror just so. She whispered strange words in my ear. The words and her voice sounded like crisp paper being crumbled up in a fist.

"See the shadow of your face off to the side. Don't blink. Good," she said. "Now look into the eyes of your shadow."

As she spoke, something extraordinary happened. It became very hard for me to move my eyes, as if there were weights attached to them. I searched the shadow of my own face, looking for eyes. I shrieked, threw the compact up in the air and leaped six feet sideways, filled with terror.

"My God, what was that, Ginevee?" I twirled around looking for the grotesque face I had seen in the mirror. Ginevee and Agnes were slapping each other on the back and laughing wildly at my discomfort.

"I don't look too good in the morning either." Agnes laughed, picking up the compact and dusting off the mirror.

I was trembling all over. I turned around, feeling dizzy, and threw up what little I had eaten for breakfast. I squatted down in the sand and held my knees, rocking back and forth. Ginevee brought me a cup of tea and they both sat beside me rubbing my back. I felt less and less dizzy. The back of my head was sore.

"She Who Walks With The Wind can find her shadow in the mirrors. If you stare into her eyes or the eyes of your own shadow, you can disappear just like she did."

"Disappear?"

"Yes. The quickest way to learn would be to stare into her eyes . . . if she would teach you. She knows the trail. She knows what you need."

"But I saw a grotesque face."

"That was your own shadow. The secret is recognizing your own shadow and then learning to have a dialogue with it. Then you learn to disappear," Ginevee said. She turned to Agnes. "Has Lynn always been afraid of her own shadow?" Ginevee asked, chewing on a twig.

"I'd say so," Agnes said.

"Oh, thanks. But for your information, that was not my shadow. How could it have been?"

"Let's say she was one of your shadows. You have many legends or imprints that make up your story."

"I could disappear?" I sipped some tea and felt better. My stomach was relaxing.

"You would come back, yea, but maybe not here, but somewhere. What does it matter," Ginevee answered me.

"Oh, that's just what I need. Listen, you could warn me next time before I disappear." I was dismayed at the thought of disappearing. I stared at Ginevee, trying to understand what she had meant. "You know, Ginevee, I did feel like I was going away into a kind of lighter place. I was scared out of my wits. I had a sort of sinking feeling. I didn't like it. I felt like I was fading."

"Gee, Lynn, can I borrow your compact sometime? I think I'll start wearing makeup, too, so I can disappear." Agnes and Ginevee laughed and started tickling me. I spilled my tea and finally I started to laugh, rolling around in the dirt with them. Finally, we stopped, gasping and holding our sides.

"Ginevee, seriously," I said, still gasping for air, "did that woman really disappear like you said?"

"Black Wolf Sister, what do you think?" She touched the sore place on the back of my head and watched me with shining eyes. I winced. I closed my eyes for a moment and knew that she had indeed disappeared. What was even more frightening was the fact that I knew I had been close to doing the very same thing. The face, or shadow, that I had seen was of a very old woman with skin like melting wax.

"She glared at me impatiently," I said to Agnes.

"I can see why. I wouldn't like you screaming at me that way," Agnes said, refusing to be serious.

"It was better for you to take your visions into your own stomach. Digest them and then we will talk."

Ginevee briefly placed one arm around my shoulder and put her other hand on my belly. I nodded that I understood.

You must make a decision to learn to help yourself.

—Agnes Whistling Elk

❖

CHAPTER EIGHT
❖❖❖❖❖❖
A CIRCLE
OF AGREEMENT

We piled our goods back in the Land-Rover, which by now was encrusted with dirt. We drove until the sun was high overhead, when we found ourselves on a stretch of road that was sparcely populated. Our stomachs were growling.

I saw a café and we pulled off the road in a swirl of dust. We were starving! The sign read "Kangaroo Café International." The wind blew mercilessly through the branches of a stunted fruit tree we had parked under. A froth of pink flowering branches showered dozens of petals over my shoulders as I struggled to open the jeep door against the gale. I picked off one of the blossoms before they blew away. It felt moist and plump with spring life between my dry and cracking fingers, much like Agnes' words often felt to me when I was lost in the emotional deserts of my own dry chaos.

The café was bright and filled with slanting sunrays. White dotted chintz curtains ruffled over the windows. Wall hangings from Bali and Java covered the maple-stained plywood walls. The three of us, dirty and tired, plumped down in Naugahyde chairs, grateful for the stillness of air. We said nothing as we absorbed the sudden quiet and leaned our elbows on the brightly colored tablecloth. It was red, and a small basket of yellow and white plastic flowers covered a fraying hole in the center of the cloth. Ginevee moved the basket over to completely cover the hole. She winked at me as I watched her careful fingers.

"For a minute or three, permit me to enjoy the perfection of this small table," Ginevee said.

Agnes and I smiled at her intention. We sat in a warm silence for several moments.

A young girl burst through the kitchen door. She was white, sixteen, with brown stringy hair and a friendly smile. She wore a blue flowered blouse made out of polyester. She did not seem to mind the odd mix of female characters confronting her. She brought us steaming cups of coffee and tea. We ordered croissants, jam, and cold cereal.

Blue and yellow irises dressed the brown Formica counter and plastic trays displayed chewing gum in yellow, green, and white wrappers. A green plastic basket proudly displayed orange-colored "Cheezies" in blue packages. A sign in red letters saying "We reserve the right to refuse service to anyone" stood out on the wall over a picture of an elderly cowboy in full finery.

Ginevee was not altogether comfortable in the café. As we ate, she eyed the sign and squirmed like a kid in her chair. I felt a sadness at her discomfort.

She threw me a darting glance and tittered, "Tsa, tsa, tsa. I'm used to it, my daughter. Not to worry, not to worry. Everything is as it should be, yea. The mirror of suppression is a great teacher," she said.

"How can that be?" I asked.

"It makes us humble, and then power comes to us," she answered.

"Anything else?" the girl asked as she began to clear our dirty dishes. Her arms and hands fluttered over the table gracefully.

"You a dancer?" Ginevee asked the girl.

"Why, yes, or rather I'd like to be," she said, surprised by Ginevee's insight.

"Go to Sydney. You'll be very popular." Ginevee's face lit up with kindness.

The girl was truly touched and pleased. She took the check and money and returned with the change without uttering a word. As we prepared to leave, we heard her tenuous little voice say, "Thank you." We turned to look at the young girl; a smile animated her entire face.

"Stay strong," Ginevee said, and we left the café.

The mysteries remain,
I keep the same
cycle of seed-time
and of sun and rain; . . .

> I keep the law,
> I hold the mysteries true,
> I am the vine,
> and branches, you
> and you.

—H.D.

CHAPTER NINE

✦✦✦✦✦✦

KEEPER OF THE WOMAN'S HEART

The next two days we spent traveling. We did little talking. The two shaman women were lost in their own thoughts and were very distant from me. This left me much time to think back over my experiences and visions. She Who Walks With The Wind had truly disappeared before my eyes. I knew that to be true; I could feel it in my solar plexus, as a kind of pulling sensation. Once before in the Yucatán I had slipped into a crack in time and what I had thought was real had vanished. Now I had the same eerie feeling. Agnes was sitting next to me as I drove down a smooth section of red dirt road. I looked over at her. She was dozing.

"Agnes," I said gently.

"Hmm?" Agnes replied, her eyes still closed.

"Agnes, I have to ask you something."

"A body never can get any sleep with you around," she snorted.

"Agnes, please, when She Who Walks With The Wind disappeared, was that the same as when you, Zoila, and José vanished?"

"I can see you want me to wake up. Well, it is difficult for me to explain this to you, but I will try."

"Thank you." Clouds of dust smeared red shadows across

the windshield of the 'Rover. I took a swig of water from an old army canteen to wash the grit off my mouth and then handed the canteen to Agnes. She took it gratefully.

"What is time?" Agnes finally asked.

"Time is a way of measuring inner space," I answered after several minutes.

"What is space?" Agnes asked.

"Space is emptiness of mind," I said at last, slipping my sunglasses into my white shorts, where they left a reddish smudge.

"Oh. Then, my daughter, what is mind?"

"Mind is our process of thinking," I replied.

"Thinking is a result of mind, but, again, what is mind?" By now Agnes was drawing little pictures in the dust on the window.

"Mind is inner thought," I said, watching Agnes' brown finger as rutted by time as the road. She drew a circle around the other smudges.

"Mind and time are all within the self-lodge circle. Space and our relatedness to all life is also within the self-lodge circle. In your language the self-lodge is the ego. The ego is an entity that exists by way of an agreement between time, mind, and space. Without that agreement you would not have an ego. Without that agreement you would be outside of what you would call relativity or the time-space continuum. We talked long ago about your scientist Einstein. He was close to a great truth in his mind that shamans have always known with their bodies. We shamans have always known how to trick time. If you take any of those agreements out of the self-lodge circle, you alter your relatedness to all living things. It is an essential part of the process of healing. Each agreement between time, space, and mind adds up to ego. Do you understand?"

"I'm not sure. What would happen in a life circumstance if you take mind out of the circle?"

"If you remove mind—which is memory—you produce a kind of madness, like someone with a multiple personality."

"What about time?"

"If you change time, then you disappear."

"I see. Then what about removing space?"

"If you shift space, you get what happened in the

Yucatán. When you left us to find the butterfly Itzpopalotal, you unknowingly changed your relatedness to us. You were dreaming a different dream, so to speak. And you fell out of our circle and you couldn't find your way back. She Who Walks With The Wind knows how to play with time and she simply removes time from our relative circle. When she does that, she disappears from our dream. She has the power to change that agreement within that self-lodge circle. You see, all of us were sharing the same circle before you left us in the Yucatán. You shifted our dreaming by leaving."

"Oh, Agnes, this is complicated. How can we all share the same circle if the circle is ego?"

"Because ego is like time; it is part of each of us and yet, like a dream, it can come and go by agreement."

"But . . ."

"Your ego is only an agreement that will one day change." Agnes wiped the circle off the window. I sat for a long time watching the road ahead. Agnes watched me out of the corner of her eye.

"How do I make that agreement?" I asked after a few miles.

"The agreement is like life-force. It is part of everything you see on earth. It is as if we all agree to be here as we are. If we did not agree, then we would not see each other." Agnes took a big bite out of a red apple.

"That still does not tell me how I actually make an agreement." We lurched over a large depression in the road. The engine of the jeep groaned and whined. A plastic water bottle fell down on Ginevee, waking her.

"You people from America sure don't drive very well, yea."

I looked at her in the rear-view mirror and laughed. Ginevee was wearing several grass mats that had slipped onto her head. Carefully, she removed the mats and put them back into the webbed side pockets above the open windows. We were all covered with a fine red dust.

"I couldn't help but hear your conversation. In Australia, we have agreements, too. We make a deal with time, say. But a deal like that has a lender. The lender of time is who you make your agreement with," Ginevee said, scratching her gray head with long black fingers.

"But, Ginevee, how do I find a lender?"

"You talked with the lenders the other night. You have already begun your relationship with them. Don't tell me you've forgotten already?"

"What night?"

Ginevee glared at me.

"You mean the crystals?"

"Yes, of course I mean the crystals!"

"You used the crystals like a mediator," Agnes said. "You just didn't realize what you did."

"Talk, talk," Ginevee said. "We have more important things to do."

"But I need to know about the lenders—" I said, but Ginevee interrupted me.

"You will learn through experience. Then you will know," she said.

"But—" I began.

"No buts. We are coming to where we're going to live and I want you to pay attention."

"But I—"

"Does this girl do anything but stutter?" Ginevee laughed and poked Agnes.

Agnes shrugged. We followed the road around a bend and through a stand of tall river gum trees.

"Where is Ayers Rock?" I asked.

"Many long way, maybe a hundred and fifty miles, maybe seven or eight sleeps."

"Oh," I answered.

"Turn right over there," Ginevee said, pointing.

"There's no road, Ginevee."

The road veered off to the left and led out into the desert again. Since no one spoke, I did as Ginevee instructed and bumped off the road. We followed an almost invisible path for several miles and finally came over a low rise. Slightly below us and in a small grove of river gum and eucalyptus trees were wurleys, or grass-covered huts. They had been completely invisible from the road.

I had never imagined that a person, let alone a village of people, could live on a desolate plain such as this. Wurleys are very ancient traditional aboriginal housing. Ginevee indicated I should pull off behind some bushes to hide the Land-Rover from view—not that we had seen one car on the Gunbarrel Highway in days. Several children, nude or wearing waist strings and tassels, ran toward the 'Rover as soon as they saw Ginevee get out. They seemed very shy as they came close and huddled together giggling.

"These are all my grandchildren," Ginevee said proudly.

With this assurance, the four boys and two girls ran to her, jumping up and down, hugging her, placing little wiggling fingers and hands into Ginevee's pockets. With shrieks of joy and laughter they ran off into the trees with gobs of paper-wrapped bubble gum. Ginevee's eyes appeared glassy in the dappled light shining through the high trees. She put her arms around both Agnes and me, hugging our shoulders to her sides.

"I'm so happy that you both are here with me. Our tiny village is little known by anyone. This is a gathering place for women of high degree and their apprentices. You are the first from the Sisterhood of the Shields to visit. I am full." She touched her heart with both of our hands.

"We are honored, Ginevee, to be in your presence," Agnes said.

Ginevee knelt down and gently touched the surface of several round clumps of desert grass.

"This is a tribe of mulga grass. They are a symbol of the rain clouds that come after a rainmaking ceremony. Here, touch this grandmother gently so that she may know you."

The grass felt dry and a little bristly to my fingers. I took a pinch of ceremonial tobacco out of my shirt pocket and offered it to the spirits of the mulga grass.

"This is a village of the juraveel. It is the sacred ground of Dirrangun, our fertility goddess," Ginevee said. "It is a village of spirit magicians. I train my apprentices here. This *must* be a very secret place," she said, nodding wisely.

"Why secret, Ginevee?" I asked as she walked us down to a natural spring that widened the small, slow-moving river by six or eight feet. Several river gums and a eucalyptus tree towered above us, shading the ground we sat on. Tiny glints of light settled like snowflakes around our feet. I reveled in the peaceful quality of the setting and the luxuriant relief from the wind and sun that had relentlessly batted us for days.

"This village is for the women of the Dreamtime. It is for the sacred teachings from long ago. I am the keeper of ancient knowledge; I am keeper of the woman's heart. You will meet her one day." Ginevee placed the palms of her hands on the red earth, much as Agnes often did.

"I'm confused," I said. "When you say 'the woman's heart,' do you mean a specific woman and not all women?"

"In this case, yes. We are women of the sacred Dreamtime. There was a first woman and she was born from a spring of water. I watched over her heart. A long time ago, the tribes of Australians, most of them, became patrilineal. Many of the women's ceremonies have been diminished or lost. So much of our culture has been destroyed. We are doing our best to survive. Much of what is sacred to our people is secret to protect the knowledge from dying."

I suspected that this spring in front of us could be the first woman's place of emergence but I didn't ask. Agnes had placed her hand on my shoulder. I was instantly quiet and alert. Ginevee's eyes seemed to recede into her face, which became all but invisible in the shaded afternoon. Her body went limp with trance for several minutes. In that time there was not a sound, not a ripple from the water, not a voice from the village. I could scarcely breathe in the profound silence that occurred. Not even an errant fly dared to enter our circle. The cawing of a crow directly above broke the stillness at last.

"Agnes . . . that sounds like Crow from Manitoba." We all stood up.

Ginevee's eyes were shiny black, and strikingly peaceful. "That's Willy-D, the mascot of our village." The large crow flew down and landed on Ginevee's shoulder. He had a bubble gum wrapper in his beak.

"Agnes, are you sure that's not Crow?"

"You see one crow, you've seen 'em all." Agnes giggled and patted my back. "Crow is powerful, but even he would have trouble flying thousands of miles."

I stared at Willy-D. He cocked his head and stared back at me. There was something very strange about this crow. Willy-D cawed at me, causing an outrageous racket.

"Shush," Ginevee said, and Willy-D flew off to a high tree branch, where he bounced back and forth.

Not black, not
that terror, stupidity

of cold rage; or black
only for being pent there?

What if released in air
it became a white

source of light, a fountain
of light? Could all that weight

be the power of flight?
Look inward: see me

with embryo wings, one
feathered in soot, the other

blazing ciliations of ember, pale
flare-pinions. Well—

could I go
on one wing,

the white one?

—Denise Levertov

CHAPTER TEN

❖❖❖❖❖❖

DIRRANGUN

The sun was setting and streaks of twilight angled through the tall trees in long dust bars above us. I looked toward the several huts. I noticed that the small settlement was deathly quiet. Everyone had vanished. A dingo puppy, clumsy, brown and spotted with white, chased a rolling seed pod around the corner of a bark structure. A woman's arm reached out and she grabbed the pup and pulled him, helplessly yelping, out of sight. Ginevee's hand tugged on my arm.

"To enter our sacred village you must walk as one who is blind. You have not yet seen the mysteries of Dirrangun. The spirits of this land have not made peace with you. After one full day, after the sun is reborn and gone to its resting in one complete cycle, then your vision can be restored. You will take part in a ritual for the rebirth of your seeing."

From the creek behind us came a low buzzing sound that became louder and louder. We whirled around as the sound became an odd primal music that was at once familiar and foreboding. I saw a woman seated across the creek in the brush. She was very old and she was blowing on a three-foot-long hollow wooden branch from a tree. I was told later that it was an instrument called a didgeridoo. The sound was a deep bass tremolo that resounded in my body near my solar plexus. The old woman had curly white hair that framed her dark face in soft, wispy light. Her eyes were closed as she blew through her vibrating lips, creating a depth of sound that enveloped the clearing.

A clicking rhythm emerged from a low tree branch where two young girls dressed in white clay paint with plant fluff stuck all over their bodies played clapping sticks. They were hidden from view, so the sounds of body clapping or the rhythm of cupped hands hitting thighs came disembodied from the shadows.

From upriver there was a sudden movement as a being wearing an enormous grass headdress and mask emerged from out of the river or the ground. She did not dance, exactly. She walked to the music with a very dignified step. She swayed gently back and forth and elevated something she was holding in her hands. She held what looked like two small grass and bark masks above her head. The droning rhythm did not cease as the tall grass-covered woman slowly approached us.

Ginevee told Agnes and me to sit down. When the strange dancer reached us, her body quivering with rhythm, Ginevee took the two masks from the woman's hands. My heart was pounding with anxiety. I couldn't imagine what was about to happen, but I felt urgency and intensity in the air.

"You both will wear these masks until twilight tomorrow night. Don't be afraid. I will be near you. Close your eyes, my sisters, and prepare."

With these words Ginevee slipped a mask over each of our heads. The grass smelled sweet, as if the mask had been newly woven. I could feel pieces of bark poking into my cheeks as I felt Ginevee tie the mask under my chin and around my neck. There were two slits for the mouth hole so I could breathe but there were no eye holes. For a moment I felt claustrophobic and panicky. Then I took a deep breath and settled down.

The musical rhythms continued as Ginevee led us up toward the village. She gave us a braided rope to hang onto and used it to lead us. I moved very slowly, realizing how afraid I was to go an inch without being able to see where my feet were. There was a dark lining inside the mask, so that all I could see was inky blackness. I couldn't even perceive the warm glow of the setting sun.

As Ginevee tugged us up the path, I could hear the

voices of several children around me. They were speaking their native aborigine tongue. They seemed to have gathered round us. They were laughing, tickling us. Little hands and fingers pulled at my clothes and they pushed me almost to my knees. It was hard to keep my balance. The din became louder as more adult voices joined in, jeering at us. Something squished against the side of my head and dribbled down onto my shoulder. I tried frantically to brush it off, but when I touched it my fingers became sticky with the oozing of overripe fruit.

"Oh, great," I said.

My body was tingling with frustration. I felt like a bird with a broken wing flapping around in circles. By now the mask was driving me crazy. I hated not being able to see. Several things were happening to me. I desperately wanted to see the faces of the women and children who were taunting us. I had worked hard and had traveled a long way to experience life with Ginevee, and now I was rendered helpless with a no-see-um mask. But even more than that, I was suddenly frantic from the thought of how I was losing writing time. Strong hands held my arms and were firmly pushing me into an enclosure. My legs backed up against something. I felt it with my hands. I thought it must be a pole rack of some kind, perhaps for sleeping. First I sat down and then the same firm hands gently pushed me down to a prone position. Fat chance of sleeping, I grumbled to myself.

Music began again outside. I knew I was alone. I felt the mask, testing the knots that were well secured with some kind of hard resin. A wave of claustrophobia pulsed through me and I wanted to leap up, thrash the interior of the hut, rip off the mask, and run screaming out into the village. I felt crazed. My thoughts were fraying off into distorted visions of monsters and images of myself being burned at the stake in an ancient ritual.

"Lynn! For heaven's sake, get a hold of yourself," I hissed to myself. My own whisper sounded rasping and unfamiliar. Thoughts were whirling around inside my head. I wanted to sit up but an invisible force, perhaps my own exhaustion, held me down.

Outside the singing sticks were clicking nearby and I could hear the sound of many bare feet touching the earth in a cadent rhythm. The chanters seemed to be circling the hut. The didgeridoo sound seemed to hollow me out with its deep reverberation. Tiny specks of light, like sparks from a night fire, swirled in my brain and I dropped off into a darkness that felt like sleep.

I remembered what Ginevee had told me in Canada when we were sitting around the campfire with the Sisterhood of the Shields. She had said that a story was lurking nearby; she had said that the story would inhabit a likely storyteller, and that the storyteller was me. She warned me to prepare myself for an extraordinary journey.

That was what I was feeling now. The urgency to proceed with the plot, the journey, had possessed me; it was a need so compelling that, as Rimbaud had said, "the symphony stirs in the depths." This mask shut me off from the source of the mystery. I was no longer able to witness the adventure unfolding as it happened, and yet I still had a firm grip on a thread. I was tugging on it as if I were unraveling a ball of yarn. The thread represented the life of the story and I sensed its power jerking through my body.

It was then that I realized fully that the story had a life of its own. That it was born from the mystery and the void, and that woman carries the void. Creativity is like a great receptive womb. The seeds of an inexplicable, shapeless mass were beginning to take form. This form was a story with intent and breath and I was its instrument and its facility in the physical world. Just like a child chooses its parents, this story had chosen me. I could almost see it, but there were too many shadows. I could just see its face, a regularity of features . . . but the body of the story was confusing, like a dream remembered in the stark light of day. I was besieged by an amorphous coagulation of fleeting memories and an undoubtedly traumatized thought process. I was drifting away from reason and losing a sense of time. The awe and the anxiety, even desperation, born of the release of mind and the birth of the miraculous precluded my next thoughts.

It was night when I awoke. Now the chanters were far off in the distance. I felt the mask around my head but somehow I could now see through it. Two people were sitting in my hut. One was a very old woman. She had long gray hair that touched her waist in neat braids. She wore a simple white dress and no shoes. I could only see the back of her head and her profile as she spoke to the young girl who faced her. She was about twelve, and she also had long braids. She was blonde and wore jeans and a striped T-shirt.

"But there's so little time!" the girl said, stamping her foot.

They were unaware of me. The girl's pretty face was twisted with impatience.

"Relax, my child. You will learn soon enough. You can't learn everything in one day."

"But why can't I?"

"Because the world must become part of you, before you can then give it up. You must learn to live on this great mother earth."

"But I am living on her and I want to learn what you know." The girl was pouting.

"You chose to be born into the land of duality, a world that requires a balance between substance and spirit. Let yourself experience this separation between you and me. Become successful in the world of substance. Learn to use your resources and live with dignity. Go to school and do your homework."

"But that takes too much time, Grandmother. That will take years of training. I want to live a spiritual life and do ceremonies!" Now the child was crying.

The old woman put her arms around the girl.

"Listen to me, Lynn." I had thought the child and grandmother seemed familiar, but now I jumped at the sound of my own name. "You must first build the physical world foundation for your spiritual castle. If you were to do only spiritual work now, before your physical foundations were built, your spiritual lodge would eventually crumble in ruin around you."

"Yes, Grandmother, but it seems like such a waste of time."

"My child, in this work there is no such thing as wasted time."

The child rummaged in her pocket with her hand and pulled out a beautiful crystal. She handed it to the older woman. As the woman took it in her outstretched hand something extraordinary happened. I could hear the didgeridoo in the distance and then suddenly the droning sound was close at hand. The old woman took the faceted crystal. As it touched her hand the hut was filled with light. I could see every strand of fiber making up the tiny enclosure. The child—who I realized was me at the age of twelve—merged or disappeared into the older woman. The gray hair of the old lady began to move and change and became ropes of black hair. The woman turned slowly around to look me square in the eyes. I gasped and fell back against the pole structure. I held up my arm because the light nearly blinded me. I could feel the exquisite beauty of this woman in my own body. Her beauty and power were tangible, like sunlight reflecting off a diamond.

"My name is Dirrangun. I am the bringer of life." She held out the crystal to me. I remembered that Ginevee had spoken of this woman. I was looking at the face of the goddess. And as I thought these thoughts Dirrangun's face disappeared.

For a second I floated like a dolphin swimming in an undersea cavern, as if I were moving inside of Dirrangun. My face was barely there, but I could see hers. Her mouth opened in song, and the music that I heard was the harmony of the great goddesses—the language of the gods. I had heard it before, when I was initiated into the Sisterhood of the Shields. The moonlight shone down from above. Dirrangun's face was momentarily illuminated and her lips sparkled as if with dew. She placed the fingers of her left hand over my throat and the fingers of her right hand behind my neck. Her touch was warm and dry. The upper part of my body began vibrating and then gently contracting involuntarily. My muscles took over. It was not unlike the first spasms of childbirth. My mouth opened itself wide, and then wider, as if I would swallow all the world. My soul brought forth a song that was clear and deeply melodic and joined with Dirrangun. With each vibration—for now I shuddered again and again—I lost my sense of separateness. My mouth encompassed all that exists. My lips began to sparkle like Dirrangun's. I wondered how I could see them.

Dirrangun reached up above her. The wurley vanished and she appeared to be holding the Milky Way in her left hand. She began to tilt it and suddenly she poured all the stars in the heavens into my mouth. My body became full of stars. I stood with Mars on my right side, Venus on my left, and the Southern Cross spanning my chest. I exploded and became one with infinite space; there was only boundless nothingness, empty, dark sky forever. Everything is sacred.

I was only a part of the whole: I was a movement that somehow knotted all the pieces of life around me into a fabric of power. I was an unknown that gathered the stars about me into a landscape that then became filled with me. And as I thought these thoughts Dirrangun's face disappeared and I only heard her words. They were gentle but firm.

"You are welcome here. Take the crystal and never forget who you are."

I felt the crystal in my hand. It was smooth, heavy, and had faceted points at both ends.

Dirrangun vanished. The darkness penetrated the mask and I was aware of the grass mat and poles against my back. I stretched my muscles and legs. I was waking up from an incredible dream. It had been like a vision. I listened for what was happening outside. The music came closer. It sounded now like the clickings of wild creatures in a jungle. Someone entered the hut.

"Lynn, it's me, Ginevee." I felt a strong hand on my arm. "Hold up your crystal," she commanded me.

With great surprise and astonishment I felt the crystal between my fingers. I held it to my breast. Had I really seen Dirrangun, and had she really given me a crystal?

"Yes, my daughter," Ginevee whispered, reading my thoughts.

Tears stung my eyelids. I held up the crystal to her. There was complete silence outside. Ginevee helped me sit up. She untied the knots and slowly slipped the mask off my face. A young woman with shining, kind eyes took it away. There was a sudden clamor of excited voices outside, and the loud singing and music began again. Ginevee hugged me. She was full of pride as she walked me outside, holding up my hand with the crystal. Agnes also stood beside me with her crystal. It was morning.

"You have met with Dirrangun. Now you can learn to see in our way. She has given you a crystal. She has given you your Koori eyes."

The maker of the ceremony was an old woman with wrinkled black skin that hung down like waves of dark sand from her bones. She came over to us. Her face held a fierce expression. She pulled at our clothes with long fingers that resembled bird claws.

Agnes whispered to me, "Take off your clothes."

In moments Ginevee, Agnes, and I stood naked within the large circle of women, our clothes in a heap at our feet. Ginevee, Agnes, and the women of the village had such dark skins, it was as if they still had clothes on. I felt conspicuously naked and white. But not for long. The women, girls, and children dipped their hands into a strong smelling substance called bandicoot grease and quickly began to rub us all over with the stuff. As they did this, they touched our breasts, our faces, our vaginas, our legs. They touched us with great fascination, examining every part of our bodies, even our tongues, which they asked us to stick out. In turn we felt their bodies and examined them with equal care. Finally, after we had covered each other with grease, the elder women sat down. Agnes and I each sat down on the laps of two of the women. Then we got up and touched our bellies, each in turn, to the bellies of every person in the village.

By the end of this welcoming ceremony we were no longer strangers. We were laughing together and had a clear feeling for each other. The elder women chanted and covered our greasy bodies with ash from the fires, patting our skin with the palms of their hands. My skin felt protected from heat and cold and I noticed that when the flies, which had previously been so annoying, landed on me, I could barely feel them.

"The maker of the ceremony is Mandowa. She is my sister-in-law. She makes good ceremony, yea?" Ginevee winked at me as Mandowa's grim expression broadened into an almost childlike smile.

"Welcome," she said as she hugged both Agnes and me. "We have been told of your sacred marriage basket. That it was woven from the dreams of all women." Mandowa took two hair belts from around her waist and presented them to Agnes and me. "These belts are woven from the hair of all the women in the village. These belts are made from the women of high degree, yea, they will protect your power." Mandowa tied the hair cords first around Agnes' hips and then mine. Soon after this the ceremony ended and we went into our wurleys to rest.

❖

The moon, a grandmother,
in her independence creates
divergence from the unknowable norm.

We stretch north
urging the pulse
of riptide (which cause
rough waters)—

quicken, quicken.

—Jack Crimmins

❖

CHAPTER ELEVEN
❖❖❖❖❖❖
A QUICKENING

I didn't see Agnes again until that afternoon. I was sitting in the dirt playing with a brown puppy that looked like a baby dingo. A shadow passed over us and I looked up to see Agnes silhouetted against the vivid sunlight. She was smiling widely, her teeth glistening from ear to ear like a child's. She took her hand out of her skirt pocket and proferred to me a large faceted crystal not unlike the one I had. I gave the pup one last squeeze and jumped up in excitement.

"Oh, Agnes, let me see." I turned her crystal in my hand. We were like two children who had discovered a treasure. I showed her my crystal. We jumped up and down and hugged each other. "Did you see—" I started to ask Agnes, but she put her finger over her lips.

"Do not speak of her now in this way. You have been given a great and sacred gift. Honor her with your silence and respect."

"Yes, of course, but—"

"No buts." Agnes' voice was firm. We found a place to be comfortable under some trees and examined our crystals more carefully.

We were sitting at the bottom of a gentle rise. Three figures appeared above us, with the sun behind them. At first I didn't recognize them. Then I saw one was Ginevee. She joined us along with two young women who stood on either side of her. They wore thin cotton shifts covered with a cornflower print.

"This is Alice and Buzzie," she said, introducing them. We laughed and talked for a while. All of us were very polite, but gave each other fleeting but intense looks. We were insatiably curious about each other's shaman expertise.

I particularly liked Alice. She was my height, nineteen years old, and had black hair with reddish ends, which was shoulder length. Her sharp eyes shown like diamonds beneath her prominent brow. The smile that tugged at the corners of her mouth showed me the lively sense of humor she had. I knew we would be friends by the way we both responded to the tiny dingo puppy that was constantly chewing on my sandal and by the way we both seemed to be affected similarly by the rainbow lights of the sun shining down through the trees. We just seemed instantly to be sisters.

Buzzie, on the other hand, was cool and definitely aloof. She was close in stature to Alice, but about fifteen pounds heavier. She was about twenty-five and appeared as obviously threatened by a white as she was by the affection between Alice and myself. Agnes, however, seemed to enjoy the clever, biting insight of Buzzie.

Ginevee kept looking over her shoulder at me.

"What?" I finally asked.

"Let's you and I go for a walk. It's a lovely evening, yea," she said, imitating me.

Buzzie did not smile or even look up as we left, but Agnes and Alice laughed and nodded good-bye. I followed Ginevee through the tall eucalyptus trees and out into the desert of reddish sand and spinifex grass. Spinifex is lethal. It loves bare human skin and can give you a healthy rip if you're not careful. In this part of the desert the spinifex clumps rise to about six feet and often are no more than six feet apart.

"Walk carefully," Ginevee said. We walked quite a distance. The sun was going down and slices of crimson and orange terraced the sky above us.

Ginevee stopped suddenly and motioned for me to crouch down quickly behind some spinifex.

Almost at once I felt a rumbling in the earth and then I

saw a cloud of red dust off to the left. I heard odd animal noises that were completely unfamiliar to me. Ginevee pushed me down. To my astonishment out of the red cloud that was now blowing over us walked a large, elegant and snorting bull camel. Another bull camel followed. They must have known where they were going, because they began to trot by us just one bush over. They were wild and magnificent even if their fur was matted and filled with burrs. They appeared to be very dangerous. In moments the dust and the camels were gone, but Ginevee waited.

"Wild bulls," Ginevee whispered. "There must be others nearby."

"Are they dangerous?" I asked, still astonished. "I didn't know there were wild camels in Australia."

"Many, yea. Especially the bulls will go crazy sometimes and can even kill you. That doesn't happen often. It's best to be careful, yea," she said.

I stood up, brushed myself off and noticed that my arm was bleeding.

"You have cut yourself on the spinifex, my daughter." Ginevee looked at the small cut carefully. It burned.

"Sit," she said. "I will quicken you. I hadn't expected to do this just now, but the signs are in your favor." We sat back down in the red dirt in a patch of tiny blue flowers.

"What do you mean, 'quicken me'?" I asked.

"You can never really teach anyone about these things, but if you look into my eyes you will catch up with me a little. I have many years ahead of you. I will quicken you like a river heading toward the rapids."

"I don't understand," I said, looking into her eyes. They were like dark pools reflecting the crimson from the sky.

"I don't want you to understand. You cannot love with your mind. You will listen from your heart." She touched my chest with her knuckles. "If a camel is walking down a path and another camel passes him, the first camel will go faster to keep up. That is how we work. I don't want you to learn anything; I want your spirit to quicken, to keep up with me."

Ginevee took my arm, smeared some blood on her finger, and then held it to her heart. The burning from the cut began to connect to my heart in some mysterious way. Ginevee's eyes looked through me. She did not blink. I was lost in an ocean of noise that had begun to circulate wildly through my system. My pulse rate increased tremendously, filling my entire body with sound. I blushed hot and had to exercise all my control just to sit still. I was seeing vision after vision, one more horrible than the next. I don't know how long we sat there.

Suddenly I realized it was dark and the moon was shining full and bright. I blinked in disbelief as Ginevee spoke. What had happened to the sunset? I wondered.

"Do you feel the big speed in your blood?" she asked.

"At home 'speed' is a nickname for a drug." I laughed. I collected myself quickly, noticing her impatience. "Yes, of course. It felt like a freight train going through me." I was utterly exhausted.

"It's good to speed your blood."

"What do you mean, Ginevee?"

"Your blood tells me of your many lives on this earth. You are a very old soul, I'd say."

"My blood?"

"Yes, your history is in your blood. When I make you go fast I am working with your past and I am clearing away whatever monsters I find."

"It's funny you say that, because when all that pulsing began I saw horrible things. They made me blush—I could barely look at them in my mind. It was as if I lost control of my thoughts completely."

"Yes, my daughter. You will not see those monsters again."

By the light of the moon we walked back to the village. I fell onto my mat and covered myself with a blanket. I slept well into the next day.

As I came along in the Dreamtime,
I left my impression on Woman's Rock.

—Ginevee

CHAPTER TWELVE
❖❖❖❖❖❖
THE MOTHER STONE

I was awakened by Ginevee's foot nudging my shoulder. As I sat up sleepily she thrust some bread into my mouth.

"Come, my lazy daughter, I have something to show you."

I scrambled up, my curiosity instantly aroused. "What is it?" I asked, choking down the bread and pulling on my shorts.

"We will not talk. Just follow me."

I had a feeling that this meant a long walk. I put on my tennis shoes. We journeyed some distance from the camp in silence. I struggled to match Ginevee's long stride. The desert sand was soft and tough going. I was thankful when we reached a deep crevice in the earth and began walking down the rocky sides of a canyon.

Ginevee sat me down atop a slab of rock and left me to observe. A giant, faceted rock jutted up out of the surrounding jumble of stones. It looked dangerous and sharp against the rounder, softer, more voluptuous rocks nearby. She returned an hour or so later.

"What did you see, my daughter?" Ginevee asked, sitting down next to me.

"I saw the moon and the sun in the sky."

"And what did you hear?"

"I heard the owl and the green mulga parrot. I heard the wind. The stones called my name. I heard the language of life on the wind."

"Did you learn anything, my daughter?"

"I learned who I am."

"It is good that the stones are here, that you are here. It is good, yea."

We got up and walked along the side of a cliff, standing and picking our way carefully. Finally we stopped and rested in a rocky crevice.

I looked across the windswept valley. The wind wooshed through the spinifex grass and buffeted against my ears, making them sensitive. Directly across from us was a smooth, sheer face of pinkish rock. It plunged up out of the earth and leaned to the right, forever petrified into a ponderous global dance. The sun reflected hot white off the sandy surface. Ginevee sat cross-legged behind me and placed both her hands on my shoulders. Her grip was hot and I squirmed a little.

"Sit still, girl," she commanded. She turned my head a bit to the right and then to the left. Very slowly, as we watched, a dark shadow began to move across the rock screen on the other side of the valley. It was the floating image of a large bird in flight. It moved strangely for a bird, almost as if it were moving like a fish underwater. Ginevee gripped my shoulders.

"Watch," she whispered. "Who lives in that shadow?"

I looked for the source of the shadow. There did not seem to be one. I was drenched in a cool foreboding. The shadow drifted to the right of the stone and then, as if attached to it by some finite glue, it rippled over a jumble of boulders and disappeared behind the rocks. I gasped and, reaching back, grabbed Ginevee's arm. She was snickering to herself and speaking in her own language.

"That's Two Hearts. He is very good," she said in English.

"Who's Two Hearts?"

"He's the tall sorcerer in your dream."

"What do you mean he's good? It sounds like you admire him," I squeaked, my throat gone dry. She wouldn't let me turn around.

"One always admires a clever use of power," she hissed in my ear.

"Oh." I was unsure of her meaning.

"Two Hearts is like these rocks. That's why he plays here. It is lonely and windswept, like he is. Our people say that when a sorcerer is about to be born, he struggles like those rocks to resist form. Three months before a sorcerer is born, the fetus begins to dream. If an unborn child is of good medicine, she dreams of her future life. If the fetus is evil and a sorcerer, she dreams of ways not to be born. They hate life and dwell in the land of death. They strive to die at birth and to destroy their mothers. They complicate the birth and cast themselves sideways in the womb, just like that rock over there is sideways between the other two. See how the life flow is interrupted there? The energy is forever crossed."

"Yes, I see." I was struggling to keep up with her thoughts and searching the rocks with my eyes.

"See the peacefulness of the surrounding desert? Now feel the eruption and power of these particular rock formations," she said as I studied them.

"That's why we call them the Sorcerer's Stone Hill. No good can come of climbing those stones. They are the home of the evil ones."

"But why did you bring me here?" I was shocked.

"Because you must know the territory, yea. You do not want to give them more power than they already have, do you?" She squinted at me as I turned my head to look at her.

"Of course not. How would I do that?"

"By being afraid to look at them."

"Oh," I said, diligently looking at the Stone Hill.

"You see, the stones tell us many things. They tell us of the sacred ones, our ancestors. They are the canvas for our sacred paintings. They are our mother and they tell us of danger to warn us. That was the mother stone telling us of Two Hearts' whereabouts."

"But I thought you said that was his shadow."

"It was, but it would have been invisible to us without the face of a mother stone. Because evil and good are not separate. The mother stone embodies all good and all evil. She walks above good and evil and becomes the pure face of truth."

"I see."

I looked back at the rocks and then at the dark face of Ginevee. She had receded into her private thoughts and we got up, dusted ourselves off, and began our trek back to the village. The sun was beginning to slide down beyond the rim of the world. A blood-red sunset smeared across the sky, throwing dramatic patterns of pink and dark purple light onto the desert floor.

The earth does not belong to man,
    man belongs to the earth.
All things are connected, like the blood
which unites us all.

           —Chief Seattle, 1855

CHAPTER THIRTEEN
❖❖❖❖❖❖
A GATHERING OF POWER

The next week we spent getting acquainted with the village and the women living there. There were about twenty-five women inhabiting various kinds of wurleys or bark huts built around a central ceremonial ground. The tall eucalyptus trees framed the sky overhead and the faint sound of running creek water could be heard from any point in the camp.

Five of the women, including Ginevee, were very old. Each was a powerful medicine woman in her aboriginal tradition and each was responsible for three or four apprentices, who were girls in their teens. A few of these girls had come with their young children who scampered around the camp like small wild creatures, getting into everything.

The atmosphere was intense, because everyone was present to work. I was reminded of the mystery schools of ancient Greece, but this gathering was without the support of its own culture. The teaching was shamanism, so many different tribal teachings were represented and shared. Each woman had come to learn about the various energies of the universe. To be able to use these energies properly, each apprentice had to evolve at her own pace. She was taught techniques of healing and secret mysteries known only to the women of high degree. The purpose of this gathering was to rescue ancient female ceremonies from obscurity. An apprentice was introduced into the extraordinary world of the sacred Dreamtime with its crystals and sacred ancestral figures. She was trained like an athlete going for the Olympics, but winning to her was to master the art of magic by wandering through the vast, mysterious dimensions of the universe, dimensions unknown to most human beings.

Every day was different. Women would disappear for days and then suddenly reappear. This was normal. No one was concerned with anyone else's business and yet a great bond united us all; that bond was the primal power of woman and the knowledge that we were all learning ancient and nearly forgotten wisdom. This wisdom had been kept secret through thousands of years of suppression and was now having a chance to re-emerge in this tiny camp in the Outback of Australia.

Every day I awoke with a sense of anticipation and excitement. Learning and perfecting my abilities was becoming the greatest joy in my life. Willy-D, the crow, had become attached to me, much to my dismay. On this particular morning he decided he needed the ribbon that was tying back my hair. I awoke to the flutters of wings on my head and the ribbon being yanked from my ponytail. I could hear Ruby Plenty Chiefs' voice in my ear.

"Get up, you lazy girl, and help me find breakfast. I'm starving!" I sat up, dazed, startled and wondering why I was hearing Ruby.

"Willy, you rascal! Give me back my ribbon," I yelled at the crow, who was hopping on a branch twenty feet above me.

The red ribbon glinted in a satiny sheen against the peeling bark of the tree. I stood up, my hair now falling in my face. I swept it back, scowling at the thief above me.

"Why, Lynn, what a nice hairdo you have this morning." Agnes leaned her body against the opening to my sleeping quarters.

"Hmm, Willy's such a pest! For some reason he reminds me of Ruby," I snorted, glaring at the shiny black tyrant who was now leaving shreds of red ribbon all over the ground.

I found two bobby pins in the bottom of my bag and pulled my hair out of my face. It was already getting very hot. All I wanted to do was to sit under a shade tree. Agnes had wandered off and was talking to one of the younger girls. I turned around as Willy-D cawed violently from the tree branch and found myself face to face with Buzzie. She glared at me for a moment. I was stunned by her fierceness.

"Ngaya," she said emphatically, jabbing her chest with her thumb. I knew that in her language of the Pitjantjara of the Western Desert "ngaya" meant "I" or "me." Buzzie usually spoke English, so I knew she was trying to communicate something very important to me by using her tribal language.

"Nyantunya," she said, pointing to me. I knew "nyantunya" meant "you." I nodded that I understood. Buzzie squatted down on the ground and cleared a circle of earth. She took the strings of ribbon that had fallen from Willy-D's beak and a pile of strips from what looked like a stringy bark tree from farther north. Buzzie looked at me. I could feel her heavy dislike. She placed her hand over her heart.

"I want not to hate you," she said softly.

"I want not to hate you," I repeated with my hand over my heart. I didn't know what else to do, so I reached into my pocket and found a feather. I placed it on her pile of stringy bark. Her frowning, inky black face softened for a moment and the sunlight burnished her cheekbones with gold. In halting English she began to speak with me.

"You wonder why I talk my language to you?"

"Yes."

Buzzie curled her hand and touched her knuckles to her stomach in sign language. "This means 'water,' " she said. "To me it is water for my spirit that we-two feed each other. Then maybe I cannot hate you."

"Why do you hate me?" I asked. Buzzie looked up at the tree branches above. She was trying not to cry. A gust of warm wind shook the leaves.

"Your people—whites—have destroyed my people. There are few of us left to live the old ways. You have broken my heart." Large tears rolled down her cheeks. I reached out slowly and touched her cheeks with my fingers. I took her tears and mixed them with mine on my own cheeks.

"That's why we are here," I said, placing my palms on the earth. "The mama earth is in great danger of dying. I want to join you in the Dreamtime. We can begin to heal her—together."

Buzzie stared at me, then she took the feather and stroked

it over her chin. "I speak my language to you. It is my give-away. In our ceremonies we speak special language for special time."

"I understand," I said.

"This is special time, yea," Buzzie said, indicating the circle in front of her. "It is very bad to use the wrong language at sacred times. So I teach you one sacred word for our ceremony. This is not for we-a-lot-of-us. This is only for we-two."

"Okay," I said.

"Nyangunanta," she said softly to me, her emphasis on "nyangu."

"Nyangunanta," I repeated.

Buzzie smiled at my pronunciation and I repeated the word with her several times.

"It is good. Now I make you something." She pointed to the pile of fibers.

"What does the word mean?" I asked.

Buzzie chewed on a piece of grass, then answered. "It means 'I saw you.' " For the first time she smiled. But the smile was so full of knowing that it made me uncomfortable. She grinned from ear to ear, but her eyes were still cold. She gathered up the ribbon shreds and bark strips. As she started to walk away, she turned and very gently said, "I still hate you." Her wicked smile was gone and there was an after-glow of caring in her eyes. She left. I sat in the dirt. I felt like I had been collected somehow, like a butterfly pinned to the wall.

Agnes came up behind me with Ginevee. "You make her something, too," Ginevee said.

"Yes, I would like to. But what can I make, Ginevee?"

"How about something that smells good?"

"Like a potpourri?" I said.

"A pot-purring—sounds funny to me," Ginevee said, giggling with Agnes.

"Come, we'll gather some sweet-smelling grasses and stuff. Then we'll put it in something, yea. Buzzie can put it in her pocket. It will remind her of how good you whites smell," Ginevee said, slapping her thigh and laughing. For some reason she thought that was really funny. Agnes and I laughed, too, but mostly because she was so amusing.

"Buzzie saw you," Ginevee said, a twinkle in her eye.

"Yes, I guess so."

"She was with her teacher last night in the Dreamtime. She learned many things. She saw your moods making owls. She saw your story, the one that lives inside of you. It is begging to be told. She killed you."

"What do you mean 'killed me'?"

"She perceived you completely. She caught you in every shadow. She is a warrioress and she killed you, because she knows you now."

I was stunned by her words, but I knew she was right.

"That's why a warrioress becomes invisible to the ordinary world. She learns to blend with every color of life. To be known is to be vulnerable. So we must teach you to be invisible not only in everyday life, but in the Dreamtime as well." I stared at Ginevee, then we walked down the path toward the river.

We found a widening in the tiny creek that formed the most beautiful placid pond I had seen in a long time. Great sweeping trees towered overhead and trailed their branches into the pond. No better water for reflecting than here, I thought, settling myself down comfortably at the pond's edge. I could still see Buzzie's face in my mind. She was a very unsettling person to me. Several fish touched their noses to the surface of the pond, snapping at bugs. Tiny bubbles floated to the outer rings and made ripples of dark green water. The glassy surface of the pond was a mysterious mirror for the life surrounding it. Shadows and elongated, rainbow-colored birds passed in and out of sight. Something that looked like reeds and cattails edged around the sides and black and white magpies and green mulga parrots gripped the reeds that floated and rubbed together in the wind. One section of reeds in front of me stood up knife-like with two clumps on either side bending down into the water in a perfect fleur-de-lis pattern. The grass smell was pungent and the coolness refreshing.

"Here," Ginevee said, handing me grasses with little furry pods on the end. "Smell," she commanded. I sniffed the grass and it reminded me of sweet grass from South Dakota.

"My favorite," I said. "What is it?"

"It's a sister of the mulga grass. Come, I'll show you." I followed Ginevee into the reeds near the water. We knelt down over some similar tufts of green, brown grass, the mud oozing up around my ankles.

"Like this," she said. She cupped her fingers around a clump and snapped several long blades off with her thumbnail. I tried to do the same, bruising the shaft of the grass. After several tries I was snapping them off just like she was. Ginevee took out her dilly bag and we filled it with the sweet-smelling pods of grasses of all kinds. I would dry them properly when I returned to camp. I knew this pond was a power spot for me. I felt I could lay in the reeds near the now darkening surface and dream with the obsidian black color of its water. Like the long extended finger of Narcissus, a drooping leafy branch swept down close to me and gently touched a mirror-like reflection of clouds on the surface of the water. After a while, we walked back to the village in silence.

❖

Black sounds
knowing, with eyes.

    Twilight voice
    be forewarned.

In the darkening
stones

    agate, jasper
    you move

never wait
emerald, gold

        roaring

    blue-black fire

wolf.

    —Jack Crimmins

❖

CHAPTER FOURTEEN
❖❖❖❖❖❖
THE HEART
OF THE WOLF

I walked around the camp. Alice had found a wild dingo that had hurt his back hip joint. She put it in a cage to heal. He was pacing back and forth with great pain inside the makeshift enclosure. Alice had put it together from woven dried bark strips and every other imaginable scrap from the camp. There was even my diet cola can flattened out and acting as a hinge for the little gate. The poor creature was wild-eyed and frightened. He was in agony, but was nevertheless sniffing the ground and the fence for any possible hole through which he could escape. There was something about the terror in his eyes that I related to. I knew he would never surrender. I was sitting between Agnes and Ginevee, watching him. The trees swayed back and forth above us in a brisk easterly wind.

"That's what marriage was like for me," I said. Agnes and Ginevee laughed, thinking I was joking.

"No, I mean it. Look what he's doing. He's making himself sick trying to understand a confinement that is alien to his nature."

"My little pup," Agnes said. "A wild thing is forever wild." She noticed the tears in my eyes and put her arm around my shoulders.

"But no one understood what I was going through in

those days—not even me. I thought it was lack of communication between my husband and myself, or so many other things. But actually it was just my nature, wasn't it?"

"We have spoken before about the difference between a nurturing great-mother type of woman who is a caretaker for her family, and a rainbow-mother type of woman who is so different because she inspires her family! That is one thing. But the dimension that our concept of 'animal medicine' brings to your kind of psychology is important. Do you know why?"

"Yes, because we then can relate to the animal kingdom through behavior patterns."

"Fine, but there is so much more." Agnes had a partially made basket with her and was weaving it as we spoke. "It's like the interrelated strips of this basket. Alone they are weak, but woven together they are strong and can hold many times their own weight. You see these vertical strands? They are called the warp. They define the form of the basket. In weaving a blanket you have the same principle. The warp is like your psychology, your physical form in life. It is your strength. It represents how you enter the world as a woman." Agnes slowly turned the basket to illustrate her point. "You see, the design, the color of the weave is the woof or the horizontal strips. They are like your spirit, the voice of your soul in life. But without the warp, the woof would have no structure on which to build. There would be no life, only madness and dissolution. There would be only a useless pile of strips."

"I see. What you say helps me."

"Why?" Agnes asked, looking at me sideways.

"Well, because I can see the balance that is needed between spirit and substance."

"Yes, because you can touch my explanation with your fingers not just your mind." She handed me the basket to finish. I began to weave the fibers slowly.

"Your medicine, your animal counterpart is the black wolf. A wolf is many things. She is a hunter by night. She hunts for food, but she also is a teacher. She goes into alien and unknown territory to search out knowledge and brings it back to teach. She may be gone for many moons, but she always returns. She would not have the heart to struggle with new ideas and terrain and enemies if she didn't know that there was a den waiting for her as protection or comfort. She mates for life, but her nature is predatory. She is wild.

Even a tame wolf is wild and her eye is on the horizon. The greatest instinct in a wolf is for survival. Survival to her means life, food, and the freedom to live out her destiny as a wolf. If a wolf fell in love with a mouse there would be great problems."

"Yea, the wolf would eat the mouse," Ginevee said, laughing.

"Maybe not in this case. But the mouse would scold and complain because the wolf was always going out in search of new ideas, new trails of inspiration to bring back and teach. How can a wolf understand a mouse? The wolf is a predator. It's your wolfness that made you so unhappy, my daughter. You loved your home, but you needed to come and go. That's hard for many people in society to understand. You are a born fighter. Many people do not understand the spirit of a warrioress. The whole world will seem to be against you, but you will never surrender. You will shift and move down alternate trails and become invisible in the wilderness, but you will fight to the death to protect your destiny." I looked up at her, my fingers fumbling with the basket.

"You're not a basketweaver." Ginevee took the basket and very nimbly began to finish it.

"Wolves hate to fiddle with close-up details. They have a far vision. That's why it is good to make you do it—good for you." Agnes smiled and poked my ribs.

"Agnes, thank you for understanding. You make me feel much less lonely."

"I understand more than you think. Now go fetch some water for that poor dingo before he dies of thirst."

There are more invisibilities
to be attained

—Philip Lamantia

❖

CHAPTER FIFTEEN
❖❖❖❖❖❖
THE BUTTERFLY WOMAN

That night as the sun went down, I perceived the whole village of women as being one giant animal preparing its food and curling around the central fire in contentment. We worked so well together. After preparing the bread and billy tea, Agnes, Alice, and I sat down to eat. Then we began to make music. As the last dusty rays of sunlight faded from the treetops, we were sitting around the fire using our singing sticks. The sticks I was using had been shared with me by Ginevee. They felt worn and smooth in my grasp. I clacked them together with short jerks of my wrists. I looked across the fire at the chanting faces and felt pulled across time into ancient history. I still had the feeling that I was some part of the anatomy of a large primal creature with many glowing eyes. We all seemed to move and experience the rhythm of the music in unison. I looked across the fire at the shiny, dark face of Ginevee. Her black skin was burnished blood-crimson by the dancing flames. She was looking at me intently, but as if her thoughts were far away.

Unexpectedly someone stood up in the shadows near Ginevee. I recognized the slender figure wearing the red print dress. It was Buzzie, and she was carrying something. Her expression was so intense it was almost ominous. Everyone kept on singing as Buzzie walked around the fire and knelt in front of me. She was carrying a basket. She offered it up to the sky, held it to her heart, and then held it out to me. There were tears in her eyes.

"For you, Lynn, so we not hate each other."

I took the basket. It was finely woven of bark strips and the pieces of red ribbon that had been shredded by Willy-D. It was beautiful. She had made it so quickly! The potpourri of sacred herbs I had made for Buzzie was also ready. I was carrying the pouch of red material in my dilly bag. The herbs had dried in the desert air. Reaching into my bag, I pulled it out and offered it to the sky and mother earth and then I held it to my heart.

Buzzie seemed very uncomfortable. Everyone was singing. The village was filled with their constant, rhythmic voices. Still holding the bundle to my heart, I said, "Buzzie, this is with deep gratitude and in hope that we may share friendship and knowledge."

I held the bundle up to her face so she could smell it. Her eyes softened and for a split second she smiled. The potpourri was wonderful. It smelled like a mixture of lilacs and sweetgrass. After a moment she took it slowly and held it to her belly. Buzzie and I looked so different and yet we were so connected by our will to learn and our interminable shyness.

"How can we be friends? But there is much to learn," she said, looking at me. The seriousness left her face. I examined the basket with admiration and delight. This pleased her and she left my side of the fire.

That night I slept fitfully, dreaming of fruit orchards. Many of us were picking peaches all day in the hot sun. By the time I woke up I was exhausted. I lay on my mat and listened to the sounds of early morning. The wind was up a little, blowing in warm gusts from the north. I could hear the children playing down by the creek. It was a restful sound—the wind in the swaying treetops. I felt secure and insulated from the troubles of my usual life. For a while I entertained the luxury of simply remaining there forever.

With sudden trepidation, the hackles rose on the back of my neck. I knew I was not alone. I turned around, leaning on my elbow. Sitting cross-legged in the dirt behind me was Ginevee. The look in her eyes was fierce. She was staring past me. I had never seen her like this. I was stunned by her presence and simply gawked at her. She frightened me.

Finally I asked, "Ginevee, what's wrong?"

"Your story is ready to be told," she said. Her voice sounded hollow and far away. I remembered the meeting in the dream state of the Sisterhood of the Shields in Canada months ago.

"Your moods make owls," she had said.

"Your story, which inhabited you then, is becoming impatient to be heard," she said now.

"And what if I decide not to tell the story?" I asked. Ginevee shifted her gaze to me.

"You have no choice. Just as power chooses you, this story has chosen you. All you can do is prepare yourself for what is certain to come."

Something about the tone of her voice scared me. It suddenly dawned on me: I was like a woman possessed. Perhaps I hadn't chosen to come here. Perhaps this "story" had driven me here.

"That's ridiculous!" I blurted out in anger. Ginevee just looked at me. "I came here because I wanted to, and I like being here." I was scared.

"What makes you think that this story is stupid? It is not. It is very clever. It is so clever that if I hadn't told you about it, you would never have felt its presence. But I want you to learn from this something that you have always needed to know."

"What do you mean, Ginevee?" I was sitting cross-legged on my mat.

"You will see. This story has much to teach you. We will prepare all day for a ceremony tonight. Come, we will tell the others. Then I will show you how to prepare the sacred ground."

I was in a complete muddle. My thoughts were scrambled like the eggs we made for breakfast. I kept trying to throw off fits of superstition. Finally, by afternoon, I was so busy with my digging stick, preparing snake-like mounds in the dirt with Ginevee, that I stopped conjuring disastrous pictures in my mind and just concentrated on my work. Agnes had not been around all day. By nightfall I was getting worried. I spoke to Ginevee, and she told me that Agnes had borrowed the Land-Rover and had gone with Buzzie to get supplies.

"What?" I was horrified. I had pictures in my head of the Land-Rover mangled around a tree. I knew Agnes and Buzzie would be fine. But Agnes was no driver.

"Stop worrying!" Ginevee ordered, giving me a stern look.

"Yes, ma'am," I said, still worrying.

Agnes returned late that night as we were all silently preparing for the ceremony. Each apprentice was being painted by her teacher. We were using red and yellow ochre. Agnes approached, dangling the car keys from her long fingers. There was a silly grin on her face.

"The car is in one piece, right over there," she whispered in my ear, pointing to a clump of bushes. She disappeared into the shadows. Now I could concentrate. Ginevee was dabbing red ochre over my heart and covering it with dots of emu fluff.

"When I see you," she said, "I see a woman who leaks power and energy through her heart. So I close these holes with feathers and ochre, so that you will be more powerful in the ceremony. I use emu fluff, because the emu flies in the Southern Cross." She pointed up to the sky. "See those four stars? That's its head and neck. See off to the left where it's dark? That's its body and wings."

"Do you mean that paint helps me hold my energy in?"

"Yes, sacred paint helps you hold your power." Agnes sang in her language and kept dabbing paint on me. All I could see were her cheekbones and her fingers in the flickering darkness. There was only a fire for light. Finally she told me to lie down and dream.

"I will return for you," she said.

I don't know how long I slept, but when I awoke it was morning. I looked down for the paint and feathers, but they were all gone. Then I remembered that I had been washed in the creek. Or had that been a dream? I was terribly disoriented. I lay back and closed my eyes. My head was throbbing.

I remembered waking up very late the night before. I had heard the sounds of bones crunching and had felt the earth moving as if in an earthquake. Ginevee led me out to the prepared ground, which was covered with mounds that looked like a great serpent coiled in a spiral under the surface of the earth. The back of it glistened with a crystal-like shine in the moonlight. All the women—dark shadows slapping their thighs with cupped hands and chanting—urged me on with their sounds.

Ginevee had placed me in the vortex of the spiral and pushed me to a sitting position. She was nude and covered in paint and feathers. Her face was almost unrecognizable through the curling designs of the red and yellow ochre. I felt as if I had been drugged, the ceremonial ground was so potent with energy. Slowly and carefully Ginevee set out a design of crystals over the mounded earth. She spoke to each crystal and sprayed them each with moisture from her mouth. The crystals woke up with electric rainbows emanating from within them. This took a long time. Ginevee attended the ground, the crystals, and other sacred carved objects as if this were her world altar of power. Her care and precision was stunning. Then she settled herself in front of a huge, round quartz crystal. She waved her arms and chanted like a prehistoric bird. This went on for at least an hour and then she stopped in a trance. She sat still and silently for a long time, and then she asked me to sit beside her.

Doing so, I looked into the crystal and saw a kaleidoscope of movement within it. I was enchanted by the vision and the exterior world seemed to pass out of my consciousness. Ginevee repeatedly smudged me with smoke and feathers. Inside the crystal I saw a figure taking shape. Slowly I recognized her; I was very excited. It was Butterfly Woman. I had not seen her since my experience in the Butterfly Tree three years before. Ginevee placed her hand on the back of my neck and gripped me. Again I heard the sound of grinding bones and the wind howling around corners. Inside the crystal, Butterfly Woman's hair was covered with butterflies. Butterfly Woman beckoned to me and I entered the crystal where a tiny beam of light pierced the darkness. I felt as if I were standing in front of her and the eyes of Ginevee were outside watching.

"Ginevee will teach you more about crystals." Butterfly Woman smiled at my astonishment.

"I want to learn," I answered.

"Crystals are simply the chips off the throne of the Great Spirit," she said. "We are all one in our sacred wisdom. But I am here to warn you, my sister."

"What do you mean?"

"There is someone in the village who wants to harm you. She is not what you think. Beware of a man with two hearts." Then she reached out her arms. They glittered like diamonds and then became like butterfly wings covered with shiny satin colors—blue, red, and gold. She gently fluttered her wings over me and disappeared.

Instantly, I was sitting next to Ginevee again. I was stunned and disoriented. A man with two hearts? I remembered the sorcerer in the eucalyptus tree that I had seen with Agnes in my vision in Santa Barbara.

"Look," Ginevee said, pointing to my body. I looked down and saw that I was covered in the red, blue, and gold designs of the monarch butterfly. My whole body looked like I had been tattooed in a butterfly design. It was beautiful and I was conscious of Butterfly Woman's wise presence within me.

"What does it mean?" I asked Ginevee, who looked at me intently, her eyes shining.

"It means that the story is no longer impatient. It has begun to be heard. You have begun your journey into our ancestral gardens in the sacred Dreamtime."

When the grapes become wine
They want our ability to change.
The stars revolving around the north pole
    long for our changing consciousness.
Wine gets drunk on us,
Not the other way around.
The body came out of us,
Not we from it.
The body is a beehive
And we are its bees.
And cell by cell we made the body.

—Jalaluddin Rumi

CHAPTER SIXTEEN
❖❖❖❖❖❖
THE BORDERS
OF ILLUMINATION

Usually after a ceremony I am exhilarated; I feel centered and at one with the universe. But on this morning I was in a depressed state. I didn't want to get up or do anything. The pleasant sounds of the village and the smells of breakfast cooking did nothing for me. I was not hungry. I rolled around on my mat, tears stinging my eyelids. My sense of loneliness was intense. What was worse, everyone left me alone, even Willy-D.

Hearing a bark and a whine, I looked over at the corner of the wurley. There stood the spotted dingo puppy that I loved, his tail wagging and his head tilted questioningly. His owner, a little girl named Polly, had named him Spot.

"Come here, Spot," I said. At the sound of my whimpering voice, his tail dropped. He whined and left my wurley.

"Oh, great," I said to myself. "I must be in pretty bad shape if the dogs run from me."

Big tears streamed down my face. I looked at the basket that Buzzie had made for me. A glint of morning sunlight was reflecting off a strand of shiny red ribbon. The basket was hanging on a hook near my head. I took it and held it against my stomach. I closed my eyes and remembered the marriage basket. The marriage basket had brought me to Agnes in the first place. I had first seen it in a photograph, an old McKinnely print taken a hundred years ago. I had become obsessed by its beauty and unusual dolphin-like design. When I had finally met Agnes, the keeper of the basket, she had explained that the basket was a symbol of the male and female balance within us all and that it was woven from the dreams of all women. It was sacred.

Now, I examined Buzzie's work. The basket was perfectly executed. I ran my fingers over the close weave and for some reason felt even more listless and sad. The marriage basket had contained my dreams and I always felt its spiritual presence within my solar plexus. Now I was only aware of the emptiness of this basket and its correlation to my own mental state. Even the marriage basket seemed very far away. At the moment I could hardly remember it. I closed my eyes and slipped into a dark sleep.

I awoke in the late afternoon. I opened a tired eye to find the sun was low in the sky. It sent slanting rays of dusty light through the grass-laden walls of my shelter. Looking around, I saw Agnes sitting at my feet, frowning. Her bronze face was deeply furrowed in the rosy light. Ginevee sat beside her. She was humming softly. There was a concerned smile on her face.

"You don't look so good," she said.

"Thanks," I muttered, opening the other eye. Ginevee placed the palm of her right hand on my stomach and slowly started to rub in a circular motion. I watched her face, which seemed dark and remote. She closed her eyes. She began humming louder and making clicking sounds with her tongue. Finally she opened her eyes and rested her hand, still and heavy, on my stomach.

"The bugeen has come to visit you," she said.

"Who is the bugeen?" I asked, my stomach muscles tightening involuntarily.

"The bugeen is like your devil." My eyes opened wide. I looked at Agnes, who was still frowning. I heard a shuffling of feet outside.

"I knew I'd find you still sleeping." I whirled around on my mat and fell off the poles onto the dirt at the sound of Ruby's voice.

"Ruby, my God, where did you come from?"

"Speak of the devil," Agnes said. We all stood up and

hugged Ruby. Ginevee stayed back, and then placed her hands on Ruby's shoulders.

"Welcome, Ruby Plenty Chiefs. It has been many long time since we have stood together, yea."

"How did you get here?" I asked, sitting back down on my mat. My head was throbbing. I was delighted to see Ruby, but, as always, her presence frightened and disoriented me.

"Same way you got here, only I spent two weeks in Tahiti first." Ruby laughed and then her face became serious. "Money is always given when the journey has great meaning," she said.

Ruby stood in a pool of sunlight. She was wearing a long denim skirt and a blue shirt. The red-beaded shield hanging from her neck glinted and sparkled in the sun. I thought I must be dreaming. Along with Agnes, Ruby has been my teacher for the past twelve years. She had traveled all the way from the Cree reservation in Manitoba, Canada, to join us. She is blind, but she gets around better than anyone. She has been a powerful influence in my learning as a shamaness. Now, though, I was astonished to see her. But I don't know why. We are all part of the Sisterhood of the Shields.

"Where's July?" Agnes asked.

"I wondered if you'd remember me." July stood behind us at the entrance to my wurley. She held Spot in her arms. She wore a yellow skirt and blouse, her long black hair hanging to her waist. She was twenty, a full-blood Cree who had been Ruby's apprentice for many years. She was not part of the Sisterhood yet, but she was learning.

"Oh, July, I'm so happy to see you!" We hugged each other and laughed.

"July has to take the jeep to go get supplies for us. She'll be gone several days. Alice is going with her." Ruby spoke as if she'd been at the village all along. I looked at her strangely. The depression I felt was overwhelming. July gave me a kiss on the cheek and was gone. Alice looked in for a moment to wave good-bye.

"Well, I can see you're glad to see me." Ruby snorted and sat down next to Agnes.

"Oh, Ruby, I am—I'm just not feeling too well."

"If you'd work harder, you'd be okay," Ruby said.

Nothing seemed real to me. Ginevee smiled at Ruby and then placed her hand back on my stomach.

"This bugeen has been sent to you," she said.

"What do you mean, Ginevee?"

"I mean that if the bugeen or the devil comes to visit you, you should welcome him and make him your ally."

"Just how do I welcome the devil?"

"Just like you welcomed me," Ruby interrupted.

"You don't want to have an enemy to fight with, do you?" Ginevee said.

"No, I sure don't."

"Lynn always likes to fight," Ruby said.

"I do not. I hate to fight," I said, still wondering if I were actually seeing Ruby in the flesh. Ginevee pressed down on my solar plexus. My muscles collapsed under her hand like an empty hammock.

"Miwi is very low, yea," she said. "Here, feel this, Agnes." Agnes pressed her fingers into my navel.

"Nothing," Agnes said, looking worried.

"What's miwi?" I asked, feeling weak.

"It's your energy. The energy that gives you psychic power. Your miwi is usually strong."

"Oh," I said.

"I knew I'd arrive just in time for Lynn to give up the ghost." Ruby giggled and elbowed Agnes. I glared at Ruby. Australia had not changed her a bit. Ginevee pressed my fingers into my navel.

"You should feel the pulse of the miwi living here at your center. We have to dig very far to find yours." She pressed my fingers practically into my backbone. I felt a very shallow pulse beat.

"What's happening to me?" I started to cry.

Ginevee rapped my forehead with her knuckles. "You better start using your noodle," she said. "A bad apple is playing games with you."

Ginevee pulled my arms up above my head. "Stretch up," she ordered.

Agnes grabbed my feet and started pulling down on them. "Lynn, breathe in deep. That's right. Now hold it and push down as if you're having a baby. Push hard."

I pushed down and felt my head pound and my face getting red.

"Now let your breath go. All the way," she ordered, pressing down on my abdomen. "Now push again."

I did this several times until she let me stop.

"Good, your spine is trying to wake up," Ginevee said, pressing my solar plexus again. "Your miwi is the heartbeat of your ability as a shamaness. If a bugeen wants to fight with you he will lull your miwi to sleep so you cannot shield yourself."

"How does a bugeen do that?"

"By making you depressed, of course," she said.

"Depression is self-indulgence," Ruby said, fingering the basket Buzzie had given me. "Where did this come from?" Ruby asked.

"A nice girl named Buzzie made it for me."

"Mind if I borrow it?" Ruby asked.

"Don't lose it," I said, and Ruby left. I was beginning to feel better.

"You will never get rid of all the bugeen inside of you, if you fight this enemy," Ginevee said.

"What do you mean the bugeen inside of me?"

"This bugeen is part of you. You have made it your nila-nila, your mirage."

"How have I done that?"

"Who is the bugeen in your life?"

I thought for a moment. "I guess Red Dog is."

"Who is Red Dog?" Ginevee asked.

"He is an evil sorcerer that has fought with me for twelve years," I said.

"Good. If you had honored him and made a place for him in your camp, he would not be your enemy."

"Ginevee, that's impossible!"

"My daughter, do you want the evil spirits to throw the bones of death on you?"

"No," I almost screamed.

"Then use your noggin." She rapped my head again. "And learn something, my daughter."

"I don't understand," I said, curling up on my mat.

"Now the bugeen has arrived. What will happen? This bugeen is the spirit of evil; he is playing games with you. He is a trickster, the ultimate coyote in your language. He can disguise himself in very pleasing ways. He is a shape-shifter. He can take any form. I could be the devil. Maybe Spot or Ruby is the devil. Maybe he's a camel or a dingo or something that pleases you. He tricks you and can make you destroy yourself. That's why we call him a sorcerer."

"Why is that?"

"Because he makes you kill yourself. He likes to keep his own hands clean."

"What do we do?" I asked sadly.

"We make him our friend, yea."

"What's this 'we'?"

Ruby came back with the basket full of spicy-smelling leaves. "This devil is Lynn's problem."

"That's true," Ginevee said, "but Lynn is a daughter in my village and I will teach her how to befriend the bugeen. It is law and you will help, too," Ginevee said, scolding Ruby. Ruby handed Ginevee the basket of leaves.

"Lynn, you will build a wurley to welcome the bugeen. Show him you are his friend. Inside of you will be a big storm. This will change you. Then the storm will go away and come back only to bring nourishing rain. The nila-nila, the mirage of evil inside of you, will fade in the light of day."

"He is your worthy opponent. He is a warrior come to visit and even if he is evil you must honor him. Build a wurley and honor him," Ginevee said as she funneled pink sand through her fingers.

"Build a wurley and honor him?" I was incredulous.

"Yes, we will go to the Dreamtime and visit Oruncha. If you are lucky you will visit with this medicine spirit. Oruncha of Chauritzi will make a Koori shamaness out of you," she said.

I knew that Koori meant aborigine. I sat horrified and confused by my mirage of evil.

"Lynn, remember all that we in the Far North have told you about the evil being called the windigo?" Agnes asked, seeing my consternation.

"Yes, I remember, Agnes."

"The windigo usually freezes the hearts of his victims. He enters a village most often in the winter when the People are cold, hungry, and afraid. What Ginevee calls the miwi, or the pulse of your psychic ability, is very low for the People at that time. It's a quiet time, when a lot of ceremonies are done, but it's also a time of survival. If ever the darkness of one's own soul will present itself, it is during the long winter."

"I understand," I said.

"You are in a time not unlike our long winter."

"How is that?"

"You know a lot, but you still don't know." Agnes pursed her lips and chewed on some grass.

"What do you mean, I don't know?"

"You don't know the borders of your own illumination." I watched Agnes and the play of silvery shadows on her face as she paused in thought. She picked up a tin can and ripped the label off.

"This is a tin can, right?"

"Yes," I said. Agnes held it up to the light.

"Is it a complete whole?"

"Yes, I guess so—in the world of tin cans."

"That's right. Now describe what you see when you look at it." Ginevee was sitting with her back against the wurley and Ruby was snoring softly. She was sleeping while she sat straight up.

"Well, the sunlight is reflecting off of one rounded side. The shine is brilliant. Then there is a beginning grayness of shadow and then the back of the can looks dark because there is no light reaching it."

"This can is like you. Can you see that?"

"Not exactly," I said, bewildered.

"Lynn will never admit that she looks like a tin can," Ruby said with her eyes still closed.

"You have just described how we see things. We see things because of light. If there was no light then we would see nothing. Perhaps then nothing would exist. Perhaps then all there is is light. That's one way to think."

"Yes, I guess so."

"I bump into lots of things in the dark," Ruby said. "Things exist in the dark."

Ignoring Ruby, Ginevee just watched attentively and was smiling to herself over Ruby's remarks.

"Let's make an agreement," Agnes said. "That you are this tin can, okay?"

"Okay."

"Then you are reflecting light from one side and not from the other."

"That's right," I said, nodding my head.

"You see, you are half light. Darkness defines the borders of your light. It is that darkness that you are still unfamiliar with."

Agnes started turning the can so that the shaded part

was now illuminated. "See, the dark side is now light and the light side is now dark. That's all. Everything is a circle. One side supports the other side, so that a whole can will be born. It's very simple and nothing to be afraid of."

"We'll just light you up, honey, where the sun don't shine." Ruby was humming softly.

"You're saying that my dark side resembles that tin can, in that it is only dark because the light doesn't reach it?"

"Yes, but then what do we mean by your light?" Agnes' direct question made my mind go blank.

"Lynn, you stare at that can like a dog wanting her dinner," Ruby said.

"Ruby, will you please stop it," I said, wondering how she knew I was staring.

"Your light—what is her light, Ginevee?" Agnes held the can up toward her.

"Her light is her knowledge as a warrioress," Ginevee answered, looking up at Agnes from under her prominent brow.

"Yes, Lynn," Agnes agreed, turning back to me.

"Your light is your wisdom and understanding. The darkness on this can is formed by the absence of light. In your case, and I know this sounds all very simple—but it isn't, in a way—to understand your dark side is really only a process of turning the can."

"I understand, Agnes, but my mind doesn't feel very clear," I said.

"Let me see that can," Ruby said.

Agnes handed it to her. Ruby felt it with her fingers for several minutes.

"So this can represents Lynn and even you and me, right, Agnes?" Ruby asked.

"In a manner of speaking," Agnes said.

"Good," Ruby said and walked outside holding the can up over her head. Agnes, I, and Ginevee looked at one another, shaking our heads as we heard Ruby calling all the kids in the village. In moments everyone was in an uproar of laughter.

"Let's play kick-the-can!" Ruby called out.

To go in the dark with a light is to know
    the light.
To know the dark, go dark. Go without
    sight,
and find that the dark, too, blooms and
    sings,
and is traveled by dark feet and dark
    wings.

—Wendell Berry

CHAPTER SEVENTEEN
❖❖❖❖❖❖
EATING OF
THE DARKNESS

The next few days were spent pulling and collecting spinifex grass for the bugeen's wurley. Ginevee was careful to show me how to bend the grasses over and pull them out without hurting myself.

"These grasses are all part of a tribe. Honor them with your prayers and your intent. Remember with every movement who you are building for," she said as she sang to the grasses, and I hummed along with her.

After much playing and laughter, mostly at my expense, I learned to balance a coolamon on top of my head. In the coolamon, which is a long hollowed-out vessel carved from the gigi tree, I tied and carried the spinifex grass.

"We make the Bull Roarer from a mature gigi tree. It is hardwood. From the younger tree we carve the clapping sticks. It is warrigan, very sacred," she said, giggling to herself as she watched me attempt to balance the coolamon on my head. At first the grass I placed in it fell everywhere, but by late afternoon I was beginning to get the hang of it.

In the evening Ginevee, Agnes, Ruby, and I were isolated from the rest of the village. We slept in my wurley and sang together. We did not eat onions or meat. In fact we ate very little in preparation for a ceremony in which Ginevee said I would meet Oruncha, the medicine spirit. I was so filled with apprehension that I was no longer depressed. When Ginevee felt for my miwi, she was pleased.

"That's why Ruby likes to make you angry. Fear or anger are a good way to wake up your miwi," Ginevee said, winking at my disgruntled expression.

"Terrific," I said. "I'll remember that."

The next morning Ginevee got me up just before dawn. We went over to a small hill and sat down facing east. A silver streak of light sliced the blue-black sky into thin layers over the horizon. The sand felt cool beneath me and a soft wind from the south caressed my cheek.

"It is good," Ginevee said, looking at me intently.

"What?"

"You feel better, hmm." She placed her hand on my solar plexus. "Wonderful," she said. I couldn't help but giggle. When Ginevee said "wonderful," the word had a lilting quality. Her words, with the Koori and English accent mixed, sounded different and refreshing.

"This is the Dreamtime." Ginevee indicated the sunrise. "We pray together for peace among all peoples, yea. This peace could begin in Australia. We Koori people know how to live in harmony. We are peace-loving people. You have an enemy within yourself. You make that enemy, hmm. We all have enemies inside us. That's why we have enemies in the world." Ginevee was using her clapping sticks very softly to accentuate her words.

"What is my enemy?" I asked.

"Your enemy is your imbalance, yea."

"What kind of imbalance, Ginevee?"

Ginevee was wearing an old blue skirt and a flowered blouse. The light was reflecting crimson and violet across her broad nose and cheekbones. Her eyes were so deep set that I could not see them for the shadows.

"You have worked a lot with this, but I will teach you more. There's a man and a woman in you. They are out of balance. The world as you see it has not accepted your completeness and the world suffers from this. You suffer from this. In ceremony we will go to the Dreamtime and Oruncha will teach you once and for all."

"But how is being out of balance my enemy?"

"Because you don't see the world as it really is. When you're out of balance you attract the bugeen, the darkness, and you suffer. People suffer."

"Oh," I said. The sky was now ignited in orange and lavender fading into blood-red. Ginevee, using her clapping sticks, sang softly. I hummed along with her as the sun rose over the desert. The south wind made little whirls of sand around us. Then Ginevee lay her sticks in her lap.

"Today we will cut the small trees for the wurley. From now on just follow me, but keep silent. Remember that this is your last day with your enemy. Honor him with silence and no eating. Just drink a little, hmm? It's the law of the spirit." She smiled at me and pinched my cheek.

The rest of the day I spent with Agnes, Ruby, and Ginevee gathering saplings and more spinifex grass. Occasionally, I would catch sight of Buzzie watching us from behind a ghost gum tree, then she would disappear. I was too busy to wonder much about her.

"I can't imagine Lynn keeping her mouth shut all day," Ruby would taunt me as she folded the grass over and pulled it out of the ground like a true Koori woman.

"If it weren't for Lynn, July and I could be back in Tahiti wearing grass skirts and sipping piña coladas on the beach." Ruby poked Agnes and they laughed. Ginevee just shook her head.

To set up the wurley, we curved the saplings and tied some at the top. The structure was very simple and not unlike the sweat lodges of the American Indian. We secured the branches into the ground. We beat the porcupine grass, as the Koori called it because of the way it prickled, to get the dust out and then began to weave it. We wove it in and out of the saplings, singing all the while. Then we just lay branches of grass over the top.

The wurleys in the village were built a little higher and bigger than usual. This allowed for the small pole structure on which we put our mats for sleeping. I was glad to be up off the ground, because the air was able to circulate underneath. The grasses on the wurley also kept the air free from dust inside. At night we would take two small logs and put the ends together. In this way, by burning just the ends, the logs lasted a much longer time and the inside of the wurley stayed warm.

Ginevee had a habit of whistling while she worked. She didn't talk much, but taught me two short melodies that I kept whistling over and over to learn them perfectly. One melody was to announce that she was leaving, but only going a short distance. The other tune was a little longer and signaled that she was going farther away. Sometimes she would bend down and create a mournful song by blowing on a blade of grass. At those moments she looked like a young girl with a twinkle in her eye.

We finished the wurley toward evening. The demeanor of the medicine women changed. They became very unapproachable and serious. Ginevee stopped talking completely and began singing. She pointed off into the distance and began whistling the longer tune and pointing at me. I whistled the longer tune back. She nodded. I understood that we were going somewhere.

Ginevee and I built a small welcoming fire at the entrance of the wurley. She taught me a short sacred song that can only be translated in a vague way. It was a song of good and evil and it called in the great medicine spirit of Oruncha as the mediator. Ruby, Agnes, Ginevee, and I sat around the fire and we sang welcoming songs to the warrior who was about to visit. Then Agnes and Ruby moved off to opposite corners and continued humming and playing the clapping sticks that Ginevee had given them.

The fire had an odd quality to it. All the fires that we had built in the village would dance and crackle for several hours. This fire had an intense orange fireball at the center and practically no other light around it. It drew my attention.

"Watch the middle of the fire," Ginevee said.

I was spellbound by the slow flickerings of red-orange flame.

"What do you see?" she asked. She had taken something out of her clever bag. Ginevee and the other older women of high degree wore fairly large clever bags made out of kangaroo skin. They hung on fur string from their necks and under their left arms. She was working something in her fingers, but I was too fascinated by the flames to shift my gaze.

"I'm seeing what looks like a long face," I said. I have seen many things in a fire but never anything like this. The face in the fire had stolen my eyes. Then for a moment I saw the face of the tall sorcerer. His head was broad and his wild, matted hair hung down to his shoulders. His face was smeared with red ochre and white encircled his eyes, which shone blazing red like the predatory eyes of a leopard hunting in the moonlight. I gripped Ginevee's arm and gasped as the fire went out as if water had been thrown onto it. Tendrils of smoke filled the wurley and momentarily obscured Agnes and Ruby from view. Agnes rekindled the fire, keeping silent.

"When you see faces in the stones, the trees, or in the fires, you know that the spirit is there. It is up to you to sense if those spirits are good or bad. You can see faces anywhere. You must train yourself to see," Ginevee said, still holding something in her hands.

"This was not good. That sorcerer looks very evil," I said, finally letting go of her arm.

"You see, he knows now that you have welcomed him. He made the fire his own. He had to do that, yea. That confuses him and that is good. For the Koori people it is often punishable by death not to follow certain sacred laws. He must accept your welcoming fire, but he doesn't know what it means."

"Neither do I," I said.

Ginevee began to rock back and forth. Her eyes were closed and as her fingers traced the finely carved markings on a teardrop-shaped piece of flat stone she began to speak the language of the Dreamtime. She indicated that I should watch her hands. Ginevee's dark fingers were deeply creased. Gray ash had settled into the lines, accentuating them. With great reverence she touched the grooves in the stone with the softer pad of her forefinger.

"These designs are the secret eyes of our people. They take us to the sacred stories of the Dreamtime. I want to give you secret eyes." She took my hand and placed my fingers on the spiral on the stone face.

"You are the first white one ever to touch this sacred gooma. Look east to the morning sky and put your bare feet down on the shores of the red desert. Take this gooma for seeing and hold its light in your spirit. You will journey a long way with the eyes of a new leader. Look up to the sky and drink from the waters of the seven sisters and let them feed you from their unnamed river, yea. We will journey together, because we have met. Our feet will leave no path to follow, for we are children of the stars." She pressed the stone into the palm of my hand.

"You keep her and never lose her. She will help you find your way. Come now. We have an appointment with the Dreamtime."

I started to look around for my dilly bag.

"No. There is no need. Come quickly, it is time."

Ginevee grabbed me by the scruff of the neck and urged me forcefully to my feet and out of the village. She ran slowly with an easy, steady gait that I had been trying to imitate for weeks. It wore well in the red sand. But she had much longer legs than I did and I became tired much more easily.

The moon above was nearly full and illuminated the desert with elongated purple shadows. I was grateful that I was wearing my tennis shoes and a jacket. We set off in an easterly direction. This area of the land was unfamiliar to me. Very quickly it became more rocky underfoot. I stumbled often trying to keep up with Ginevee. Once I almost dropped the gooma. Ginevee must have felt it and looked around at me sharply. Finally we came to a gully and we slowed to a walk, picking our way down a slippery incline. The granite rocks that loomed up around us shown silvery-gray in the moonlight. From time to time Ginevee would explain to me who a stone was and which ancestral figure had left her imprint from the Dreamtime.

This gully had a strange unearthly feel to it. The boulders strewn around the walls and floor of the gully made it look like a valley on the moon. I walked very close to Ginevee. We went a long way as the moon climbed higher in the sky. She signed to me that I was to be quiet and approach this place of power with reverence. Then we turned a corner around a flat-topped boulder and Ginevee seemed to walk straight into a low bush and disappear. I panicked.

"Ginevee!" I cried out, but there was no answer. Frantically I walked over to the bush. A hand reached out and grabbed me. Ginevee stood in a crevice in the rock behind the bush.

"Shush," she said sternly, holding my arm. "Naked," she said in a quiet tone.

"What?" I whispered.

"Naked into the Dreamtime." She reiterated and began to tear off my clothes. In moments I was standing naked and cold in a gentle wind from the south.

"Here. This kangaroo skin has been worn by all our sisters in ceremony. Now it is your turn." She held it up to the moonlight. It had been perforated in a celestial design.

"This is the skirt of the seven sisters," she said. The

moon shone through the skin in tiny pricks of light in the same configuration as the Seven Sister Stars of the Pleiades.

"It is with great honor that I hold this out to you, yea."

She wrapped it around me and led me around the corner on a rock shelf. Before me was the mouth of a large cave. It stood black and vacant in the night. The mouth looked like it had one large tooth, for a strangely shaped rock stood at its entrance. Ginevee took me up to the stone.

"Place your hands here on the Women's Rock," she said. Ginevee put her hands onto a long, rounded section of stone. I put the gooma on a little ledge and placed my hands on the rounded rock. It was smooth as if many hands had been there before mine. The surface was worn almost slick. At first it was cool but it quickly warmed.

"Hold on," Ginevee ordered. "This is the Women's Rock used for women's initiations." She had moved to the entrance of the cave and was building a small fire.

Hold on, was right. Touching the rock, I felt like a current of electricity was coursing through my fingers and palms.

"Feel the spirit?" she asked.

"Yes. What is it?" I asked.

"You feel it, yea. That's the spirit of the Dreamtime, my daughter. Next time you will see the spirit."

Finally the sensation became too intense and I had to let go. I picked up the gooma and sat down next to Ginevee. Striations of clouds were blowing over the moon and the gully had become ominously dark. The clouds were moving fast in a high wind, causing eerie undulating shadows to pass over the granite rocks.

"Lay down here next to the fire," Ginevee whispered. She reached into her clever bag and produced a pouch. Opening it, she covered her hands with grease. Then she opened my kangaroo skin and rubbed grease on me from head to toe and on both sides of my body. Taking large handfuls of gray ash, she rubbed it into the grease.

"This bandicoot grease will protect you from the cold and it will let Oruncha know where you are." The grease had a strong insulating effect and I quickly was much warmer. I was even feeling sleepy.

"Now, my daughter, you will sleep."

"Where will I sleep?" I asked, suddenly awake and terrified that Ginevee was going to leave me.

"You will sleep here at the mouth of the cave. I will return for you in the morning." She placed her fingers over my mouth. "Quiet." Her gaze was ominous and firm.

"You mustn't scare the alcheringa away. The spirits are shy," she whispered, and was gone as if in a dream.

I lay by the fire, smelling of charcoal and wrapped in kangaroo. My teeth were chattering from fright, but I didn't dare move. I listened for the sound of Ginevee, but I could hear nothing but the wind. It was the quintessence of silence and felt heavy in my ears. I watched the fire spit occasional sparks into the sky. I was afraid to look or think about the cave, so I just stared into the fire and finally my eyelids got heavier and heavier. I was soon asleep.

I don't know what woke me. I thought I felt something on my shoulder, but nothing was there. The fire was only a jumble of hot coals and it was still dark out.

I saw something near the mouth of the cave. There was a movement on top of the Women's Stone and I heard sharp, clicking sounds. I sat up and scared away whatever it was. I next heard scraping noises and a lot of whooshing sounds. Something threw a gigantic shadow onto the left wall of the cave. My mouth fell open to scream, but nothing came out. My gooma stone dug painfully into my hand as I held onto it as if I were grasping onto my very life. The shadow jumped up and down and then large, fringed shadows flapped like two giant wings. I saw the head of a tall crow the size of an ostrich. It was hopping to the top of the rock. It was looking from side to side until it saw me. The crow's large, reddened eyes held my gaze like a stick in a vise. The bird loomed up and flapped its huge wings in an attempt to swoop down on me. It was screaming and I was screaming too as I ran through the fire toward the dark cave. From the right came an ear-splitting yell, and I saw a spear tether the bird to a desert oak. I turned just as another spear pierced my throat. The pain was excruciating and I fell.

The next thing I remembered was a tall, bearded warrior with a red band around his head. He was covered with sur-real red-ochre designs and carried me into the cave over his shoulder like a sack of millet. He walked a long time as I drifted in and out of consciousness. I felt my blood running over my face and down onto his back and legs. I knew I was dying, but I was too weak to move.

That was the last I remembered until I awoke lying by

a river in a grassy meadow. I listened to the sounds of the water, and to the bellbirds chirping in the bush, their voices like tiny, clear chimes. When I opened my eyes, everything seemed vague and far away. The sun was shining and the sky was blue, but I knew that this was a different world and that I was dead. I was no longer frightened or in pain. The big crow was standing nearby and the tall warrior was taking several crystals out of his own chest and putting them into the wound in my neck.

He stood up and, taking his stone ax, he sliced my body open from top to bottom as if I were a rainbow trout. The crow hopped over and the two of them pulled out my heart, stomach, and all my intestines. Everything they did seemed perfectly understandable. The warrior had smoothed the sand next to me so that now as they lay my entrails onto the ground they began to form designs. The crow leaped around, joyously picking up my intestines and laying them this way and that until several spirals were formed. The warrior added sacred stones to the design.

"My name is Oruncha of Chauritzi. I am a medicine spirit warrior. I am Crazy One, the Hermaphrodite. I have killed you that you may live. This is Crow, your nari, your medicine familiar. He is a clever bird and he will guard you always. You must die to enter the sacred Dreamtime of the alcheringa. Your gooma, your teacher's sacred stone, has much power. It called me well. I will give you your own gooma now. You have earned it. For all time walk in balance on our mother. Look at the design in the sand."

My spirit seemed to rise up out of my broken body and I looked down at the multicolored patterns made by my own insides. I was fascinated by the curves and their beauty.

"Give me your fingers," he said. It seemed a normal thing to do, so I did as I was told. His long gray hair fell over most of his aged black face. Very gently I felt him take my fingers.

"This spiral is your childhood," he said. As I traced my fingers over my large intestines I went into a dream that must have lasted for days. I saw the totality of my early life.

When I returned, he directed my fingers over a large rectangular design. "This represents the birth of your daughter and the life with your family and your friends." Again I slipped away into the years of experience. When I came back I traced a star design that was my heart shaped like a star.

Oruncha's kind eyes, like burning coals, looked into me. Finally we traced the design that marked the end of this life and the next life that was coming up.

"Whenever you retrace this design on your sacred stone you will recall perfectly the dream that is you. In knowing your dream, you can kill the dream. In taking your power, you can balance your power. You see, my sister, our sacred sand paintings are the ceremonies of our sky beings, or alcheringa, but if you look closely you will see the galaxies. See, here are the Seven Sisters just as they are in the Pleiades." I looked down and saw that he was right. The patterns looked like stars and protozoa all wrapped into one picture. I realized that I was made from stars and that the universe was within me and that it had always been that way.

"If you see clearly it will come true. What you design in your inner life will manifest in your outer life. See, it is all here. These markings are the designs of your tiniest cells that make up your body. These designs are also the sacred pattern of your destiny. Never forget what is here in the Dreamtime."

Then he placed a flat stone in my hand. It held the exact design of my intestines in the sand.

"This is your own gooma stone, a spirit-haunted stone from a sky warrior of the Dreamtime."

Very carefully he took all of my intestines, my heart, and my stomach and washed them clean of sand. He took a few more crystals from his own body and a few magical objects and closed me up, using his magical shell and other instruments and leaving the crystals inside of me.

After the incision was fully closed Crow hopped over by my side. He was still very much larger and more fierce-looking than any crow I'd ever seen. He looked like a crow-eagle. He had a handful of white feathers in his beak. He dropped them onto my stomach and Oruncha put the feathers along the incision and the hole in my neck. Then he took a fire stick from the fire, called a madagor, and ran it along the cut flesh to heat it and heal it. He sang many songs into me and into the cut. The crow cawed, but it didn't sound like cawing. He wailed and cried and turned his head so it lay on his shoulder and sort of groaned. I could smell my own flesh burning and my insides moving with a new life of their own.

The only real pain I had felt was the agonizing pierce of

Oruncha's spear. When the blood had been pouring out of me, I had felt like a balloon deflating, and during the rest of my time with Oruncha I had felt very weak and hazy as if I were floating on a cloud faraway. But pain had not been part of this experience until now. Under the aegis of Oruncha I knew I could learn how to use these crystals inside of me. His herculean abilities were beyond anything I had ever known and I felt a strong bond with this being. I didn't want to return from this valley of knowledge.

Oruncha touched me gently with his hands and made sure that I was healing. I felt prickly heat and a pulling sensation, but that was all.

"I will bring you back to life now. Is there anything you want to ask me, my sister?"

"Yes, Oruncha, how do I use the sacred objects inside of me?" I said, coughing and testing my voice. I did not sound like myself.

"I have shown you how to heal someone. Your personal gooma lives in your mind. To use its power, extract it from your body through your alcheringa eye." He pointed to his third eye.

"If a fella comes to you sick in body, I have placed crystals all through you so you can help. Feel this one now."

Oruncha pressed my stomach.

"Yes, I can feel it. There's a clear feeling." I was crying with excitement. He pressed several other parts of my body and again in each place I could feel the sensation of clarity.

"If a fella has a sick stomach, use the crystal in your stomach to heal. That's why I have put magical objects all over you. Keep your sacred gooma in your clever bag. You are a clever woman now." Before I could say anything else, he had slung me over his shoulder and was striding out of the valley, toward the entrance to the cave.

The next thing I knew it was morning. I was still wrapped in kangaroo and laying at the mouth of the cave. The sun was warming my face and I opened my eyes. At first it was hard to see and I felt a little nauseated. Ginevee and Agnes were helping me to a sitting position.

Then I remembered Oruncha and I tore open the kangaroo hide. There was no scar on my midsection, but dozens of white feathers were stuck to me. Suddenly I felt sick and threw up. Afterward, I felt better and struggled to my feet but I could hardly walk. I heard a forlorn cry of a crow. I looked off to the left, but all I saw was the shadow of a bird in flight.

"Don't talk, my daughter," Ginevee said, as the women helped me back toward the village. Several hours later when we walked into camp, the whole village was there to welcome us. The children kept pointing to my left shoulder, as did some of the women. "Alcheringa eyes," they kept saying.

"You have magical insides now. You have magical eyes," Ginevee said.

"Why are they all pointing at my shoulder and looking at me that way?" I asked.

"Because they sense the nari."

"What is the nari?"

"The nari is your familiar. It is your medicine spirit from the alcheringa.

"Your nari is very unusual. It is a crow-eagle, a bird that lives only in the Dreamtime. It will protect you well on mother earth and in the sky world."

I barely made it into my wurley before falling asleep. I could feel the crow-eagle sitting on my left shoulder as I closed my eyes.

The next day I felt very remote from everything going on. Finally Ginevee came and sat beside me. She held a bundle wrapped in bark in her arms.

"You must tell me, my daughter, of your journey with Oruncha," she said, watching me patiently.

I was in no mood to talk, but I knew I must. I recounted everything I could remember. Agnes and Ruby joined us and sat quietly against the back of the shelter. When I finished, it was dark outside and Agnes had built a fire. Ginevee seemed very pleased, indeed.

"I knew you were doomed!" Ginevee said with great excitement.

"What does that mean?" I asked, scared again.

"We say that someone is doomed when an apprentice is taken to the Dreamtime and cut into pieces. Don't worry, it is good. Wonderful!" she said, patting my shoulder.

"I always knew Lynn was doomed." Ruby giggled and poked Agnes, who smiled.

Ginevee unrolled her bark bundle and took out a deep pouch made of kangaroo hide on a fur string and handed it to me. Agnes and Ruby stood around. They all hugged me and patted me on the back.

"Look inside," Ginevee said after I had placed it over my shoulder and head.

I fumbled around inside and felt a flat stone. I pulled it out and, to my astonishment, found my own gooma. It was exactly as I had seen it in the Dreamtime. The design was identical. Ginevee next gave me a few carved pieces of wood.

"These are churinga. They were also part of your dreaming." I took them and felt their designs carefully before I put them in my bag.

"Here is a red-ochre stone. You will need it for paint," Agnes said, handing me a small red rock.

"This crystal is for dreaming," Ruby said, handing it to me.

"Don't forget to put the crystal that was given to you by our goddess, Dirrangun, into your clever bag. For now, keep my gooma, too. She will guide you."

My clever bag was beautiful and I was overwhelmed by its significance. Tears streamed down my face as I thanked them. As Ginevee left the wurley for the night she turned to me, her hair framing her face like a halo.

"Now you are prepared for your meeting with the devil. The bugeen is circling nearby in the darkness. Wear your clever bag while you sleep, my daughter, and dream well." Her strange eyes held a kind of flowing light, like the reflection of the sun on a dark pool.

Ginevee woke me at dawn.

"Why are you waking me?" I asked.

"Because today you are a new woman. You are a clever woman now and you will see the world differently. Get up and follow me."

I got up, but my head still didn't feel right. I slipped on my skirt and blouse but remained barefoot and followed.

"Where is Willy-D?" I asked.

"He's right over there." Ginevee pointed her long arm. Morning light was filtering down through the trees. There was still a slight mist on the ground and the mulga grass was sparkling with dew. High up on a branch was Willy-D. He hopped around. Ginevee was watching me intently through squinted eyelids.

Willy-D suddenly lifted his wings and his shape shifted into something larger and strange. With a dull popping sound, I felt an exchange of energy between the bird and myself. I felt a tugging sensation around my navel as he became the crow-eagle. He flew down onto the top of a wurley across from where Buzzie slept. His awesome eyes stared at me. I stared back in amazement.

"That's it, that's where we go." Ginevee must have seen him, too. "This is where I want you to sit." Ginevee patted the ground and we sat down, our backs against the grass-covered structure that the crow-eagle was standing on.

"Did you see the crow-eagle?" I whispered to Ginevee.

"Of course not, he's your nari. But I can sense him and sometimes see his shadow. He knows what you need to do," she said.

"What do I need to do?" I asked, placing my hand over my navel.

"You need to read the map," Ginevee said. She began to draw a design in the red sand with her dark finger.

"Ginevee, I'm confused. What map?"

"Why the map that the bugeen has left for you. There is always a clear map to the devil if you know how to *see*."

"I don't understand." Why did I always feel like such a stupid, frightened schoolgirl when something was about to happen?

"You have traveled to the sacred Dreamtime with Oruncha, the warrior god. You have sacred gooma and churinga inside of you. Your insides are magical now."

I kept watching Ginevee's finger drawing spirals in the sand.

"You have the alcheringa eyes, secret eyes. But you must learn to use them. This morning you saw your nari, your familiar, giving you directions! He showed you the place you needed to sit. You need to sit here because you need to observe someone. Your nari knows what you need to know. No one else on earth can *see* him. If someone else feels him, that is good, but you alone can *see* him. A few days ago you saw him as the pest Willy-D. That was your agreement with him. You saw him as a pesky fella, yea. You did not see the god in him, so he could not become one. Now you can see, truly *see*, hmm?"

"Yes, I guess so, but . . ." There was something inside of me that didn't want to accept this new responsibility.

"My daughter, it is very difficult to own your power." Ginevee placed her hand over mine with tenderness.

"Yes, I am afraid," I admitted. "But why?"

"You tell me," she said.

I looked around the village. A few women were moving around, stoking fires. They ignored us, as if we weren't even there.

"I don't know," I said, watching the smile on Ginevee's face.

"You became committed long ago to the path of knowledge. You are a warrioress of the rainbow. You live with a foot in two different worlds and that's the way it will always be. You live with dignity in the physical world and as a teacher in the world of spirit. It's like being stretched between an ancient past and the future in the stars, yea."

"How do you mean?"

"You are a white woman, dedicated to the translation of an ancient female and native culture into the white paradigm. Why? Because your people and many of ours have lost their truth, the wilderness of their own spirit. They hobble like cripples of the soul through their tiny lives. They have lost their ability to find secret eyes. Whether on your Wall Street or the Gunbarrel Highway, they have lost their map to the stars. Once it was easy, because every culture had a school for the mysteries and wise ones who were honored, yea? The earth mother reflects our inability to understand and now she is in great danger. Your body reflects the outer world just like your intestines in the Dreamtime reflected the patterns in the Pleiades. The world is a process of translation: spirit into substance, powerlessness into wisdom, ego into knowledge. At each stage of learning we must give up something even if it is a way of life that we have always known. There is no free lunch, my daughter, even on the road to the stars."

As Ginevee had been speaking, her voice had healed some of the fear inside me.

"I'm afraid of being different," I said.

"But you've always been different, yea."

"Yes, I guess so."

"Well then?" Ginevee was giggling.

"You're right. I know I'm kidding myself. But I get so lonely." Tears welled up in my eyes.

"It's all a nila-nila, Lynn. It's because you don't accept who you are. It's a mirage that any of us are alone." Ginevee pointed up to the moon that still shown in the night sky. "The moon is alone shining her wisdom onto mother earth and yet she is not alone. She is held onto a path, a transit of the universe by the galaxy that she belongs to. First you must accept that you are utterly alone. That, as you know, is the first lesson of power. And then you must realize that none of us can exist without the other, girl—none of us. We are not separate, we are all part of each other. What Buzzie does over there with her little finger effects you in some way. You and me, separate, are the teaching of the bugeen. That's the devil in you and you will learn that today, once and for all." Her black face was shiny in a ray of sunlight slanting down through the wurley.

"Oh, Ginevee, I understand what you say." I sighed heavily.

"But do you understand here?" She pressed my solar plexus and I felt something different, a new solidity or strength. I looked around the camp. My eyes felt different, like I was scanning. They felt like some kind of radar. I looked at Buzzie and suddenly I knew why I was sitting here in the dirt with Ginevee at dawn. As Ginevee had been talking and drawing in the red sand I had made an inexplicable decision. Another commitment had inched me a little further down the road to being a true clever woman.

I adjusted my clever bag under my arm and nodded to Ginevee. I had decided to own the knowledge that I had been given by Oruncha. I realized that Oruncha had opened the door to power, but I had to walk through and take power for myself. No one can give you power if your spirit is not available. Ginevee and I just looked at each other. Then she smiled knowingly and gave me a hug.

"Watch her for several hours," Ginevee said.

She got up to leave. I needed no explanation from her. Ginevee knew that I had seen Buzzie in a new way. I knew that I needed to observe her carefully. I had seen a darkness around her that I had not been able to see before. She was the map Ginevee had been talking about. I didn't know how to read it, but I knew Buzzie would give me the answer if I watched long enough. Ginevee had brought the basket Buzzie had made for me. She dropped it in my lap as she left, whistling her "short distance" tune and winking at me.

I kept shifting back and forth between being a frightened schoolgirl and a clever woman. Part of me wanted to whine and run after Ginevee, asking her nonsensical questions, and part of me was real tired of that weak position in life. I ran my fingers over Buzzie's basket and realized that every time

I looked inside of it I was filled with a sticky, sweet feeling of depression, which lingered long after my thoughts moved elsewhere.

Then I heard a voice deep inside of me. It instructed me to make my next decision with great care. "Make this decision so that whatever the outcome, you are affected in a positive way. Be sure and weigh the consequences of every action before you make it."

Without thinking, I began to draw a design in the sand. The first lines told me about the beginning of my visions of the nari. The next design spoke of my talk with Ginevee. The spiral I now was drawing told of my new way of seeing Buzzie. By drawing and thinking at the same time, I enabled myself to see in a much more efficient way. The foolish chatter in my head ceased and my intent became profoundly stronger.

Buzzie walked around the corner of her wurley and stopped in her tracks when she saw me. For some unknown reason, I had expected her not to notice me, like everyone else. She looked into my eyes and I watched her belligerence turn to fear.

"Why you sit there?" she asked, nervously.

"Seemed like a good place to sit," I said, fingering the basket and smiling.

"What you drawing there?" She walked over and squatted down next to me. As she did so, I saw my nari loom above her. Buzzie saw my eyes look up above her and she shivered and stood up.

"I go get me sweater, yea," she said.

"Yea," I said, continuing to draw. I didn't know why the nari had done that, but I kept on drawing the story. It was dawning on me that the design was my map and that the nari was like an extension of my body mind. It already knew what was going to happen; I just had to be smart enough to follow.

When Buzzie came back out of her wurley she was different. Her eyes seemed sunken and very guarded. She would not look at me, but I noticed a darkness on her left side. It could only be described as a sort of blackish cloud about ten feet high that seemed attached to her in some way. I couldn't believe that I hadn't noticed it before. With a jolt, I realized that I must be *seeing*. For a moment I saw my nari jumping around on top of her wurley. I felt a surge of newborn pride.

I could *see*! When Buzzie saw the radiant smile on my face, she lurched backwards and ran into her wurley and out of sight. I heard a lot of things falling inside her place and I became concerned that I had hurt her in some way. I put the basket down and got up, going over to her doorway.

"Buzzie," I called to her. I wasn't able to see anything inside except for some vague shadows.

"What you want from me?" I heard Buzzie demand.

"I don't know," I said, walking a few steps inside. I looked around as my eyes adjusted to the darkness. Buzzie stood defiant in the filtered light. All manner of bones and odd-looking things hung from the curve of the ceiling. Too late I heard the warning scream from the nari. Buzzie had turned her body around to the right and out of the left side of her head came a vision or the real face of Two Hearts, the sorcerer from my dream. He was screaming, blood dripping from his hands as he reached out and grabbed me by the throat.

I tried to yell, but Two Hearts was strangling me. I could not utter a sound. He threw me around the wurley as if I were a paper bird on a string. I tore at the grasses and branches trying to stop the spinning. He smashed the wurley into a heap of rubble using my flailing body as a club. He threw me into Buzzie time and time again until we were both lying in a beaten heap under a mound of grass and the demolished wurley. I heard screams of alarm from the women in the village. The last thing I remember seeing was the nari flying after a dark whirlwind spinning out of the village. Then they disappeared over the hill. I heard Ginevee and Ruby as they pulled away the branches and debris.

"The bugeen, the bugeen," everyone was saying. Buzzie was unconscious. The other women tended to her. Ginevee and Agnes gently lifted me out of the mess. I was covered with scratches and I felt bruises on my throat. I was so terrified that all I could do was sob. They took me back to my wurley and set me down carefully. Ruby, Agnes, and Ginevee felt me all over for broken bones. When they realized that nothing was broken, by some miracle, they all breathed a deep sigh of relief.

"Can't leave Lynn on her own for a minute. Look at the mess she made of that poor girl's house," Ruby said, tenderly stroking my forehead.

"My God, Ginevee, what happened?" I asked.

"I was going to ask you the same thing," she said.

Suddenly there was a tall shadow in the doorway. I jumped with terror, not being able to see who it was.

"Ah ho," Agnes said as Ginevee stood up to greet She Who Walks With The Wind.

"Welcome," Ginevee said.

The tall woman came in and looked at me. I noticed that she was wearing a very old clever bag. She was very thin and her hair hung in reddish-blonde ropes to her shoulders. She smiled at me. Her front tooth was missing and she seemed very proud of that. I knew that in some tribes, having a front tooth knocked out was part of initiation. I was glad that I wasn't in her tribe.

She sat down next to me and held her long, narrow hands over my body. They seemed to calm me, or maybe it was the attention that was comforting. Whatever, I finally stopped crying.

Then she held her finger to her lips. Everyone was silent. She looked around at us all; her gaze was imposing. We watched her with fascination. She held her fist to her heart and then opened her fingers. She continued to sign in the most beautiful and graceful way. After about ten minutes Ginevee took the hands of She Who Walks With The Wind and held them. Tears were in her eyes.

"She Who Walks With The Wind says that she enters our village with love. She says that she has been watching you, Lynn, for a long time and she sees the story that lives inside you. She knows that it must be told and she wants to help. She wants you to know that Two Hearts was a feather foot in her tribe a long time ago. Power took him and made him a crooked man. Very evil, she says. He was hurt in some way and his spirit never returned. One by one he killed everyone in his village, including She Who Walks With The Wind's husband and children. He tore out her tongue, for she was the keeper of the song, and left her for dead. She says that somehow his loved ones were killed by women sorcerers and his life is spent in revenge. She doesn't know what happened that made him so evil, but she has walked with the wind ever since, following him, and trying to warn people of his evil."

We all looked at each other, wide-eyed. Suddenly my cuts and scratches were forgotten.

"What do you mean my story . . . Do you mean my

story has something to do in some intimate way with Two Hearts?" I asked, my voice sounding like a squawk.

"Yes, my daughter, I'm afraid so," Ginevee said. "But don't worry, you are a clever woman."

"Not clever enough, I fear." I tried to get up, but every bone in my body ached.

The rest of the day was spent with the other women rebuilding the wurley. My right leg was badly bruised, but I limped around. The camp women were careful to stay between me and Buzzie. Buzzie was cut and scraped, too. Nothing had been broken but her spirit. She would not look at me. I had told Ginevee, Ruby, Agnes, and She Who Walks With The Wind about Two Hearts and how he had appeared in the wurley.

"You stepped into her shadow," Ginevee said. "I thought you knew never to step into the shadow of a sorcerer."

"How would I know that?" I asked. "So what does that mean?"

"It means that you open yourself to very great danger, even death."

"Oh," I said, remembering the voice in my head that had warned me not to make a move without careful deliberation. I told them about that.

"I feel good, because the outcome was positive. Now I know that Buzzie is connected in some way with Two Hearts," I said.

"Yes, but we have to know exactly what the connection is, my daughter. You have done well. And you have learned something else," Ginevee said, rubbing her large flat palms together.

"What is that?" I asked.

"You have learned that your new abilities can get you into a kind of trouble you have not known before. We live in an earthly dimension where everything seems real. Just above and below that seeming reality are other realities. The maps into those dimensions read differently than the ones here. Never follow them in the same way. In other dimensions you can never indulge yourself in a human way; it will mean your death. The maps leading there are trickster maps. They will look the same as ours, but they are not," Ginevee said.

"What do you mean by 'indulge' myself?"

"To be a warrioress means to stand in the center of your

power and never budge. That means to be aware of everything and still be humble. Today you were supposed to witness Buzzie and discover her darkness, not worry."

"But I wasn't worried," I said.

"Lynn, think back. You were worried about hurting Buzzie. That's your big weakness. You're always worried about hurting someone and, worse than that, you couldn't imagine how all that seeing with your nari was really happening," she said.

"Yes, you're right. It was all crazy," I said.

"You were there to do one thing—observe."

"You mean I should not have gone into the wurley?"

"No, you should not have gone into the wurley and almost gotten killed." Ginevee pinched my cheek. "But it's important to understand why.

"By following her for the wrong reasons—worry and curiosity—you lost your stance as a warrioress. You took the bait. You lost your balance by moving off your center. You were no longer at ease. But it was a good lesson and you're okay. That is the important thing now," Ginevee said. I noticed that she had her bags of crystals with her, and she saw that I was looking at them.

"We're going to have a crystal seeing ceremony tonight. The village is already preparing the ground. Everyone understands what's happened and understands what must be done." Ginevee had her hands in her crystal pouches.

"What must be done?" I asked.

"You will see, yea. Just rest now. It will be a long night."

"You made designs in the sand, Lynn. May I go and look at them?" Ginevee asked.

"Yes, of course. Why?"

"Because they are an important map to the other side. They could help us tonight. Hold your miwi-miwi now, your power, you are going to need it. Watch over the crystals, my daughter," Ginevee said.

As Agnes and Ruby left with her, She Who Walks With The Wind remained, sitting with a large, rough smoky quartz crystal in her lap. She was resting against the back of the wurley with her legs straight out in front of her on the ground like long black sticks. Her eyes were closed. Her chest moved in the even rhythm of a deep sleep. I closed my eyes and was instantly asleep. Australia had the most extraordinary effect on me. I could go to sleep anywhere at anytime. And

I could sleep easily for twelve hours. The sun went down early and came up late. Some of the women told me that it was the dryness and the static electricity that made us so sleepy from time to time. Whatever the cause, I slept well and it was dark when Ginevee came for me. I felt rested, although I was stiff and sore.

"Come, I am going to paint you for the ceremony," Ginevee told me. "Better yet, I'm going to teach you how to paint yourself."

I followed Ginevee out into the village. The camp was transformed. Women were preparing the ground with a papunya painting, or ground painting. She didn't want me to see that yet, but I caught a glimpse of white dots in a spiral. The women were sitting in groups of twos and threes, preparing their bodies as a living art form.

Ginevee and I sat down with her sister-in-law, Mandowa. She was the elder woman who had been the maker of the ceremony when we first arrived. Since then, we had seen each other and nodded in greeting, but that was all. She was a large woman, heavier and bigger-boned than Ginevee, with short-cropped, gray hair wrapped in a bandana. I saw that her front tooth was missing when she smiled hello to me; her grip was like a feather when we shook hands. I had noticed that all the Koori people shook hands very lightly, to test the spirit in the other person's touch. But Mandowa's hands were like two hard baseball mitts. She had obviously been preparing colors by grinding most of the day.

"Usually, sisters-in-laws prepare each other for ceremonies," Ginevee said. "We are sisters, so we will paint each other."

We stripped down so we were standing naked in front of the fire. Mandowa took her big flat hands, covered them with white clay, and began patting my face, shoulders, upper arms and thighs.

"When you dance at night the firelight catches only the white clay and the rest of your body disappears into the blackness. Soon you will dream your own designs, hmm. For now I will put the dreaming onto your body and everyone will see you dance the dream, yea. I put white pipe clay on your thighs. The keeper of the white clay is a giant kangaroo." She wiped off her hands as Ginevee applied the white clay to her own body.

"For the red blood of our hunting and fighting ancestors

of the alcheringa, I draw this design over your heart." Saying this, Mandowa took a brush and drew an intricate design of dots and circles on me.

"I want you to remember your dreaming last night, Lynn. Take this brush of spinifex fibers full of red ochre and put that dreaming onto my forehead," Ginevee said.

I took the brush that was dripping with color and began to draw. What happened was a beautiful swirling design; I felt proud.

"Now place yellow ochre here and here," she said, indicating the sides of her face. "The yellow represents the sacred mountains of our land. It is the sacred color of Chirutja," Ginevee said, looking quite pleased herself.

"Edge that design in black ochre, yea," Mandowa said. "It is made from the fires, the sacred fires that the alcheringa used to form us."

Mandowa picked up her coolamon, which was filled with feathers covered in red ochre.

"This is portulaca bird's down mixed with ochre. It is only used in sacred ceremonies of the highest degree. For ordinary bunguls or corroborees we use plant down," Mandowa said. As she spoke, she took out a knife and before I knew it she had made a small slice on my arm.

"Ouch," I said, surprised.

She squeezed the cut for blood.

"Bird down is sacred and is held to your body by human blood," Mandowa said. In moments she had transformed my face and Ginevee's into a sculpture of feathers, making us unrecognizable. We both had white feathers across our brows, cheeks, and noses, with red fluff covering our cheeks, chins, and chest. Mandowa tied a clump of larger white feathers into Ginevee's hair at the very top of her head. Then she placed some fluff on our breasts.

"This is for the kangaroo clan that Ginevee belongs to. Because you are kindred, you belong, too," Mandowa said.

Ginevee and I began to work on Mandowa. We looked like giant, feathered ghosts dotting and smearing her body with white clay and then red, yellow, and black ochres. When we were through, we stood giggling and looking at each other. I could feel the true power of disguise and the dream designs. We were like spirits of ourselves walking an uncharted path into the ancient and timeless rituals of magic.

Several of the women had begun singing. The papunya

was finished. As we joined the circle in a shallow gully near the campfires around the sand painting, I realized that I recognized no one, not even Agnes and Ruby. The papunya painting glowed in the firelight. Several fires surrounded the fifteen-foot area. The sand painting consisted of ordered dots in spirals with swirls and designs in various areas. The design told of the Dreaming of the Black Swan. Ginevee, in this instance, was the Black Swan Dreaming. The darker designs denoted the cliff areas around our camp. Two swirls represented Buzzie and Two Hearts. The spiral represented the rest of us. Ginevee and a woman I thought to be She Who Walks With The Wind began placing crystals onto the painting. The didgeridoo was droning loudly. It was accompanied by clapping sticks. The women's singing and the instruments' music was making me quickly drunk. I danced and leaped through the fire smoke with the others in a mounting fury, as if we were in a collective dream. I pounded the ground with my bare feet, sweat shining through the white ochre.

I felt like I was taxiing down a dirt runway in a small plane. Engines were revving up somewhere inside me and the ground underneath was vibrating and throwing up sparks. And then everything started to move. The noise was deafening and my body shifted first to the left and then to the right. There were clicking sounds and a whooshing and grinding almost like a jet motor getting ready for takeoff. Light played over my body and bright flashes were in my eyes. I saw the nari as I lifted off the ground into some kind of cloud space. I could see the red earth beneath me dotted with blue-green smears of oily-looking figures that stretched for miles into the serene blue distance. There were designs, like gigantic bark paintings come to life. They noticed me, but didn't move toward me in any way. Great boiling funnels of cloud and light loomed on the horizon. I could see the nari floating on spread wings into one of the lit caverns in the distance. I knew I was to follow him. In the process of that knowing, I began to move instinctually in that direction. Lightning flashes split the clouds and I saw what could only be described as a school of dolphin spirits. I remembered that lightning was the juraveel of the dolphins. They swam ahead of me into the cloud-like funnels and disappeared.

For a short time everything went dark, and then I was

back on the ground in the circle of the medicine women and the crystals. I wondered if all of us and the entire sand painting that was our ceremony had lifted off the ground like a giant flying saucer and had been catapulted into the Dreamtime. It wasn't important. All that mattered was the information that Ginevee and She Who Walks With The Wind were extracting from the crystals.

Ginevee lifted her bare arms and chest over her huge crystal in the center of the circle. Her body was embellished with red, white, and yellow ochre swirls and dots. Her ancient skin hung in ripples from her arms, making her look like a primeval lizard with wings. Her pendulous breasts swung over the crystals like great striped clever bags, as if giving a painted and hallowed blessing from the Great Mother Goddess herself. The didgeridoo bellowed relentlessly with the clapping sticks. There was chanting and the eerie calling of the alcheringa spirits of the Dreamtime by the Bull Roarer somewhere nearby. I felt the rivers of my blood, all my past and future lives merging with the others into one great effort to understand the sorcery of Two Hearts and Buzzie.

Out of the central crystal, belonging to Ginevee, came flashes of light in clear rainbow colors. It caused my ears to fill, and I kept trying to clear the pressure it made me feel in my head. Suddenly the crystal seemed to split apart and a vision of a snarling dark monster, a human, appeared from out of its center. Ginevee was speaking to it in Koori as it slowly turned itself around. I saw then that the monster was Two Hearts himself in an almost transparent gray form. I felt a wrenching pull inside my solar plexus, as if I too were about to tear apart like the crystal. Ginevee grabbed me and pulled me next to her, presumably so I could see better.

"There, right there," she said as she painted with a stick. In a piercing ray of light I saw the Rainbow Serpent. He was an epicene creature, a male that possessed a womb. He undulated back and forth. His scales reflected rainbow hues of color. I recognized my sacred twins standing within his womb. I could see them standing between one crystal world and another, one that appeared to exist within the Serpent.

"They are waiting for you," Ginevee said.

"What do you mean?" I asked, bewildered.

"You must eat of yourself," Agnes said.

"I don't understand."

"Your sacred twins are the male and female parts of your self, my daughter. You must first eat of your male side," Ginevee told me.

"And how do I do that?"

"Reach into the crystal and into the womb of the Rainbow Serpent; take your male self. Eat him like a witchiti grub."

"Here, I'll help you," she said, watching the stunned look on my face.

Ginevee took my fingers and guided them into the crystal and into the Serpent's womb where my twins stood. My body was going through muscular convulsions; my abdomen and womb were contracting as if I were in the first stages of labor. I felt as if I were expelling the sacred twins and compelling them all at once. Zoila, my medicine woman in the Yucatán, had taught me about them. The sacred twins are the male and female warriors within each of us. They live in the crack between the worlds and they translate your unconscious thoughts so you can understand them consciously. Then you no longer have to depend on your dreams for insight, because you can meet with your Sacred Twins directly, Zoila had told me. I had met with them often since. They were strong entities of energy, but they had felt unbalanced and I hadn't known how to fix that.

"You must eat of the male side of yourself," Ginevee urged me again. "It is the only way to freedom. The only way to balance."

The singing of the women was louder now.

"But I'm afraid. I can't."

"Lynn, you must. It is the only way to rid yourself of the darkness and imbalance." As she said this, I saw a large dark cloud descend on the ceremony. I knew it was Two Hearts. Impulsively I grabbed my male warrior and popped his head into my mouth. Closing my eyes, I chewed it up and swallowed it.

"You must eat of your opposite, my daughter. You are not just a single color of the rainbow. Become like the Rainbow Serpent. Eat of the balanced fruit of his womb and carry all the colors of the Rainbow. It is the good tucker of the Dreamtime. To absorb your male, you must become a cannibal and digest all that is your opposite side. It is the law of the spirit," Ginevee said. I placed the whole of his body into my mouth like I had seen Kooris eat grubs and I swallowed. He went down easily.

"Now you must eat of your female warrior. It is good," Ginevee said.

I could see that Ginevee was also aware of the dense blackness that had entered the circle. As I reached for my warrioress I felt the blackness try to get behind me. I knew it was trying to stop me; I didn't understand why. I grabbed her and swallowed her quickly. It was much easier to eat my warrioress, because she was more familiar to me. I saw the cloud try to envelop me, but it grew smaller as Agnes and Ruby protected my backside with their crystals.

Then an even stranger thing happened. I had always experienced my maleness and femaleness as being part of me and yet outside of me, or perhaps outside of my control. By eating them, they became absolutely a part of me. It was almost sexual, as if they had mated in an ultimate way and somehow through my own digestive process had become truly one. In a sense they were gone and in a sense they were more a part of me than ever, but as a single entity. A balanced me.

I felt quite different, as if my spirit were nourished and full. When I had experienced my twin warriors with Zoila, I had first become aware of the distinct male and female sides of myself and had made contact with them. Now I realized that the sense of imbalance that I had felt was because of their need to be mated or merged. I looked into the crystal where the Rainbow Serpent was moving.

"You have eaten of my blood, sister. Now you must eat of my body. I am your alcheringa, your teacher in the Dreamtime. I too must become one with your body. Become a cannibal and eat your sky warrior."

These were the words of a Koori voice I heard in my head, but somehow I knew it was the voice of the Rainbow Serpent. "Consider this well. You are already dead. You have already been eaten by me, the Rainbow Serpent."

The women had started to dance again around the sand painting. Ginevee, Agnes and Ruby and I still sat in the center with She Who Walks With the Wind. I heard the ever increasing whirring of the Bull Roarer. The sound seemed to be emanating from inside my head. I kept staring into the crystal. The Rainbow Serpent was moving in a spiral circle, faster and faster. Out of the center of the circle a face began to emerge. I recognized the face as that of Guboo Ted Thomas, a seventy-year-old elder from the Yuin tribe in the south. I have known him and his family since he visited California two years before. He is responsible for preserving many of the sacred lands and traditions of his people. Now, as my eyes met his, he smiled at me. In one hand he held Buzzie and in the other he held Two Hearts.

"Eat of the highest master within you. I am here to tell you this. There must be no separation between you and Ginevee. Ginevee is your Koori mother. Become one with her by eating the Rainbow Serpent."

He held the Serpent out to me. I let it curl around my fingers and then ate it quickly.

"Only now can you mate with the All Mother." Guboo's face was radiant and pleased. He wore a red headband and his gray hair touched his shoulders. "This is your teaching on this ancient Koori land. That is your gift from the Rainbow Serpent. I hold two warriors here who have fallen into evil ways, yea. You have been called across many seas to help us. It is your task here. In absorbing your own dividedness you will help cure theirs. Many Kooris have lost their dreaming because of your people. Return the sacred Dreamtime to Buzzie and Two Hearts."

"But how can I possibly do that?" I asked. My voice was a whisper.

Guboo handed me two white feathers. "Take these to Buzzie and have her look at you through them. You will know what to do."

Guboo smiled at me and was gone. The music around me was deafening. She Who Walks With The Wind brought Buzzie into the sand painting circle. Buzzie sat down across from me. For the first time, she slowly looked at me. I saw anger and fear in her eyes. Her whole body was painted with black clay. I handed her the two white feathers. Buzzie took the feathers and held them over each eye.

"Look at me," I said.

Buzzie looked at me through them. She became even more fearful.

"Tell me what you see, Buzzie."

"When I look through the feathers I only see you as transparent, yea. I see only your skeleton, your spirit self," she said.

"Give them back to me," I said. Her words had, as Guboo had promised, told me what I was to do. I looked at her through the feathers, putting one feather up in front of each eye. I could see that there was a spirit spear thrust into her solar plexus and I knew it belonged to Two Hearts. I gave one feather to Ginevee. She put it up to her eye and I could tell she could see the spear as well. I reached out to take the spear, but Ginevee stopped me.

"Remember, you must never change the destiny of someone's life without permission," she said.

"But she has been possessed by something very evil," I answered.

"My daughter, that may be her destiny."

"But how could evil be anyone's destiny?" I asked.

"We are only on this earth to become enlightened, to reach the All Mother in the sacred Dreamtime. It is possible that she needs to live through this evil on her own and to learn something from it that is none of our business. We must stop the ceremony now and wait. The Dreamtime will give us a sign. Power will tell us what we are to do. I'm sorry, my daughter, it is law."

Ginevee and I had been whispering. No one else, not even Buzzie, could hear us. I took the feathers and wrapped them in a bark bundle. Ginevee smugged Buzzie and everyone with smoke from sacred herbs and wrapped up her crystal. We sang a while longer and then began to sweep away the sand painting. Buzzie looked bewildered and relieved. Everything was back to normal, or so it appeared. We went back to our wurleys just at dawn, after we had washed each other in the creek. The river bled red and yellow as the light of the rising sun began to reflect on the waters.

❖

The self, anti-self in dire embrace.

—Theodore Roethke

❖

CHAPTER EIGHTEEN
❖❖❖❖❖❖
A SORCERER'S FOOTSTEP

When I awoke around midday, I heard the usual sounds of the villagers. The children were playing with dingo pups and I could smell cooking on the fires. I felt good as I put on my skirt and shirt, as if I had come home after a long journey. Everything I touched felt different, as if my fingers were more sensitive than usual, as if I was gently vibrating with an innate life force.

I was looking in the shadows of the wurley for my sandals when, for an instant, the darkness seemed like the pupil of a large eye and the filtered light coming through the spinifex grass was the iris. The iris contracted and the pupil expanded and opened. For a moment I was pulled into its vision. I knew without a glimmer of doubt that all things in the universe were connected by a living truth that would not relent its continuing search for wholeness until every form of life was united.

"Thank the Great Spirit, Sleeping Beauty has been kissed by the toad and miraculously wakes up," Ruby said, coming into my wurley in a huff.

"Ruby, you have your fairy tales mixed up," I said, giving her a quick hug.

"Well, at least we're going to something called a station.

I can't wait to be around some normal people. We've been waiting for you, you know." Ruby stood with her hands on her hips.

"What station and where?" I asked.

"How should I know? I suppose it's somewhere in the Outback of Australia." Ruby sat down, made a face, then pulled one of my sandals from underneath her and threw it to me. Ginevee came in carrying her granddaughter Skeeter, who had been named after the mosquitos. She was about four, with short blonde hair, black button eyes, and a big smile. All the children seemed to call Ginevee grandmother, but Skeeter was her favorite. Often they would sleep together or play string games in the morning or evening.

"She has the spirit," Ginevee would say, pinching the little girl's black bottom.

Skeeter loved to sit at my feet with her dingo puppy and watch me write. I would give her an extra pencil and some paper and she would draw pictures of Spot the pup or draw big circles with lots of squiggly lines representing my blonde hair. This would make us both laugh and she would roll around in the dirt with Spot barking. We all loved Skeeter. She was wise beyond her years. Her eyes held the story of her people. She would one day be a clever woman of high degree.

Agnes, Ruby, and I gathered our dilly bags as Ginevee led Skeeter back to her mother. The four of us uncovered the jeep, pulling dusty branches off the hood and fenders. After getting in and brushing dust off the seats I turned the key in the ignition. As always, I was amazed that it started. The mechanism of engine and car seemed surreal after the essential, primitive life of the village.

For the next two hours, I navigated the Land-Rover down an old dry riverbed.

"Just take it easy," Ginevee said from the back seat. She was sitting next to Ruby, and Agnes sat next to me in the front seat.

"Just follow that deer track, now, off to your right. That's it, just take it easy. It gets pretty rocky round the bend, so better slow down a bit."

She wasn't kidding when she described the road as a deer track. I could barely see any road at all. Mostly there were just patches of mulga grass that had been flattened down. Once I stopped the car and got out to test the softness of the ground ahead. To my surprise the sand was very firm.

"Not to worry," Ginevee said with a big grin.

"Well, I'm glad everyone's in a good mood," Ruby said. "It's about time, what with flying wurleys and sorcerers jumping out of perfectly good crystals. I just don't know how to take all you bush folk. It all seems pretty wild to me." Ruby split some long curly strands of grass as she spoke.

"What are you doing with that grass, Ruby?" I asked, looking in the rear-view mirror and almost hitting a tiny spinifex hopping mouse that jumped frantically out of the way.

"That nice Buzzie is going to show me how to make a basket when I get back from the station. Isn't that nice of her?" Ruby had started to shred the grass all over Ginevee and the back seat. She was giggling wildly to herself, her gray hair sticking out in all directions.

"Ruby, could you try not to make such a mess?" By mistake I hit a big rut and Ruby and Ginevee were thrown against the front seat. Pieces of grass went everywhere. I started to sneeze from the tiny bits catching in my nose.

"These pieces of grass just happen to be from your basket." Ruby stared toward me bug-eyed in the rear-view mirror. "Didn't it ever occur to you that your depression had something to do with the basket Buzzie gave you?"

I looked at Agnes, then back at Ruby. I was driving slower now.

"No, it never occurred to me," I said.

"Well, it did to me. Here's your red ribbon back. See, old women aren't just useless. We're good for something, yea?" She laughed at the silly sound of her own Aussie and Koori accent. We all laughed as we pulled onto a better dirt road and saw a few cars and what looked like a store in the distance.

Ginevee abruptly became silent. Her happy expression disappeared under her protrusive forehead; her eyes closed and she began to sing with her clapping sticks. She had a dark brooding look.

Agnes and I looked at each other and shrugged our shoulders. In a few miles we had reached Matthew's Station. Several desert oak trees stood around the lonely windswept buildings. The bark on the oak trees was several inches thick, like heavy fish scales.

"If a bush fire comes through here those trees are the

only thing that will survive, because of that bark," Ginevee told me as she glanced at a police car that was parked nearby.

"Yunga," she said under her breath.

"What do you mean?" we all asked, almost in unison.

"Means octopus," Ginevee said, indicating the cop car. "If I'm in the water and an octopus puts an arm around me here," she said, making a sweep with her arms, "and then he puts an arm around me there, and then he got ya, yea. Yunga means 'octopus' or 'police.' Police so crooked they can't lay straight in bed around here," she said, taking my arm as we walked toward the building that said "Supermarket" on a red and white sign over the door. Ginevee stopped and looked at the small square building, covered with bent tin. Very quietly she turned to us. She made a round sweep with her arms.

"This is the shape of the universe—round, not like this square building." Her tone was strange.

We entered the store, not knowing what to make of the obvious change that had come over Ginevee. Inside were close, dimly lit aisles of grocery goods. Flypaper hung from the ceiling, covered with hundreds of dead flies. Two white children ran around through the aisles and a fat man and woman stood behind an old cash register at the checkout counter.

Agnes, Ruby, and I made for the refrigerator in search of ice cream and soft drinks. The woman with short dark hair and a dirty white sweater watched us over her spectacles. She was elbowing her husband with an aghast look on her face. We must have been a sight. I looked down at my skirt and shirt, which were layered in red dirt, and then I caught sight of myself in the chrome molding on the refrigerator. I looked like an imposter of myself. My eyes had the wild look of a wolf and my hair was the same color as my kangaroo sandals and hung in semi-mats about my red-smudged face. I started to giggle. Then I heard clapping sticks and a forlorn song coming from the heart of the store. We hurried down the aisle and around the corner. There, sitting on the floor, her legs crossed like fire-making sticks, was Ginevee.

The shelves of canned tuna fish, Q-tips, Tampax, and motor oil towered above her as she sang a Koori song with tears rolling down her dirt-covered cheeks, leaving little shiny rivers of black skin. We went over to her, not knowing what was happening. We sat next to her in respectful silence until she was finished with her song. When she was through, Agnes asked her why she was singing there.

"This is the place where our alcheringa ancestors entered the Dreamtime. They climbed up our sacred tree. It was a giant ghost gum that had been here forever. For thousands of years our people came here every year to honor our ancestors that gave us our life. One day the government came in and wanted to put a station right here on our sacred ground. And they called us clowns," she said, wiping her tears, "as they cut down our tree."

"Why clowns?" I asked.

"Because we are, we are all clowns. To us we are the clowns. Can't make a world without clowns. You go to a circus and the clowns make you laugh. The government laughs at us. They keep us good. Like you give a dingo a bone to keep him quiet, you give him just a little. We are clowns. Circus no good without clowns, yea?"

We agreed with her and didn't know what else to say. We sat on the floor with her for several minutes.

"In our way, the clown is very sacred. The clown makes everyone laugh, but the clown also does one very important thing," Agnes finally said.

"What's that?" Ginevee asked.

"The clown walks into all the sacred rounds, even the ones she's not supposed to be in. She tests the people and the ceremonies to see if they are true. She is the highest one," Agnes said and then hummed to herself. She took a pinch of tobacco.

"So that our people may live," she said and let the tobacco fall to the floor with a circular motion. Ruby and I did the same. Ginevee's face brightened.

"The clown is sacred—the same for us, yea," Ginevee said. "It is good that we speak the same language, hmmm. Let's get some of the billabong candies for my granddaughter. She loves those so much," Ginevee said, getting up and starting down the aisle.

I looked at the large wooden fan on the ceiling, the rows of cellophane and plastic packages in bright colors, the fat whites and the ancient native women with their weathered skin like the aging crust of the red earth center of Australia, and I wondered. How much of the ancient wisdom can we preserve if a tribe that has been on the earth in harmony for possibly fifty thousand years was not allowed to save even one sacred tree against the churl of civilization? What are the sacred sites without living tradition to support them?

For a moment I wanted to get desperately depressed. Then a voice inside me said, "We are only at the beginning of a new way of life. The once sacred ways of nature and the All Mother will merge with science and space and the pebbly rivers of the Milky Way will run with the rivers of ochre and the blood of our ancestors in the sacred Dreamtime. The best is yet to come." It was the faraway voice of Guboo Ted Thomas, the elder of the Yuin tribe I had seen in the crystal ceremony.

"Are you going to sit there pissing and moaning all day, girl, or you going to help me find a toy for Skeeter?" Ginevee said, giving me a hand up and smiling at me. She gave me a friendly poke in the ribs.

"I'm here," I said, feeling spirit and substance colliding into a big jumble in my head. "What about those wind-up kangaroos over there?" I said, pointing to the counter.

"Hey, wind up sacred warrigan. Wonderful! We'll take one of those kangaroos," Ginevee said, taking a cellophane bag of wrapped candies and emptying them into her pocket.

"All them kiddies love these red ones," she said, handing the fat woman the bag.

We all piled everything we wanted onto the counter. I dug into my pockets and put several bills into the pudgy soft hand of the proprietor. A look of surprise crossed his face. I'm sure he thought we had no money. We got a tank of gas. I had the extra gas cans filled, got the tires and oil checked, and the front window cleaned. We were in good shape and in high spirits as we left the station.

It was late afternoon. By the time we were back on the deer track we were all gaily singing a song Ginevee had taught us about playing a game of "two-up," where two heads on two coins won.

"Billy go banga lee geema Billy go banga lee geema masta kee," we sang at the top of our lungs. Ginevee and Agnes were accentuating the words with their clapping sticks. All of a sudden, a shape about five feet tall loomed onto our track from the bush on our left. I slammed on the brakes and went broadside, stopping in a flurry of red dust. We all looked in astonishment as a stately emu bird walked right in front of us.

"I didn't know there were any emu birds left," I said. "Around here anyway."

"The emu walks like a clever woman. Stately and proud," Ginevee said. "She leaves her tracks in the Milky Way." Ginevee was frowning. "She walks from the left. It is not a good sign." Ginevee gripped my shoulder and pointed to the horizon. We gasped in unison. A dark whirling funnel spiraled up into the evening sky. The twister looked like it was right over our village and moving at a fast pace away from us.

"Something terrible has happened," Ginevee said as I throttled full tilt down the deer track and onto the dry riverbed. We hung on for dear life as the 'Rover lurched and leaped from one pothole to another. The car that had been so neatly packed became a mass of upside down shopping bags, with gear all over the floor.

We got back to the village just before nightfall. We could no longer see the dark swirling funnel of the whirlwind. But we could see its effects on our wurleys. Grass and thatch were strewn everywhere and the women, children, and dingos were running in every direction picking up their broken things. At the sight of us, Mandowa came running. Tears of anger and terror were running from her eyes.

"Skeeter, Skeeter," she screamed. "He's taken Skeeter!" Ginevee and Agnes quieted her and got her to sit down. Ruby was holding my hand.

"Out of the ground came the big wind, yea. It smelled of the bugeen. It was a dark whirlwind that just came up out of the sand. I was holding Skeeter on my lap. I was teaching her bark painting, hmm. Next I knew the wind came and swept her up out of my arms." Mandowa was crying with big sobs that shook her shoulders.

"No one else was taken," Mandowa said.

Ginevee hugged her and said, "We'll find her, my sister." Ginevee grabbed my arm and looked at me.

"Come," she said as we started off to the village. She Who Walks With The Wind joined us.

"Buzzie has taken very sick," she signed. Ginevee translated as we walked straight to Buzzie's wurley, which stood unharmed. We walked inside and found Buzzie lying on the floor moaning.

"It was Two Hearts," she whispered. Ginevee leaned down to hear her and pulled a branch off of her stomach.

Ginevee placed her hand on Buzzie's solar plexus. The girl winced in pain. Ginevee looked at me.

"What should we do?" I asked, knowing she had felt the spear.

"Nothing yet, until we find Skeeter," Ginevee said, looking at Buzzie.

"Where is she?" Ginevee demanded.

"I don't know. Please believe me," Buzzie was crying.

"Why does he do this?" Ginevee asked.

"He say he wants Lynn, Agnes, and you or he will kill the child." Ginevee's anger made her face seem to blacken and her eyes to turn a deep red.

"It is time, Buzzie. You tell us, now, who you really are and what has brought you here disguised as a sister. We took you in with good heart." Ginevee pressed her fist to her chest.

"Now tell me who you are or I will kill you." Ginevee lifted up a stone ax that rested on the dirt floor. Buzzie's eyes went wide and she began to shake and cry.

"I never meant to hurt anyone," she said. "I will tell you." She Who Walks With The Wind helped to prop her up a little.

"I come from the north. The sorcerer you have seen in your visions, Lynn, is my husband."

"You mean Two Hearts?" I asked.

"No, the other one," she said. "His name is Booru."

"I don't understand," Ginevee said, now very, very angry. We were all frightened.

"Long time ago Booru and Two Hearts were doing bad things to the people because they had been betrayed. Many people died and suffered. Then Two Hearts saw my ability as a clever woman and he wanted me for himself. Two Hearts never told Booru. I didn't want to be with either of them. I was very afraid. Until now, I believed the things they had told me about the evilness of power women. I came here as a spy for both of them. They are still friends together. My husband doesn't know that Two Hearts has been here. Two Hearts, his medicine is very strong. He works with the whirlwind. He came here to take me away and to kill you. When he didn't find you, he took Skeeter instead. I wouldn't go with him. Now my husband will know what has happened. I am very afraid. Ginevee, I am sorry from my heart and my spirit. This is a good camp. You help the people live. I am so ashamed."

Buzzie reached for Ginevee's hand. Ginevee brought the ax down with great force into the ground. I looked at the ax buried in the hard ground and winced.

Ginevee took Buzzie's hand and looked at her in silence for a long time. The blackness in her face faded a little. For some reason she looked very young. None of us dared to speak.

Then, with tears in her eyes, Ginevee said, "The deepest sadness of my life is when one sister turns against another; then they are being like men. Men often turn on one another and cheat. Women know better in their hearts. When women assume their power on this mother earth and remember that they are the warrioress of the All Mother, that they are the goddess, then something like this can never happen. If you had stood in your power circle, Buzzie, your husband and maybe even Two Hearts could have learned how to live from you. Men need women for that or they are lost. They lose their direction and they forget why they are alive. They lose their Dreaming. I saw your darkness when you first came here. For some reason Dirrangun accepted you and gave you a crystal. There is goodness in everyone, just like there is a dark side. You still have a heart, I think, hmm. But we just have to find it." Ginevee got up quickly. "We will prepare for ceremony."

I walked outside, following her. Agnes and Ruby joined us. I turned and saw a big smear of red ochre across Buzzie's wurley. I showed Ginevee.

"Kudaitja Man, Red Ochre Man. He can smell you like a fox. It is the mark of Two Hearts," Ginevee said.

"What ceremony are we going to do?" I asked, shivering.

"We're not. I just wanted Buzzie to think that we were. Two Hearts will be following her thoughts. You, Agnes, and I are going into the bush in the old way. It's time you learned to live as a true Koori, my sister."

Ruby stayed behind in the village with She Who Walks With The Wind. They would cover for us and watch over Buzzie. Ginevee, Agnes, and I left the village on foot under the shadows of darkness. Each of us wore two kangaroo skins laced together. Agnes and I also wore kangaroo sandals, but Ginevee went barefoot. The bottoms of her feet were hard pads like those on a camel. Ginevee had made us leave our other clothes as if everything were normal.

"We cannot wear anything that smells of you, like our regular clothing. You can wear your clever bags and things made out of kangaroo, because we are of the malu or kangaroo totem. We are protected by the Malu."

Each of us carried a long spear with a carved stone tip, a coolamon, and a digging stick. We had no food or water. Ginevee had said that Two Hearts would return for us and smell us out.

"He will never kill Skeeter without finding us. It would give him no power. Power is all he really wants. We will find a way to get Skeeter back and destroy Two Hearts as well," Ginevee said, showing us how to walk toe first, so as to leave absolutely no trace. I was fascinated by the acumen and endurance of these two seemingly elderly women. Their faces appeared to be unfurrowed, their eyes reflecting the moonlight like faceted diamonds. I ran between them carefully through the patches of spinifex grass. A growing fear was welling up inside of me. We moved through the bush toward the Peterman range of mountains, which stood before us in the distance, for many long hours. Ginevee knew where she was going. How could we survive without food or water, I thought to myself, but I said nothing. Late in the night we arrived at the campsite. There was a small stand of desert oak trees and vines of paddy melons grew over the ground.

"Paddy melons give you a sick stomach, yea," Ginevee said. They lay like strings of iridescent pearls in the moonlight. We put down our spears and things and gathered porcupine grasses for a shelter from the wind.

I looked around at the vast wilderness in all directions. The wind was blowing harder now in cold gusts from the south. Ginevee cut some saplings and in a half hour we had a completely hidden shelter built between two trees. I was desperately thirsty.

"Come over here," Ginevee said. There was a low cliff over to our left. Fortunately there was enough moonlight to see by. Ginevee walked over to a large round rock laying on the ground against the cliff.

"Help me," she said. The three of us rolled the rock to the side, revealing a deep hole in the ground.

"What is that?" I asked.

"It's a Koori water fountain," Ginevee said, laughing at

the look on our faces. We all lay down on our stomachs and cupped water into our mouths with our hands. When we were through we rolled the rock back.

"I'll show you something else." We followed Ginevee over to a shallow cave.

"Lynn, reach up there and see what happens," she said.

Hesitantly and very cold from the wind, I reached up onto the rock ledge and felt with my fingers. I produced two fire sticks, a flintstone, and a long flat red stone with carvings on it.

"That flat stone is a churinga. It's called a dingo's tongue. It tells of the dreaming of this sacred place. You can put that back and give me the sticks. Everyone in our tribe knows of the water holes and sacred caves where tools are left for those in need. It is our way in the desert. We'll make a small fire, yea. Agnes, help me. And, Lynn, you go find us two small logs for the fire."

In a very short time we were huddled by the flames. Ginevee had caught two lizards. Agnes and she each held a lizard on a stick, roasting it over the fire. I was starving, but it was all I could do to eat the lizard. When I finally did, it was really not bad, only a little chewy perhaps.

Ginevee took out her pouch of bandicoot grease and we rubbed it all over ourselves and then rubbed the white fire ash into the grease. Again, I was amazed by what a marvelous insulation it was against the cold wind. We lay on our sides like three pups huddled together under our wind shelter and fell fast asleep. One or the other of us would wake up during the night and stoke the fire. Just before dawn Ginevee got me up and put my digging stick and my coolamon in my hand.

She took a ring of braided human hair and placed it on top of my head. She took my larger and deeper coolamon or piti and positioned it on top of the ring like a regal crown. She grinned at me. The bluish light of early morning made her skin look as gray as her hair. I walked carefully behind her. My earlier practice now helped me to at least keep the piti from falling.

We came to the round rock and rolled it back, lying on our bellies to drink deeply from the well. Ginevee showed me how to take a handful of grass and wad it up really well until it would sit in the bottom of the piti. I filled up the coolamon the best I could with water and left the grass in bottom to keep the water from splashing. Ginevee helped me settle it on my head. No mean trick, I found, as little trickles of water dribbled down my shoulders. I actually got the water back to the fire and set it down in front of Agnes as if it were the grand prize. Not much had spilled. Agnes cupped her hands and drank carefully.

Ginevee and I set off with our digging sticks and a coolamon to find breakfast. The heat was already coming up out of the desert. Heat waves shallied on the horizon and the grasses smelled sweet as the morning dew quickly evaporated. My body felt strong and my stride was more confident. I was very hungry.

Ginevee spied a gnarled tree with bent roots coming up out of a dry and pebbly riverbed. She beckoned me with a crook of her arm and we both sat down with our legs straddled around the tree roots. Holding our digging sticks upright we started digging a fairly deep hole following two different roots. Eventually Ginevee found what she was looking for—a nest of wichiti grubs. In crevices along the roots we found a couple of dozen big fat juicy grubs, which were whitish in color and about two inches long. We pulled them out with our fingers and placed them in our coolamons. I couldn't believe that I was hungry enough to think about them as breakfast. I decided to convince myself that they were shrimp. Ginevee giggled more than once at the expression on my face as we worked.

"You'll lose that," she said poking my stomach.

I laughed to myself at the vision of hundreds of women coming to the Gibson Desert to eat wichiti grubs and lose their fat stomachs. I looked at the little critters in my coolamon and was determined not to be squeamish.

I noticed a strange glimmer in Ginevee's eyes. She reached out and touched my arm. We listened to the vast stillness around us. It was heavy in my ears. Her eyes darted from one place to another.

"Do you hear a sorcerer's footsteps?" she asked. I listened, my neck bristling.

"No," I whispered.

"A sorcerer's footsteps sound different than the footsteps of power or an ally. Listen carefully, my daughter, you may never hear this again." She lay down with her left ear to the ground. She motioned for me to do the same. We lay there for some time. I was straining to hear something. Then

I heard it. It was not like a footstep at all, but more like a Bull Roarer with a definite beat, as if it were walking.

"What is that?" I asked. The sound had truly come up through the ground.

"Power is stalking us and it has been sent by Two Hearts. You are learning, my daughter. You heard that because you stopped that incessant chatter in your head. The subtle language of magic can not be heard unless you can be still inside and out," Ginevee said, resuming her digging.

"What do you mean, Two Hearts has sent it? And what is it?" I asked.

"You know enough about dreaming to understand that this is impossible to explain. All I can say is that the sorcerer is trying to dream us. You have just heard the footsteps of his dreaming. I can also tell that he is a long way away," she said.

"How can you tell?" I asked.

"Because the steps sound very far away," she said, laughing at me.

"Oh," I said. Ginevee turned back to her work, but I found it hard to concentrate on finding grubs. I kept listening for that sound.

"You can only hear the footsteps of his dreaming through the ground," Ginevee said, looking at me out of the corner of her eye.

"How is that?"

"Mother earth has a lot to do with dreaming. Your connection to her is important, how you have honored and given away to her. Many of our people think when you travel above the clouds and you look down and everything is white, they think everything is the same, you know? People of the spirit understand each other around the world. The gods live in the sky. They speak the same language. Power is in the rocks and the earth. That means that when we take something from the earth, our mother, we must return that energy in a ceremony, with honor. Then the power stays happy and never leaves. Power only leaves when you take and never give back," Ginevee said. "Power knows me, she helps me. She's beginning to recognize you, too. You're living close to her now. She just gave you a sign. A good sign, yea?"

"I guess so," I said.

"What do you mean, you guess so? You hear the footsteps of dreaming every day?" she asked.

"No."

"Be grateful, girl. Wonderful." We picked up our coolamons full of grubs and started back to camp. Ginevee had put the strings of her dilly bag around her forehead so that the bag itself hung down the back of her neck. With her coolamon on her head, this left her hands free to use her digging stick. Ginevee stopped in front of a low rock and knelt down on one leg.

"Look," she said to me. What looked like seeds were stuck to the side of the rock. "Those seeds are from the koilpuru," she said, running her fingertips over them and catching them in her palm.

"How did they get there?" I asked.

"They were left by a bird-fella sharpening his beak. Look there at those tiny scratch marks. Koilpuru is our tomato of the desert. Must be plants nearby. Let's look," she said as we set off in a slightly different direction. About forty yards away we came across a cluster of plants growing on the ground. We pulled several and loaded up our coolamons. Ginevee taught me how to hum a short melody to give thanks to the spirits of the witchiti grub and the koilpuru for abundance. Happily and with our stomachs growling, we headed for camp.

"It's about time," Agnes said, placing several grubs onto coals in the fire. "I'm starving. What do these taste like?"

"They taste just like an ice-cream cone after the ice cream is gone," Ginevee said.

Agnes and I both held a toasted grub gingerly in our fingers. We looked at each other. Agnes winked at me and put the whole grub in her mouth.

"Tastes like pork . . . sort of," she said, a little wide-eyed as she chewed.

I ate mine whole, trying not to grimace. It really did taste like pork. I knew the Koori thought of these grubs as a delicacy, and now I could see why. Ginevee burst out laughing and rolled around on the ground, slapping her thighs and saying something in Koori. I told her she was being rude.

"We heard the steps of Two Hearts dreaming," Ginevee told Agnes, who was taking a bite of desert tomato. Agnes was instantly alert.

"And?" Agnes asked.

Ginevee patted the ground. "Listen for yourself. Perhaps he is still dreaming."

We all lay with our left ears to the ground. I tried to clear my thoughts, but was unsuccessful. I could hear nothing but the buzzing of flies.

"It's very faint," Agnes said.

"He is very far away," Ginevee agreed.

"My daughter, pull all your miwi into the pit of your stomach. Collect all your psychic power like water in your coolamon. Make your miwi and your thoughts be as one. Strengthen the power within you. Clear your mind and be still with power," Ginevee said, placing her hand on my solar plexus and closing her eyes. Agnes put her hand behind my neck and my thoughts instantly ceased. I still heard nothing but flies.

"Remember the crystals of Oruncha? Try placing the one from your stomach out onto the ground and let it perceive for you. Visualize the crystal moving out from you on a luminous fiber. Concentrate all of your force and you will hear the dream," Ginevee said, encouraging me to keep trying.

This time I heard it. Sending the crystal out of my body psychically produced a strange sensation in my gut and down into my knees. My lower body felt like it had turned to water and I became seasick, as if I were floating on waves. As I heard the very dim sound of Two Hearts, I had an automatic reaction of wanting to swim and throw up at the same time. But my clarity of hearing was true. I retracted my crystal into my stomach and the weird sensation went away. As I came out of my daze, I saw Agnes and Ginevee watching me intently. They slapped me on the back and made me walk around. My legs were stiff and sore, as if I had run twenty miles.

"If you could ever relax you would be a powerful clever woman," Ginevee said.

We sat quietly in a circle pulling the twigs and leaves out of each other's hair. Now that I knew we could find food and water, I was beginning to enjoy the incredible feeling of being able to live off the land with virtually nothing. I felt a freedom and self-reliance that I had never known before. I understood on a much deeper level the need for a gracious exchange with the powers of our earth mother.

Somewhere
the crystal flame
leaps

into bare hands
and she cries

I am not burned
I am mad for colors—

bright moon, jasmine, weathering the
    dark.

—Jack Crimmins

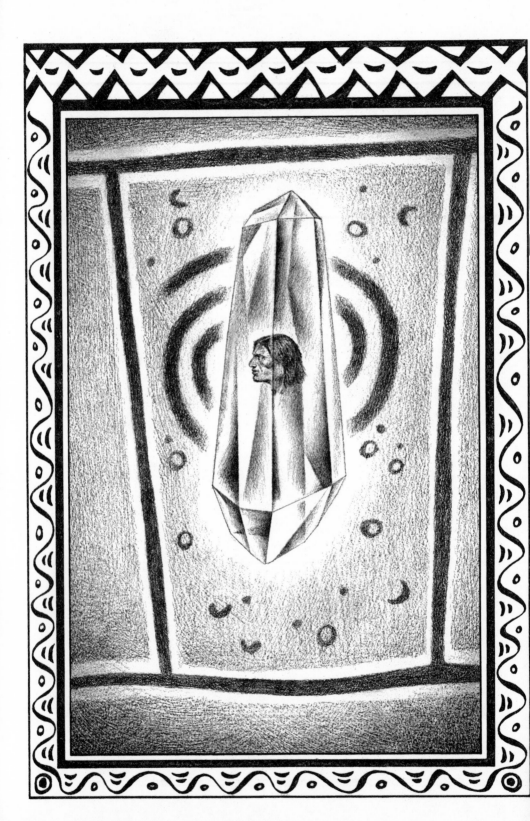

CHAPTER NINETEEN
❖❖❖❖❖❖
GOOWAWA
DREAMING

The bluish tinge in the morning light had melted into an orange, golden glow over the quiet desert. The leaves and the shiny bark on the eucalyptus trees looked like they had been burnished in bronze and the red desert sands were covered in a satiny iridescent sheen. I noticed that with our bodies protected with ash and grease we looked as if we had nearly the same color skin. Agnes, Ginevee, and I shared an intense moment of kinship, a feeling that our souls had merged into that of one woman. Our eyes became filled with tears as we briefly held each other's hands. We would survive. That is the goal of a clever woman.

"What now?" Agnes said, looking from me to Ginevee.

"Tonight we will work with the crystals and the goowawa, the little people," Ginevee said.

"I saw their tracks this morning over near the waterhole," Agnes said.

"You did?" I asked in amazement. "Are they like the menehunes in Hawaii and like our little people?"

"They're like your fairies, yea. They live in a cave near here. That's why I brought you to this camp. They help with the dreaming. Tonight we will leave food for them at the mouth of the cave. If they have taken the food by the time the moon is high in the sky, then that means they will work with our crystal dreaming," Ginevee said.

"What happens if they don't take the food?" I asked.

"Oh, they will. They're always hungry," Ginevee said, winking at Agnes.

"The goowawa are very good, but you have to be careful of them. They're very emotional and they can have bad tempers. You don't want to make them mad."

"What makes them mad?" I asked.

"Lots of things. You must never lie to them and you must always keep your word. As I said, they get very hungry. Some of these witchiti grubs are for them. That's their favorite meal."

"It was a big mistake for Two Hearts to steal Skeeter," Ginevee said.

"How do you mean?" I asked.

"The little people will see her tracks first. They like children because they're childlike themselves. Little people and children understand each other," Ginevee said, a wistful look on her face.

We all had many unanswered questions. Each was aware of the vital concern in the other's heart. Our eyes would occasionally meet and hold for a moment, speaking unsaid words of encouragement and strength. We knew that as warrioresses who must survive, we had to conserve all our energy for the task at hand and for what lay ahead in the next few days. It was not unlike being in the eye of a storm. We sensed our world raging around us in tumultuous flurries while we sat, for at least this moment, in an unreal but magnificent state of camaraderie and peace.

That afternoon Agnes and I gathered more food, firewood, and some berries, as Ginevee instructed us. As we performed our tasks, my excitement mounted. I was eager to work with the crystals again and the goowawa.

"Hold your power, my daughter," Agnes said, touching my arm. "This is a time for pulling back the bow. Collect your arrows." Her voice sounded dry and guttural. We began our late afternoon walk down the low gully escarpment to the camp.

The tall eucalyptus trees stood like towering sentinels guarding the cavelike entrances to the lower world where the goowawa lived. It was getting dark. It was the time when the world changes. Our purple shadows preceded us as Agnes and I returned to camp.

Ginevee looked up in welcome. She had been working with her crystals and had made a most extraordinary sand painting. I lay down on my stomach on the red sand and propped my chin on my hands, regarding it.

"Ginevee, please tell me what this means. It is so beautiful," I said.

"It is called 'Little People Dreaming,' " Ginevee said proudly. "For a papunya to be powerful it has to have the spirit; it will be full of muru muru, or full of life. Do you feel it?" she asked.

As Agnes and I held our hands over Ginevee's extraordinary work, we both unmistakably felt little tingling waves. We shook our hands and smiled at Ginevee. She was pleased.

I smelled meat burning. I looked around and to my surprise I saw a dead euro, which is a cross between a kangaroo and a wallaby, roasting half obscured in the coals. Ginevee was working with the point and edge of her boomerang and pulling the large tendon out of its back leg. I moved to help her.

"Why are you doing this?" I asked her.

She dropped the leg of the euro and picked up her spear. "The sinew will be used to repair the point on my spear, which came apart when I pulled it out of the euro. Now I will fix it with his tendon. He gave away that we may live." As Ginevee spoke I noticed that she had collected some of the euro's blood in her coolamon.

"Here, we will all drink of his blood and offer it to his spirit living in the Milky Way. Drink with thanks."

Ginevee took a drink and held the coolamon up to the setting sun. She began to sing and handed it to me. I drank, the best I could, and held it up to the sun, as Agnes did after me. Agnes sang the lightning song that Ruby always sang to the spirit of the deer. I joined her and then sat down again next to the sand painting.

Agnes and I sat watching as our Koori sister tended the euro, her black, agile body twisting and turning in the waning light. Her movements were accomplished. To watch Ginevee do her work was a lesson in being a warrioress. Everything was well thought out in advance. She surrounded herself with all that she needed. She prepared the ground and, without a wasted motion, executed her task. In no time she had extracted the tendon and twisted it into place tightly around the stone tip and the spear. She had already collected and melted resin from the spinifex grasses and secured the whole operation in place. Once she was done, she looked up, ready to prepare food for the goowawa.

Ginevee took the euro meat that was nearly raw, scraping the fur off with her boomerang. Agnes and I decided to wait a little and just watch. I kept looking at the rectangular sand painting. As the sun settled into the horizon the red, mauve, and yellow sand particles reflected the pearlescent beige and pink tones of the sky and brought Ginevee's designs to life. I was fascinated by its subtle shifts in hue.

"The many small circles in the center represent the goowawa. Those three half-circles are us. The many dots up there are the goowawa dreaming. Here in the center spiral is their sacred ground, and these red dots mixing with their dots represents a combination of all of our dreaming together," Ginevee said, her fingers holding a piece of euro meat dripping with grease. Ginevee looked up at a bush behind me.

"The goowawa are hungry, yea. I'll finish fixing this coolamon of food, and you, Lynn and Agnes, will place it at the entrance of their cave."

I slowly turned around to look at the bush. A branch moved almost imperceptibly, but I saw nothing else.

"The goowawa are about waist-high," Ginevee said, tearing off a piece of meat. "When I was visiting my cousins on the coast, we would wake up in the morning and hear little voices calling 'heh, heh, heh.' We were just kids and we'd sneak over to the rocks near the ocean and watch them little fellas trying to catch an eel. That's why eels are sacred to many of the people, because they know that the goowawa like them, yea. The eels bring the goowawa. The goowawa are a race of forgotten people, hmm. They are wonderful and they know many things." Ginevee handed us the coolamon. "We will eat when the ceremony is over. Just follow those baby tracks, you'll find them behind that bush," Ginevee said.

We took the offering and went over behind the low tree. I became so excited I almost dropped the food. Agnes and Ginevee grinned at me. I saw little tiny baby tracks leading off to the right. I touched them with my fingers.

"Follow those tracks a little bit, until you get to the cave, then just leave the food on a rock," Ginevee said, smacking her lips and wiping the euro juice off her fingers.

We followed the tracks quite easily to a low cave or rock shelter. There was a scraggly green bush with yellow flowers covering the entrance. If we looked carefully we could see the tracks going inside. We set the coolamon down and sang a song by a small ledge of stone. Then we returned to our fire.

"What's in that wooden dish?" I asked Ginevee, who was resting.

"That's the last of the grass I used for making resin. Look," she said, picking up the dish and shaking it. "If you rock the grass back and forth and get out all the dust and stuff—see—then the good stuff, the resin, comes down like this a little. It separates and then you melt that resin into a cake and you fix your spearhead or your chisels or whatever. Wonderful. See, you thought I was just sleeping this afternoon when I was really preparing for war." Ginevee pinched my arm. "Come, let's sleep a little with the crystals and get them ready for ceremony."

Agnes, Ginevee, and I crawled under the grass shelter. Laying on our sides, we each cradled several crystals to our bellies and snoozed for an hour or so, as Ginevee's ancestors had done for fifty thousand years.

It was dark when I awoke. Agnes and Ginevee were already working with the crystals. They had placed them onto the sand painting. Agnes was sitting across from Ginevee. I stoked the coals of the fire and sat to Ginevee's left. Ginevee took a white flower out of her hair and sniffed its fragrance.

"This flower has a wonderful smell," she said. "But if I were to pull this flower apart I could not find the how of that beautiful smell. It just is. Am I right?" She handed the flower to me.

I took it gently and sniffed its sweetness. The atmosphere around both of the medicine women had changed. They had both moved into their places of power. I struggled to collect myself and catch up with them.

"Yes, I'd say you're right."

"And what about this big crystal, my daughter? It is made up of minerals and many things, yea?"

"Yes, it is."

"It has many parts. Your scientists would say that this whole crystal is the sum of its parts. Am I right?"

"Yes."

"Wrong. I'm going to teach you a big secret of our Dreamtime. If you can understand this, you understand who I am," Ginevee said, and she began to sing. She handed us some singing sticks and we beat on rocks. Ginevee began looking over her crystals. The tempo and rhythm of her ceremony slowly began to grab me. After singing several songs and becoming immersed in the tempo of the clapping sticks, I was swept into a different dimension, a place of blue light and soft winds. The crystals became like living rainbow lights in front of us.

"One of the crystals will ask for you. She will show you her colors. Dream with her and follow her with your eyes," Ginevee whispered. I found my crystal and stared into her pink, crystalline world. It had a mesmerizing effect.

"The crystal you are seeing has great beauty, my daughter. The crystal is made up of physical things. It is part of this earthly world. But it has beauty, too. It has something more, just like the mountains do. Your scientists say that one and one equals two and that's that. We say in the Dreamtime that the Great Spirit is forever and that we are forever. You might say that if I took a chip off that crystal it would be less. In a sense yes and in a sense no. The world might blow up, but it would still be part of the Dreamtime. You say that if I take something out of the crystal it will be reduced, but I say that the crystal is part of the whole, therefore it never can be reduced. Its beauty is the key, my daughter. The crystal is more than the sum of its minerals and things. Beauty is the essence—it is part of the higher arithmetic of the Dreamtime. Certain things add, one, two, three—regular-like. When you enter the Dreamtime your concept of arithmetic must change. There is beauty in this sand painting, but there is also the sacredness of life. Do you understand?" Ginevee asked. Her eyes were closed.

"I think you mean that numbers are just part of an idea and that when you travel in the Dreamtime that idea changes. You become aware of more than just, say, a tree as bark and branches. The tree has beauty and spirit and qualities that can only be measured by a different set of values," I said.

"That is good. Now watch the papunya. Watch how the colors begin to move." I watched and, indeed, the sand painting began to move. First the colors sparkled and then the wavy lines began to undulate back and forth.

"The name of this papunya is Goowawa Dreaming. As I said, the goowawa are a forgotten race. Inside each of us is a forgotten person. That person is represented also by the dots that represent the goowawa. Because whatever is outside is inside. Each of these dots is part of self-unrealized. The painting helps us to realize and bring together what has never before had life. For this ceremony to work and have power there must be intuition and insight, self-realization. That's more food for the little people. So they can be remembered. See this dark edge around the painting? It is the abominable darkness. We fall into that darkness when we fail to see the inward whole, when we fail to balance our inward intuition with our outward actions. See, the moon is high now. Let's ask the goowawa to join our ceremony." Ginevee began to sing.

Fleetingly, I looked across at Agnes. Her face and eyes were very remote and she looked arcane in the flickering firelight. A hot wind was coming down from the north. Suddenly our close circle felt overly warm. The heat became oppressive. I began to drip with perspiration. I noticed that Agnes and Ginevee were also experiencing the sudden rise in temperature. Rivulets of sweat began to run from our foreheads.

I again had that familiar feeling, as if we were taxiing down a runway directly headed into the Dreamtime. Invisible engines revved and the ground beneath us became unstable. I wanted to hang onto something as I lurched forward and backward. Then I felt an enormous shoving down and inward of some unnamed pressure or force. It felt like gravity or depressurization in a spacecraft. My head was thrown back and for a moment everything went black.

The first thing I saw when I came to was tiny baby tracks moving at a good pace around the edging of darkness on the papunya. The empty coolamon was in front of Ginevee. I could have sworn I heard a burp. I wanted to think that I was seeing things. The baby tracks led over to Ginevee's big crystal and stopped there. I couldn't see what was making the tracks.

"If you doubt, my sisters, he will not show himself," Ginevee whispered.

"Welcome, my friend," Ginevee said, smiling into the

crystal. Her eyes sparkled; she was obviously seeing someone or something.

"Yes, I know we're in great danger. That's why we've
come," Ginevee said, spraying drops of water over the crystal. I could see what I thought was the profile of a tiny face
in her crystal. It moved around, as if the goowawa were
talking from inside. I was hypnotized and astonished. I studied the baby tracks and looked back at the crystal and listened. Ginevee began translating for us.

"He is giving me pictures. I will tell you what I see,"
she said. I strained my eyes, but I couldn't quite see into her
crystal. To do so, I would have had to move, but I didn't
dare.

"There is much confusion at the village. Two Hearts is
lurking nearby. I see Skeeter. She is frightened but okay.
Yes, I know, my friend. It's a fine mess, yea. What's that
over there? Oh, I see. Oh no. Buzzie has been hit by the
bone. But it's not from Two Hearts, it's from her husband.
He is not too far away. He is dark and angry. He found out
about Two Hearts. He'd kill him if he could find him. What's
that? That's She Who Walks With The Wind and Ruby,"
Ginevee said in a trance-like voice. I could see sparks, actual
sparks, around the crystal.

"They say that Two Hearts will trade Skeeter for Buzzie's
life. If Buzzie dies, the child dies. They've been looking for
us. My friend, now I owe you one," she said.

I could have sworn I heard a rasping giggle. I saw footsteps leading out of the papunya and off toward the cave.
They vanished. I put my fingers on the sand where moments
before I had seen baby tracks. There was nothing now but
flat red sand.

We sang and Ginevee came out of her extraordinary
trance. Her face had turned dark and strained with renewed
anger. When the sand painting was erased and the crystals
put away, Ginevee gathered us around the fire. We ate hun-
grily and spoke about the ceremony. She explained the message again in case we hadn't heard it.

"What did he mean when he said that Buzzie had been
hit by the bone?" I asked.

"In every society there have to be laws, my daughter.
In our tribal world from long ago our ancestors set down
laws for the people. Some of these laws are very sacred. For
Buzzie to go with another man when she is married is against

her tribal law. The upholders and the executioners for these laws and for those who break them are the Red Ochre men. They are a society of executioners. This man of Buzzie's is a Red Ochre man, so he is acting on the law by throwing what we call the bone. It will kill Buzzie within three days unless we go to her and save her. This is also permitted. I don't know how strong Booru's medicine is, but it's my guess that it has been weakened," Ginevee said, swatting flies with a leafy branch.

"Why would his medicine have been weakened?" I asked.

"Because he has turned to evil ways. He's forgotten that his power comes from woman. Even a Red Ochre man can go wrong. He has killed many women and children. Power will leave a man like that," Ginevee said, gathering her things and putting her crystals into her clever bag.

We swept the ground and left the camp as if no one had been there. I left a pinch of tobacco for the spirits of place and the goowawa. I had, momentarily, touched the sweet face of wisdom here. I would always remember it.

Sweet stars, I'll ask a softer question:
  Moon
Attend me to the end. I'm here alone.

—Theodore Roethke

CHAPTER TWENTY
❖❖❖❖❖❖
SPIRIT WOMAN
AND TWO HEARTS

I didn't reach my wurley at the village until dawn. The three of us decided to remain together until we gathered everyone for a meeting. Curled up together in my shelter, we caught an hour's sleep. We were exhausted. No one but Ruby and She Who Walks With The Wind had seen us return. We had been as inobtrusive as a beam of moonlight entering the village. Ginevee had known instantly where Booru the sorcerer was, and by listening intently to his dreaming we knew how to avoid the powerful psychic radar of Two Hearts. During our trip back, I had become intensely afraid. I had felt I was running blindly in the dark within a system of magic that was foreign to me. I slept so deeply once we were safe, I think I must have passed out from fatigue.

Ginevee nudged me awake. A gentle wind caressed my face. I lay still, sharply alert, listening with every pore of my body. I looked into Ginevee's eyes questioningly.

"I have spoken with the other elders," Ginevee said. "The crystals never lie. It is just as we thought. Buzzie has been hit by the bone and we are the only ones who can save her. We must go to her now—there is no time to spare."

Ginevee, Agnes, and I walked to Buzzie's wurley, which

still had a smear of red ochre on it. The village was quiet, as if deserted.

We stepped inside to find Ruby and She Who Walks With The Wind tending Buzzie. Buzzie was lying on her mat on a pole structure. She looked up at us and shook her head. The three of us sat around Buzzie's head. Ruby touched my shoulder and I squeezed her hand.

"It's the bone. I will waste away," Buzzie whispered.

"Buzzie, we are going to heal you. But you have to help us," Ginevee said.

"My husband's medicine is too powerful . . . it's no use . . . I'm dying," she said. We all looked at each other.

"Nonsense. When were you hit?" Ginevee asked.

"Yesterday," she whispered weakly. I took a rag and wiped off her perspiring forehead. Some of the other women came into the wurley and began taking Buzzie's belongings. They took her coolamon for carrying water and started taking her few clothes. I stood up horrified.

"That is the custom, my daughter. If someone is sung by sorcery, even her family will leave her. They take the person's things and leave her to die without food or water," Ginevee said.

"Well, she's not going to die," I said angrily.

Buzzie opened her eyes and looked at me.

"Buzzie, I know you believe in the power, is that right?" I asked.

"Yes." She nodded.

"Then if you have the faith, you know in your gut that we can heal you." I pressed her abdomen and she flinched. "The power can kill you, but it can be turned around onto its source and you can be healed. Do I speak the truth?" I asked, my voice firm.

"Yes, this is true. But I have been sung and the bone was pointed at me. It is law, yea," Buzzie said in a whiny tone of voice.

Agnes was holding a coolamon of cold water that she had just gotten from the creek. She stood up and in a split second threw it hard into Buzzie's face. For a moment Buzzie forgot her illness and was startled out of her maya, her own state of illusion. She spluttered and almost sat up. Agnes grabbed her hard around the waist, lifted her up in the air, and shoved her back against the wall of the wurley.

"You are a warrioress. There is no telling why you have

been chosen for this great path or what stroke of fate has brought you to this learning, but you are a sacred one and you have the power within you. Your man has fallen off his path. His power is weakened and we are strong. Ginevee sees the tracks of that bone and she will send it home for you. You are the goddess, you little fool. By forgetting that, you could have died. Wake up and remember who you are," Agnes said, slapping Buzzie twice across the face.

Ginevee was a flurry of motion. She cleared the ground and propped Buzzie up in a half-sitting position. Buzzie was now wide-eyed and gasping for air as if she were having an anxiety attack.

"My daughter, you extract the spear. Use your white feathers," Agnes told me. She seemed to know what to do, as did the others. Clapping sticks came out and a low, monotonous chant began. We could hear the others outside and the fire was being stoked near Buzzie. I left and came back with my ranga, white feathers, and my clever bag. I felt as if sharp currents of electricity had replaced my blood. I sat in front of Buzzie and after singing my power song I brought my medicine energy and thoughts down into my solar plexus. I could feel the crystals of Oruncha inside of me. I can only explain it by saying that I could begin to see from the vantage point of various aspects of my body, as if my body were made up of words, and put together, the words made a coherent paragraph. I held up the two white feathers that Guboo had given me in the dream. I looked through them at Buzzie and saw the spear in her stomach. I could not see it without the feathers. Then I gave both feathers to Buzzie. She took them and looked back at me. She started to cry.

"Why do you cry?" I asked her.

"Because when I look through the feathers I don't see you, I only see a spirit woman," she said.

"And that is what I am. And I see a spear in your stomach. I saw it before, but it was not time to take it then. It was put there by Two Hearts to hold you. May I take it now?" I asked. I was in a hypnotic trance, my concentration was so intense.

"Yes, take it," Buzzie said, crying again.

Then I did something I'd never done before, although I'd seen it done by medicine women in the Far North. I leaned forward and I put my physical fingers around the spirit-spear by burying my fist into her stomach. There was a split second, a tear in time, when my body was pulled across into the dimension of the soul and I felt the ridged spear that existed out of time and space, and I yanked it with all my strength across into the relative world. I fell back onto the ground amidst cheers from the women and a wild-eyed Buzzie. I sat up holding a tiny, bloody spear with a stone point. I think I was more astonished than anyone else. I gaped at the thing in my hand. My whole body was shaking. I went over to Buzzie, who kissed my arm, tears streaming down her face. I felt her stomach. It was bruised, but there was no wound. Agnes and Ruby grabbed me as Ginevee re-entered the wurley. She was covered with fluff and black-and-white-ochre-dotted designs in swirls. She was magnificent. She held out a coolamon rubbed in red ochre.

"Put the spear here, in this," she said.

"Wash in the creek, my daughter, while I prepare with the singing." Ginevee immediately began to circle inside the wurley. She was trotting, lifting her knees exaggeratedly high and singing with her clapping sticks. Swinging around, I was rushed off to the creek, where Agnes and Ruby dunked me and rubbed me with sand. She Who Walks With The Wind held my head as I vomited on the creek bank. My stomach convulsed only once or twice. They rubbed the arm and hand I had used to extract the spear. They tingled and hurt badly. Then we rejoined the ceremony. I was wrapped in my kangaroo skirt.

Ginevee was hopping in little circles and began screaming. She brandished a spear above her head. By the firelight, she looked like the angry skeleton of a giant spirit bird—the personification of her power medicine, the swan. Her performance was awesome, her head swaying and her arms spread like wings. She approached Buzzie and, suddenly immobile, she stared at her for a long time. Then she backed away from Buzzie and leaped into the air, screaming an unearthly cry. Bending at the waist, Ginevee jerked her arms outward to their full length toward Buzzie and tiny flecks of light or sparks shot from her fingers and entered Buzzie's body. I knew these sparks were like healing stones being projected into her. Ginevee repeated her original high-stepping dance, which led the others into a fury of song while she twisted characteristically into the air.

Finally, after an hour or so of this frenzied dance, Ginevee stopped in midair, landed on the ground, and screamed like an eagle or a wild swan. With one dramatic action she leaped toward Buzzie, who was obviously in a state of absolute terror. Ginevee bent Buzzie almost in two and grabbed her hair as if she meant to pull it off her head like a wig. She placed her open mouth onto Buzzie's neck and began sucking. There was a sudden, almost deafening sound of the whirring Bull Roarer. After a minute, Ginevee fell backward into Agnes' arms. Her mouth and face were covered with blood. Everyone gasped as slowly and deliberately Ginevee pulled a long, hollow bone out of her mouth and held it up for all to see.

Buzzie was sobbing with joy. I took a cloth and wiped her neck. There was only a bruise. I could not begin to explain what had just happened, but we all knew that Buzzie would live and Skeeter would be returned to us.

"Lynn, we will return this coolamon full of evil to Two Hearts and Booru ourselves," Ginevee said.

"We will?" I asked, whirling around to see Ginevee disappear into the night. There was no time to sleep. I knew that Ginevee was worried about Skeeter. Buzzie was so pleased to be alive that I could tell she didn't care who she had to live with, even if it meant going to Two Hearts. I felt badly about her going to a man she feared, but, after all, she was the one who had almost brought disaster down on all of us. As it happened we had all learned a great deal and as in all experiences in life, we had grown.

Buzzie knew where Two Hearts was, so carrying the ochred coolamon with its spear, Ginevee, Agnes, Ruby, and I followed her out into the red desert. Buzzie was very weak. After such an ordeal, she should have rested for many days. As it was we had no time to lose.

The night sky was dense with cumulus clouds. When the moon was covered, a blackness would descend upon us, drawing a curtain of vague shadows that merged into each other until we could hardly see to walk. Ginevee and I each held one of Buzzie's arms to steady her. She was not doing too well. She was not even as strong as she had thought. The porcupine grass kept needling and scratching her legs as she tripped over unseen rocks and branches. But we kept on going, knowing that we had little time to spare. We went a long way up a dry creek bed that was filled with round flat stones that looked like shiny silver dollars in the occasional light from the moon. Off to our left two rounded hills loomed up from behind the red river oaks. They looked dark purple and forbidding. The night was strangely silent, as the atmosphere often is before an earthquake. I didn't want to go any farther. We were scratched and overly exhausted.

"How much farther, Buzzie?" I asked. We sat down under a ghost gum tree.

"We go until Two Hearts chooses to be seen," Buzzie said.

"He is with us now. He is watching our movements. He is preparing his ground," Ginevee said. "He wants to see our firmness of spirit and make sure that we want only an exchange."

"Pakaria!" Buzzie cried, pointing up at a shooting star blazing across the sky. I was surprised to see the immense fear in her eyes.

"Why does that shooting star frighten you?" I asked.

"Pakaria is a sorcerer flying through the air to come down and do his evil magic. He is dropping his firestick to kill us, yea. It is Two Hearts," she said.

I looked to Ginevee for an explanation, but she just nodded and chewed on a twig. Finally she said, "It's a good sign—he is telling us that he's near. Most times it would not be good, but now we need to meet with him. We keep going, hmm."

We lifted Buzzie to her feet and walked on up the riverbed. It was not long before Buzzie pointed to a deer track going up the riverbank to the left.

"I don't know where he is, but something tells me to go there."

So we struggled up the bank. The track led up between the rounded hills into a narrow gorge. I had to force myself to keep moving. Danger was in the air and in the ground under my feet; I could taste it. It was like green mold on my tongue. There was something familiar and yet horrible about a buzzing sound way distant on the outer reaches of my hearing. I looked to Ginevee again.

"What is the buzzing?" I whispered.

"Just night bugs," Buzzie said.

"Nope. It's a warning. Just keep walking, slowly," Ginevee told us.

I could see Ginevee's body tense. She was like a wild animal, her focus of attention stunning to witness. I wished I could stop shaking. I heard a distant thumping. It was slow, deliberate, and maddening. The moon was hidden abruptly behind a cloud. For a moment we could see only dark masses, then a shaft of moonlight broke through the clouds illuminating the cliff of red sandstone on our immediate right. We stood in the middle of the gorge and could nearly touch both walls with our hands. Carved into the gorge walls on our right were deeply rutted symbols. There were X symbols and long wavy lines with circles on the ends. The markings were strange and ominous for some reason that wasn't clear. Then I realized that they depicted circumcision. They were symbols of power that drifted like sidereal dust across the face of the stone. I was at once fascinated by the strangeness of the drawings and wanted desperately to run away from this place. The thumping sound was becoming louder or closer. I looked up and saw the painted face of the sorcerer in my dream. He was standing above us, his face and body still painted in the white snake design. He looked ten feet tall.

I opened my mouth to scream, but I was completely mute. He danced above us, circling and undulating his body like a snake. He sang his power song, the gorge echoing his guttural voice.

I see through stone
I have the secret eyes
I come from where the grass people bow their
    heads
They stand with their heads bowing before the
    wind, patient
and obedient . . . do not be afraid

He sang with great force, then he repeated the song very softly. His voice had the power to hypnotize your spirit and pull your insides out. I had experienced that sensation years before with the sorcerer named Red Dog, who had stolen the spirit of July and had nearly taken mine with the magic of his flute music, so I was ready for Two Hearts. I shielded myself instantly and focused my creative energy in my solar plexus. I took a deep breath and shoved the energy down and then I let it float back up to my shaman eye in my forehead. Instinctively I knew that unless I looked at him only through the crystal that Oruncha had placed there, I would never survive.

I sensed that Ginevee had taken her power stance, but

Buzzie was lost. Either she did not know how or she chose not to shield herself. In minutes she was straining against our grasp in her need to go to him. Two Hearts' song created a force field around us. Ginevee pushed me gently on the arm.

"Sit now," she whispered.

We grabbed on to Buzzie and made her sit with us. Because we had been standing, we had not seen the circular sand painting in front of us.

Now that I looked at it carefully I realized it was not like the other papunyas I had seen. It was all in white and there was a slash of broken lightning drawn with white clay sand through the center. I thought of the juraveel of the dolphins; lightning was their sacred helper. Thoughts raced through my mind; I was confused. I knew this all had something to do with my vision in Santa Barbara. Two Hearts had worn my face as a mask over his own.

I heard a high-pitched scream of warning. I looked up to see my nari. Suddenly I knew that Two Hearts was trying to scramble my mind. He was attempting to enter my thinking process. He knew how to jump into the crack between the spheres of intelligence, the conscious and the subconscious. If he found his way to my sacred twins, my male and female warriors, he could split me in two forever by holding them apart and isolated from each other.

The mistletoe that he wore in the dream and was wearing now is the king of the trees. It is part of an ancient language known by good and bad sorcerers. Mistletoe lives off even the greatest of trees; it sucks their life force and kills them. It is a parasite. That was the key. Just like Red Dog, the sorcerer in the north, Two Hearts must live parasitically off the power and spirit of woman. Perhaps he meant to trade now, but my guess was that he wanted us all for himself.

I didn't know exactly what he was doing, but my head felt like it was going to explode. His power came in the form of intimidation. Had I not fought Red Dog before I don't know if I could have withstood his attempt at domination. Then I saw the basket. It was large, and reached up to his knees. He kicked it from time to time. Ginevee saw it too and tensed with anger.

"Remember the laws of Oruncha," she called out to Two Hearts. She must have sensed his treachery as well.

There was silence, threatening in its pervasiveness. It

lasted a long time. Two Hearts appeared to lie down on the ledge with his head on the edge. A tree stood next to him. A whirl of flames emanated from what looked like his body. A cone of fire rose up into the sky at least thirty feet high. It looked like a fiery electric cord. We were mesmerized by the sight. Then he did something that I had heard that sorcerers of high degree could do. He began to climb up the magical cord until he reached the very top, which was on the level of the top of the tree. He sort of rolled over onto the branches and pulled up the fiery cord like a lariat. It was an extraordinary performance. The cord seemed to disappear into his stomach. Two Hearts stepped off the tree and, lying on his back, gently floated down to the ground, his painted body shimmering like a pit of silver snakes freed from their bondage, a fiery force that was untouchable. Buzzie doubled over as if she were in agonizing pain. I knew he must be using her power to perform his tricks.

Two Hearts sat down on his heels and sent out the magical cord from his belly. He tied it around the basket and lowered the basket inch by inch down into the gorge. Broken lightning zigzigs were painted on its side. He began to twirl it, like a silent whirlwind. The basket spun into the center of the clearing, throwing the white sand of the designs into the air like thousands of glowing sparks. It settled down on the ground and was still. The far-off throbbing began again, or I became conscious of it again. I realized that the buzzing was emanating from the cord. Inside the basket we saw Skeeter curled up and lying on her side.

Ginevee told me to hold Buzzie. Slowly she walked over to the basket. Standing outside of the rim of the papunya, she took off the lid of the basket and pulled Skeeter out. She was unconscious but alive. Ginevee put the coolamon with the spear into the basket. She lay Skeeter down in front of me. Buzzie seemed to be in a trance. She sort of shuffled over to the basket and stepped into it, but she managed to turn around to me.

"Oruncha works in strange ways. Funny a basket should separate us again. I hate you no more." Big tears spilled down her cheeks.

She began to hum and Two Hearts pulled her up to his ledge and they were gone. Ginevee cradled Skeeter in her arms and we walked, then ran, out of the gorge and back into the red desert.

The moon was shining full force and we made our way back to the village in half the time it had taken us to reach the gorge. It was almost dawn, but everyone was waiting for us. We were greeted with great excitement and laughter. Mandowa and Ginevee tended to Skeeter, who had been given some kind of herbal drug by Two Hearts. She had been badly frightened, but she was unhurt. I don't even remember crawling into my wurley and going to sleep. The experience with Two Hearts had been terrifying, but I slept well because as darkness defines the light I knew very deeply inside of me that we were fending off the dark forces of the world.

Remember Midnight.
That was our hour
our time for magic
for dreams that
made life real.

For awhile
I thought we were forever.
Midnight held
onto our hair like rain.

—Steve Bailey

CHAPTER TWENTY-ONE
❖❖❖❖❖❖
IGUANA SPIRIT

That evening we were all so drunk with our success in returning the spear and Buzzie to Two Hearts and having Skeeter back among us that we decided to throw a huge feast. We gathered food and all had a hand in stirring coals and roasting meat or vegetables. We chewed on pitcheri, an herb that has a mildly intoxicating effect, and danced and sang.

I sat between Ruby and Agnes at the fire.

"You seem quite nice tonight, Lynn," Ruby said, tweaking my kangaroo skirt, which had places where hardened blood and river sand were ground into the fur.

"And you too, Ruby. Your makeup is just too divine," I said, touching the smears of red ochre and pipe clay swirling over her cheeks. We giggled together as we shared a piece of euro meat and a few berries.

I looked at Alice, who sat across from us. She winked at me, her hair frizzed out in a yellow-reddish fan around her face, which was completely covered in ash and white ochre. We had had so little time together. She and July had just returned from their long expedition to Alice Springs, because their jeep had broken down and they had had to wait for parts. When July saw me looking at her, or I should say trying to recognize her, she came around the fire.

"I'm so happy to see you," she said, giving me a big kiss and leaving a smudge of white that felt gritty on my lips. Her face was ringed in white ochre.

"I was so afraid for you, when I heard you had been in the bush," July said. "I seem to miss everything, don't I?" She smiled. "But I did get to Australia and Alice will be a lifelong sister." She was full of joy and bounced back around the fire.

Ginevee was sitting next to Mandowa, with Skeeter asleep on her lap. I watched Ginevee, who had washed away her paint with creek water. She sat proudly, with erect posture. She had an eye on everyone and made sure that the whole camp was cared for before she was. I had known another matriarch like her long ago whose name was Opel. She, too, had had swan medicine. I had loved her and I felt her presence now as I watched Ginevee surveying her flock with immense dignity.

"Does this gathering remind you of a Beverly Hills party?" Ruby asked, giggling into her yellow-painted arm.

"In a way it does," I answered.

"How's that? Must be the catering service," Ruby said.

Agnes smiled as she ate a grub and listened.

"Everyone is wearing their finery," I said. "And women are like women everywhere. We all love to talk about the events of the day. Of course the subjects might be a little different."

"Your world makes it very difficult to be unique," Ruby said, smacking her lips.

"Yes, that's true," I said.

"It takes great courage and a true point of view, wouldn't you say?" Ruby said.

"I guess so," I answered, nodding.

"Each woman here is painted in her own way—not with makeup, which so often disguises. These women are animated shields painted with the designs and colors of their particular knowledge. What a great sacredness that is. Tonight we personify our shields. I can't see you all, but I can *see* you and it makes my heart full to be a part of this powwow. And may I say, Black Wolf, your work the last few days makes me proud. Of course, let it not be forgotten who taught you everything you know. Here, crack these nuts and make yourself useful," Ruby said, handing me a handful of brown nuts.

She complimented me so rarely that tears stung my eyelids. I looked at the nuts in my hand. So many, so close together. I gave them back to Ruby. I got up and walked away from the fire. Turning a corner around a wurley, I leaned against the poles and woven grass and wept. I felt as if a dam within me had burst. Suddenly nothing I had ever done in my life made any sense. Especially being in Australia. I didn't know why my mood had changed. I heard the dancing and singing and I thought, That's right, that's just like life—it's going right on without me. So what if I make a difference or I don't? Nothing makes any difference anyway. If I try to be a shaman or a secretary, I'll botch it up somehow.

By now I was sobbing hysterically. If I could have found an ocean to drown in I would have. The beauty and truth and sacredness of these women meant so much to me, but so what? What did the world care? Most of all, I was desperately, agonizingly, and stupidly unworthy. I felt as though I were in a state of demented depression. I sat down in the dirt and sobbed quietly to the moon, to my family, to all the people I had ever known and let down, and there were many.

After a while I felt the silent and gentle presence of someone sitting down next to me. Out of the corner of my swollen eye I saw Agnes. She said nothing; she just let me cry. Once my tears had slowed a little, she lay her hand on mine in a way that was very kind.

"You are so terribly frightened and no one knows," Agnes said.

"Oh God, yes I am," I said, gasping for breath.

"No one has ever known how frightened you are. You never tell anyone," Agnes said, still touching my hand with tenderness.

"It's true," I said, getting a hold of myself.

"Remember, long ago, I told you about a warrior named Poor Cow?"

"Yes, but tell me again, Agnes. I never really understood it," I said, sniveling.

"Well, Poor Cow felt very sorry for everyone in the camp. He saw Many-Horses, who had a broken leg, and he said, 'Oh, poor Many-Horses, how will he get through the winter with a broken leg?' Then he saw Amy White Buffalo, who could have no children, and he said, 'Oh, poor Amy, what will become of her?' And so Poor Cow was sad for everyone and felt pain for them all. Then one day he noticed that he had lost his shadow. He went to the medicine chief of the camp and asked him, 'Oh, Great Chief, I am sad, for I have lost my shadow. What shall I do?' The Great Chief said, 'Poor Cow, that is very sad. Why don't you go into the sweat lodge and find your shadow?' And that's just what Poor Cow did," Agnes said. By now I had stopped crying.

"What happened in the sweat lodge? I forget."

"Poor Cow found his shadow and he died," Agnes said, watching me with her strange eyes.

"I never did understand why he died," I said.

"Of course not, because there's a lesson here for you."

"Please teach me, Agnes. I feel miserable."

"Never walk in the shadow of a sorcerer or you will die," Agnes said.

"There are many ways to die," she went on. "In a sense you have been living in my shadow as my apprentice. There comes a time when that is dangerous. There comes a time when you have to own your own shadow. Poor Cow lost his shadow because he was weak. He feared too much for himself and others, for a good reason," Agnes said.

"What was that?" I asked.

"Because he couldn't own his own power, let alone his own shadow. He wanted to fix others, so he didn't have to focus on fixing himself. When he entered the sweat lodge, which is a symbol of sacredness, his physicalness merged with his spirit and he was healed," she said.

"But he died." I looked at Agnes.

"Yes, he died to what he had always been—a weak and divided person. He emerged from the sweat lodge a new man."

"I never understood it in that way," I said, wiping my nose and my tear-stained face.

"There are many ways to understand a good medicine story. I'm glad that it helped," Agnes said, giving me a squeeze.

"It helped. Thank the Great Spirit that you are here with me." I hugged Agnes and we went back to join the others.

The next afternoon Ginevee and I were sitting on the ground in front of my wurley. We were resting in the shade and I had been talking to her about what had happened with Two Hearts.

"Ginevee, I don't understand how a person, no matter

how powerful they are, can produce a magical cord that they can climb."

A flicker of a smile lifted the corners of her mouth. It was that sardonic attitude that she had that always put me on edge. I wished I hadn't said anything. Ginevee closed her eyes and took a long, lazy breath.

"Why are you smiling?" I asked.

"I think we should take a little stroll," she said, not answering me.

"A stroll?" I had never heard her say "stroll" and it sounded funny. "Okay," I said as we got up.

I walked stiffly for the first few minutes. Almost everyone in the camp was resting; even the dingos had been noticeably absent. We meandered down by the creek and over by a stand of ghost gum trees about twenty minutes from the village. Ginevee walked quietly as if she were paying particular attention to our surroundings. She was up to something. At one point she stopped quite suddenly and cocked her head to the side like a crow listening. I watched Ginevee's face, which was etched severely against the afternoon light. She looked so ancient and mysterious, like a high priestess from some arcane and forgotten time. Every wrinkle was even more deeply furrowed by the shading from the trees. She appeared wiser and older than I could possibly imagine anyone to be, even in my most remote dreams.

"Stand very still," Ginevee said in a sharp whisper. "Don't move."

I couldn't imagine what she was doing. I stood still watching and listening. I saw a darting movement, a blur near Ginevee's foot. I was surprised to see an iguana, a large lizard-like creature about a foot and a half long, going along his way between us. I had always seen iguanas posing very still on hot rocks or scurrying off away from me.

"Don't move, whatever you do," Ginevee said again as she moved behind me. I watched the iguana as he stopped to look around. It was as if he hadn't even seen us.

"This is a test of your warrior spirit. Don't move," Ginevee whispered to me.

I couldn't imagine what was going on, so I stood very still, alert. I watched the iguana make a decision. He walked over to my left leg and placed one little scratchy foot on my toe.

"Be a tree," Ginevee whispered.

It bothered me that I couldn't see her. Suddenly, with a scurrying rush, the iguana ran up my leg and back. I felt the pulling and scratching of his tiny claws as he went right to the top of my head. As usual, two thoughts pervaded my thinking. On this occasion, I thought both that I provided a good lookout for this iguana, and that I should be shrieking and flailing my arms.

"Hold your power," Ginevee hissed at me. "He just thinks you're a tree. Hold still, yea. That's not bad, Lynn. You surprise me with your control. Your new hat is quite appropriate for a clever woman."

I closed my eyes and stood still, clenching my fists and gritting my teeth. After a few minutes, Ginevee moved toward me and then with boisterous affectations she moved off to my side. I could feel the iguana flinch. He fled down my back and ran over toward a ghost gum.

I breathed a sigh of relief. Ginevee moved over to another ghost gum. The movement of the iguana caught my eye. He started to run and disappeared abruptly into the tree. I started to walk closer to see if he had gone into a hole in the tree trunk. There was no hole. Another movement to my left startled me. I turned and Ginevee was gone.

"Ginevee," I shouted, getting very agitated.

"Lynn, you don't have to yell and hurt a poor old lady's ears," Ginevee said, stepping out from the tree or from behind the tree.

"Ginevee, what are you doing? I couldn't see you," I said, lowering my voice.

Ginevee looked old and ethereal, almost transparent in the shafts of sunlight penetrating the clearing. She walked toward me, smiling slightly. Then, turning her back to me, she walked deliberately and slowly right over to the ghost gum tree that the iguana had gone to, hit the tree once with her fist, and was simply gone. I blinked my eyes and ran over to the tree and looked all around it.

"Ginevee, darn it! Stop this. You're making me crazy." I was yelling. When I stopped, I heard my own voice echo in the trees. The iguana walked out from the tree on the other side. I rushed around. The iguana didn't run but walked slowly away from me; he turned his head around to look me in the eyes as if he were human. I started to scream, but a hand on my shoulder stopped me. I turned and jumped at the sight of Ginevee.

"I told you an old lady's ears are sensitive," she said.

I whirled around to look for the iguana, but he had vanished.

"Ginevee, you disappeared into that tree, didn't you? And so did the iguana." I was almost in tears.

"Let's just say that I was trying to answer your question," Ginevee said, sitting down and leaning up against the tree.

"I was giving away time, you might say. Perhaps that is all I have." She was chewing on a piece of grass.

I was completely flustered, so I sat down beside her. "You mean you were answering my question about the magical cord?" I asked.

"Yes. Power is a question of your use of time. I wanted to show you how I play with time. A medicine woman knows how to arrange time. As you know, much of what you see in life is an agreement that something is in fact true. You can't imagine that I could give away five minutes."

"No, I can't, and who would you give it to?"

"I just gave you five minutes."

"What do you mean?"

"I gave you five minutes from the Dreamtime, as we say in Australia."

I pondered Ginevee's words. My body and mind were feeling very odd, indeed. "You mean you really disappeared?"

"I simply switched time on you. I took five minutes from our agreement of what time is and switched it with five minutes in the Dreamtime."

"But how can you do that?" I asked.

Ginevee picked up another twig and snapped it in two pieces. "There are two different areas of time." She lifted up one stick. "There is the relative world of time," she said. Then she held up the other twig, saying "And then there is the Dreamtime." She watched me.

"If that's true, which I guess it is, then how can you do what you did and why can't I do it?"

"You can and you nearly did with Oruncha. You brought back a piece of time in the churinga, the sacred stone with the design of your dream. You didn't understand it, but that was an exchange of our time with the Dreamtime."

Ginevee drew circles in the sand with her finger.

"But how can you step in and out like that?"

"It's a power that you develop. It is good to focus your attention on one thing in life, just like in becoming a clever woman, yea. You become very good at one specialty. You become an expert. In the process of becoming an expert you finely tune your whole being. You collect the important parts of yourself and you begin to live the life of a warrioress. You rid yourself of attitudes that are not essential to your task. I have learned to step around all the sides of time like you walk around that ghost gum. Just like She Who Walks With The Wind can disappear or Two Hearts can climb a fiery magical cord. If you believe in magic you can learn to do wondrous and magical acts, hmm. It's just a matter of practice, yea." She laughed at my glum look of consternation.

"But I want to learn to do something special," I said.

"But you already have a speciality."

"No, I don't. I can't disappear."

"Oh, no?"

"No, I certainly can't."

"That iguana didn't see you."

"That was because I was disguised."

"Well?"

"Well, what?"

"We are all disguised."

"That's different."

"Is it?" Ginevee said, looking at me.

"And what about that iguana? How did he disappear? He certainly doesn't practice disappearing."

"The iguana was a disguise, too."

"What do you mean?"

"Don't you know that my medicine ally is an iguana? He lives inside of me. When I want to know things I send him to check things out. I also have the black swan, but she stays near me."

I knew that everyone has allies in the spirit world or the Dreamtime. "But I didn't know that people could see your allies?"

"If you have the spirit strong inside you people can see your ally if you want them to," she said, grinning.

"Oh," I said. Thoughts and pictures were colliding in my head. I stood still, looking stupid.

"When you were with Oruncha getting your crystals in the Dreamtime we came back for you and you had disappeared. We didn't see you until dawn when you appeared again."

"Really? Is that true? How come you never told me?"

"Because, you never asked." She smiled and got up. "Come on, let's go help with supper. I'm starved, yea."

"Yea," I said absently, as I struggled with this new information.

"I have a task for you, my daughter." Ginevee started talking as we walked. She had a leafy branch in her hand and she was slapping her shoulders with it to keep off the flies.

"What do you want me to do?" I was eager to understand.

"I want you to become aware of time, every moment as it passes."

"But I thought Koori people didn't think much about time."

"It's true. I want you to become more Koori." She was saying all of this with a strange twinkle in her eye.

"I don't understand."

"I want you to put on your watch, yea, and be aware of what time you do everything. Watch the sun, the moon, and the transit of the stars. Find out what time the Southern Cross is lowest in the sky before dawn. I want you to be aware of your own cycles, when you get hungry, when you sleep. You white-fellas are already obsessed with time; now I want you to *become* time." By now we had reached the village. Preparations were underway for supper and the sun was low in the sky.

"I don't want to think about time," I said, wanting to pout.

"As a warrioress, this is your task for the next many days," Ginevee answered sternly. As she walked away toward Mandowa she whistled her "going away for a short distance" song.

Wounds are shadows
great heaps of dark
space.

Between two valleys
trees swim like rivers
orchestrated in wind.

Old man and dragon
clouds ride shotgun
on blue northern sky.

Very few have been here.
Turkey buzzard, white-tailed deer,
Miwoks a hundred years ago.

The void is like this centering place.
Beyond wounds it is a canal
of birth

deep into uncharted avenues
where a path of truth covered
with overgrowth lies

attending to the reservoir of dust.

—Jack Crimmins

CHAPTER TWENTY-TWO
❖❖❖❖❖❖
AN APPOINTMENT WITH TIME

For the next few days, I did as I was told. I put on my watch and became totally obsessed with capturing life in terms of a clock. It was awful. I became regimented, irritable, and closed to anything spontaneous. Even though I spent a lot of the day complaining, I became aware of patterns in my habits and moods.

I decided to draw my own papunya. I cleared a patch of ground in my wurley so no one would bother me and I designed a sand painting of my life inside of time. I divided the painting into four colors of sand for the four periods of time during the day: red, black, yellow, and white. Then I made symbols for the stars, food, praying, and other activities during the day. Small white dots of sand represented the Dreamtime flowing in and out of the red dots that symbolized everyday time.

By the third day I was fanatical about looking at my watch and being exact. Making the papunya was kind of like fashioning an altar. Besides all of the other sacred aspects, it was like a microcosm of my inner and outer life. It enabled me to extend out of myself what was intangible inside of me and make it tangible in the papunya. Then I could see it and experience its density of color. Best of all, I could clearly see the design and symbology of aspects of my life.

One afternoon Ruby walked into my wurley. "Well, well, what have we here?" she asked.

I told her about the task that Ginevee had set for me. "Being Koori, why do you think she wants me to be so involved with time?" I asked.

"Because you're always worried about one aspect of time or another."

"So?"

"So if you're obsessed with something like sex or time or anything, it's better to explore it than to deny it. Then you come out on the other side with some kind of understanding. If you bury yourself in time thoughts maybe you'll get sick of it," she said.

"Oh." I nodded.

"What's all this sand in here?" she asked, shuffling her bare feet around.

"I made a sort of papunya for time and I've been gathering different colors of sand."

"I thought most normal people swept sand out of their houses instead of bringing it in! Of course, everything is backward Down Under," Ruby said, sneezing from the dust her moving feet were creating.

I started to sneeze, too. "Ruby, please, I'm trying very hard to stay disciplined."

"No one likes to have a blind old lady around. You're just like everybody else. You just want to get rid of me."

Ruby stomped her feet and raised more dust until the air in the wurley became a murky tan color. If Ruby wanted to get my attention she was succeeding. The effect she was having on me was surreal. Her words were those of a disgruntled, petulant, half-mindless old lady. But looking at her was something else. She stood in the center of swirling clouds of dust. She was irritating me like the storm of sentiment that she created. At times like this her face was stern and severly chiseled as if it were cut out of stone. She stood confronting me, looking as old and mysterious as the red mountains that surrounded us in the distance. Truth is in those mountains, just like I could sense it in Ruby. Nevertheless, the process of finding that truth is frightening and unfathomable.

"Ruby, what do you want?" I asked.

"I heard you were dreaming your own papunya and I wasn't consulted," she said, pouting.

"But, Ruby, Ginevee just told me to think about time and stuff."

"And what's time and 'stuff'? What I want to know is what do you have in your sand painting that represents the unknown?"

I studied her face for a moment. My mind went blank. Then something began to open in my brain. That's it, I thought, that's it!

"That's it, Ruby, that's what has been missing. I hadn't thought of it."

"Thought of what?"

"I forgot the unknown. I will put black dots all around the outside for the unknown."

"Make them wavy lines, Lynn."

"Why?"

Ruby began to giggle to herself as she sat down across from me.

"Because you always float on the waves of acceptability."

I stared at her. "What do you mean?"

"I mean that you are very superficial."

"I am not. Just because I took your suggestion does not mean I'm superficial." She was really irritating me.

"You are superficial, because you do not take your thinking deep enough."

I started grinding up some charcoal from the fire on a stone to make black sand. I stopped and glared at her.

"What do you mean by that?"

"You think I'm wasting your time."

"Yes, I do."

"Don't forget to represent wasted time. And, furthermore, you have no respect for the unknown," Ruby said.

"How can you have respect for something that doesn't exist?"

"That's what I mean. If you leave the unknown out of your papunya, you show a lack of honor for what you perhaps cannot see. Can you see my back right now?"

"No."

"But it still exists," Ruby said, her hands on her hips.

"Of course it does."

"So things exist even if you can't see them. It's the same with ideas."

"Okay. So what are you getting at?"

"There is danger lurking around you, Lynn, and I

want you to be aware of it." Ruby squinted her eyes at me.

"What kind of danger? Do you mean that sorcerer, Booru?" I asked.

"What is evil?" she asked, ignoring my question.

I thought for several minutes. All kinds of ideas flitted through my mind. "Evil is inflicting harm on another person," I finally said.

"What if the harm that someone receives helps that someone grow and eventually become enlightened? What if the Great Spirit has designed all wars and pain so that people can learn and become realized?"

"But that's saying that sorcery and the manipulation of others and killing for ideals or whatever could all be acceptable and not evil."

"That's one way of looking at it, if you're ignorant. If we continue to talk we will get lost in our feelings, in our private interpretation of word meanings. We will get lost in our own subjective histories. So where is the truth?"

I thought a long time, feeling the back of my neck beginning to tense and hurt. "When you put it that way . . . I'm not sure."

"Is it possible that we may see only part of the truth and that part of it lies out in the darkness of space in the unknown?"

"Yes, I guess so."

"If part of truth lies in the unknown, then maybe you understand why we must have respect for the unknown."

"I see what you mean." I was mixing my black color for the dots.

"There is often great darkness in those who think they know. Great evil has been done on earth by people who think they have all the answers. They have no respect for the unknown. Do you understand?"

"Yes. But is there ever something that can never be known?"

"A human can never know with the mind what a medicine woman would call the unknowable. When Two Hearts climbed up his fiery cord and rested on his back on what you said looked like thin air, that is part of the unknowable. He was demonstrating his respect for that miraculous dimension. There is no way to describe how something like that is possible. It is part of the world of power. It is a world unknowable to most human beings."

"But then how can we know it truly exists?"

"Because we experience miraculous events as medicine women. All you can take into death is your experience," Ruby went on. "Once an apprentice experiences enough and knows that much of her thinking is centered in her will, then she can quiet her mind. She literally stops thinking so that her body-mind in her solar plexus can take over. The secret to a powerful shield is the same as the secret to a powerful sand painting. Give respect to the unknown and what is perhaps unknowable even to a medicine woman. That is what I call the back of the Great Spirit—the part of his body that is always in shadow. Your stealth as a warrioress depends on your faith in the Great Spirit. If there is no Great Spirit in your papunya, then where is your basis for any argument about good or evil?"

"I understand," I said, rubbing my neck.

"Lie down on your stomach, Lynn."

Ruby came over to me and laid her hands firmly on my neck. She pushed my face down into the sand as I lay on my stomach. "I spoke of danger."

"Yes," I said, spitting out some sand.

"If you do not see all sides of truth and you think that only what you understand is valid, then you dishonor power. You ignore much of the body of the Great Spirit."

"What is the body of the Great Spirit?"

"It is all creation. We are limited as human beings. Most humans live in a tiny little world where only their own perceptions are accepted as real. They will kill for those perceptions. I am asking you to respect what you don't see. What you don't see sees you very well. What you have forgotten to honor is living off you right now," Ruby said, giving my sore neck a twist.

"What do you mean 'living off me'?"

"You have created a darkness around the back of your neck."

"How have I done that?"

"By needing to be right. Don't you need to be right, especially about your ideals of right and wrong?"

"Yes, I guess I do."

Ruby pushed again on my neck and I sneezed once. "That darkness has been given form by your own ignorance. Your father always challenged your ideas as a kid, didn't he?"

"Yes."

"He never let you win an argument, right?"

"Right."

"Think about it. That created a need in you. That need has a big mouth. He eats that emotion of yours, your need to be right. It looks like a black cloud around the back of your neck. He feeds there and makes your neck hurt real bad. Right?"

"Yes." I was horrified at the thought of some blackness attaching itself to me.

"That's how disease begins," Ruby said. "We open our arms and bring it right in."

"How can I get rid of it?"

"By giving humble respect to what is unknown and unknowable in the universe." She gave my neck one last twist and said some words in Cree. I saw little pinholes of light in my eyes and my neck relaxed.

"Come. I'll help you put those black dots in. We'll sing a power song while we do it. I'll mix while you draw."

I looked at the eerie light coming from Ruby's eyes and the deep kindness in her face. I felt such relief in my neck that tears came to my eyes.

In the beginning of all things, wisdom and knowledge were with the animals; for Tirawa, the One Above, did not speak directly to man. He sent certain animals to tell men that he showed himself through the beasts, and that from them, and from the stars and the sun and the moon, man should learn. Tirawa spoke to man through his works.

—Chief Letakots-Lesa

CHAPTER TWENTY-THREE
❖❖❖❖❖❖
DINGO MAN DREAMING

It was dark and mysterious when I awoke the next morning. It was still cool in the wurley, as the first warmth of day had not yet spread over the desert. I watched the darkness recede slowly from the corners and streaks of dawn light begin to permeate the wurley with a soft pink glow. There was a thin sheet of fog moving over the ground of the village and settling in the hallows.

It was a good time to think, good time to chase the shadows of my mind. The web of Ginevee's teachings, woven with such care, enveloped me with delicate, irresistible threads. Each time I shifted my thoughts, another silvery fiber of truth would snare me. I couldn't escape. I remembered Ginevee handing me the talking stick at that ceremony in Canada, seemingly so long ago. With a jolt I realized that she indeed had been right. The story had possessed me. I was inhabited by a force. It felt like something shiny and fat or fecund. It filled me with longing. As I lay watching the fog slowly dissipate, I felt the power of this force magnify until my stomach ached. Ginevee was right, this story had taken me in a very clever way. To me, this story was of my own making. It had the power of making me believe that.

Lazily I looked over at my papunya on the floor. The pink light glinted majestically off the tiny mica and crystal fragments in the sand. I admired my work and then I was quickly awake. My sleepy reverie vanished with the shadows. I sat up. My papunya looked different. At first I couldn't see what was wrong. Then I realized that there was an odd-shaped hollow in the center of it. It was sort of pear-shaped. I got up and examined the sand painting carefully. None of the design or colors had been in the least disturbed except for the large depression of the sand in the center. It was as if something had slept on it or lay down on it. But there were no tracks to indicate that. Something about this was ominous. As I stared at the pear shape, I began to be frightened. A shadow of a person fell across the papunya. I jumped and looked up.

"It's a good morning, my daughter, yea," Ginevee said.

"Ginevee, you startled me," I answered.

Ginevee looked down at the sand mosaic and stared. She knelt down, obviously seeing the depression in the sand. I moved out of the way as she examined the ground all around it. Finally she closed her eyes and ran her long fingers over the sand floor.

"Hmm," she said. "So Booru the sorcerer is also Dingo Man Dreaming."

"What are you saying?" I asked. I didn't like this. The back of my neck was beginning to perspire.

"See this pear shape in your papunya?" Ginevee said, pointing.

"Yes."

"See how it looks like an animal has lain down and slept there?" She passed her flat palms over the colored sand.

"But how could an animal lay down there and leave no tracks?"

Ginevee looked at me with her light-filled eyes. "Only a spirit animal could," she replied, watching my face for my reaction.

"You mentioned Booru. Do you mean Booru sent his spirit animal to sleep on my papunya?" My voice cracked and sounded whiny.

"Look, my daughter. Many things are said to Koori people by the way an animal sleeps on the ground. We read the impression of his body in the sand. See here and here?" She pointed to a deeper imprint. "That usually means that the animal has eaten well and his belly was full of food and water.

I will show you later how to follow the tracks of an animal from his sleeping place. But this animal has left no tracks. Just like Poor Cow in your story, he has no shadow. He has lost his shadow, because he is not of this world. His shadow has been taken by Booru, the one who never dies. This is the imprint of a totem animal. This is the mark of Booru's ally. It is a dingo. Now we know that Booru is Dingo Man Dreaming. We know more about him now. It is good, yea?"

"Yea—no, Ginevee!" This scared me. "Booru has sent his familiar to me. He laid right down in the middle of my conception and dream of time, my time. What's so great about that?" I was visibly shaken. Ginevee placed a calming hand on my shoulder. She contemplated the papunya for several minutes.

"It is true, hmm. Booru has penetrated your outward manifestation of your Dreamtime. He wants you to know that. He has made a statement to you. Let's see if we can read what it is." Ginevee sat down across from me. The papunya rested serenely, a sparkling disc of variegated colors between us. A halo of morning sunshine silhouetted Ginevee's seated figure, her hair wispy and curling like cobwebs in the intense light.

"Calm yourself, my daughter. Look through your magic crystals inside you. You are a clever woman. Learn to read the imprints of the unknowable. There is no way to understand with your mind how a totem dingo of the sky world can actually journey to your wurley and leave a message for you. Quiet your silly mind and read with your body." Ginevee pressed my solar plexus with her hand.

"The totem dingo has left a map for you, yea." Ginevee hummed a chant for several minutes. I felt my extreme anxiety and tension begin to bleed away through my feet and down into the earth.

"That's better." Ginevee nodded approvingly as she watched me relax. I looked intently at the impression in the sand. I started at the beginning, tracing my hands in the air over its outline.

"It's pear-shaped and it looks like the dingo's head was here. Its feet and legs seem to have been there. It's funny. Its body left an impression like a cloud—is that right?" I looked to Ginevee for assurance. She nodded, smiling.

"And its legs, spread down like that, look like the symbol for rain," I said.

"So what does that mean?" Ginevee asked.

"Well, it means rain cloud to me. It means a sky being, a cloud being, doesn't it?" I was speaking slowly, trying to understand.

"That's right, it is the mark of an ally, a sky being, no question. The legs were positioned like that, and see the way the head moved toward its belly? That's the movement of a female dingo watching her stomach. They do that when they carry their young."

"What does that have to do with a cloud?" I asked.

"A rain cloud is female and gives birth to life-giving rain. It is good and very interesting," Ginevee said, pursing her lips and scratching her head.

"But I still don't understand," I said, feeling dumb.

"Let me tell you something about Booru. He is sometimes called the One Who Never Dies, or a sandamara."

"I wondered what you meant by that," I said.

"You see, for several hundred years the white fellas have tried to kill him. There was even a time when he hid in the mountains and all of his warriors were women. That is very unusual, yea. But now we know why. His totem is a female dingo. Anyway, the armies of the white fellas would attack and be killed by seemingly unending numbers of Booru's warriors. The white fellas couldn't figure out where they were all coming from."

"Where were they coming from?" I asked.

"Some say there was a secret tunnel to the other side of the mountain. The fighters came through there. After a while they disappeared. They say he secretly left through the tunnel. But who knows. All we do know is that the white fellas felt like they were shooting their bullets and spears into the vast ocean. Nothing happened and Booru still lives. All the white fellas died long ago, but not Booru. He understands the power of woman. That is why Two Hearts teamed up with him. It is said that after years of fighting for his people, Booru's people began to want the ways of the white fella. They wanted the drink and television and sugar. They turned against Booru and he became very bitter. He lost his shadow and threw in with the evil Two Hearts."

"What do you mean he lost his shadow?" I asked.

Ginevee started to laugh. "There's a lot of fellas around here without shadows today."

Then she became serious. "When we say someone has lost his shadow, we may mean that the person has died. In this instance, I mean that Booru has lost his spirit. His spirit has left him, because he has turned to evil ways. He has no shadow."

I stared at my sand painting for a long time.

"Look at the impression that Booru has made on my process of time, Ginevee. In a way I guess I'm fascinated. We all do that to each other, don't we?"

"Yes, my daughter, but Booru's ally was respectful of your power. He only compressed your painting slightly with his weight. If you look at most people, you see that they behave like wild dogs. They run madly into the painting of your life, throwing your colored sands of time out into space where they can never be found again. We become victims of their process and we seem to forget totally that we were even creating a papunya of our own. The worst thing is that often we step into their sand painting as if it were our own. And we leave our beautiful designs to scatter to the four winds. We let that happen. We have a name for people like that. They belong to a different tribe than we do."

"Where is this tribe?" I asked.

"This tribe lives near the water. They sit on the red sandy riverbanks under the eucalyptus trees. They never go in the water; they just spend their lives looking at it. They are the Half People, and, as you can see, they are split right down the middle. When they hear you coming they put their halves together and run and hide behind the trees. Most tribes trade goods with each other. The Half People only trade very crude stone axes or tobacco. All they want is tobacco."

"Why do they want tobacco?"

"Tobacco is sacred and the smoke from it carries messages to the sky beings in the Dreamtime. They hope that baime, or the Great Spirit, will make them whole again." I watched Ginevee's face. There was a twinkle in her dark eyes. She took my hand and held it for a moment. "I want you to come with me down to the creek. There is some very pure sand, very fine. Wear your dilly bag and bring your coolamon. We will gather sand and place it all around your papunya. Then we will watch quietly all night."

"What will we watch for?" I asked.

"We will watch to see if anything leaves any tracks. Sometimes spirits leave tracks and we can follow them back into the Dreamtime."

"I'm not sure I want to follow an ally of Booru's into the Dreamtime."

"It is time, my daughter. You have no choice. Just like power chose you years ago, you cannot back away now. It would be fatal for you. Booru's ally has come for you. We do not know the reason, but you must find out."

"How do I do that?" I was scared again. I didn't want any part of this. If it meant backing away, then I would do just that. Ginevee watched me and slapped her knees. She rolled around on the ground laughing. The more I protested the more she laughed.

"You white fellas can forget the spirit so quickly, yea. You remind me of the Half People."

"I've jumped in the water more than once. I'm not like the Half People," I said. I felt very indignant.

"Yes, you are. When they hear our footsteps and put both of their sides together, they think that their split is invisible, that they look like everybody else. Perhaps to some people they do. Just like them, you think that you can run and hide. But you can't, my daughter. This ally is evil and very powerful. He sees your power and in his way he has honored you. He has chosen you as a worthy opponent."

"Oh, great, now I'm the worthy opponent of evil. Oh, great, I can't wait. Let's put out a welcome mat!" By now I was stomping around the wurley in a fury as Ginevee laughed.

"You have already welcomed him. You have even been calling his name."

"I don't know his name . . . you mean Booru, or his ally?"

"There is no separation between Booru and his ally," Ginevee said.

"But of course there is," I said, staring wide-eyed at her. She was always trying to confuse me.

"Booru's ally is an extension of his own spirit. They are part of each other." Ginevee was making spirals in the dirt with her thumb.

"Well, we're all part of each other in some sense. But if Booru and his ally, the dingo, were standing together in this room they would appear to our human eyes as separate, wouldn't they?" My voice was squeaking again.

"No," Ginevee said. She was smiling at me.

"You mean, if I had been awake, I would have seen Booru lying on my sand painting?"

"There's no way of knowing what you would have seen. There's a reason for Booru confronting you, that's all we know, and we don't even know why. But he thinks you have power and maybe you do." Ginevee winked at me. I couldn't tell if she was playing with me or what.

"The reason he has confronted me is because the dolphins sent us a message that he and Two Hearts were trying to destroy the women's ceremonies and certainly the women of high degree. We came to help you and he somehow knows that," I said.

"Maybe, maybe not. The most important thing right now is to gather some sand, hmm." Ginevee grabbed my coolamon and handed it to me with my dilly bag.

"Did I hear that you are going to gather more sand? Seems to me there's enough sand in this house already," Ruby said as she shuffled into the wurley, her bare feet raising a cloud of pink dust.

"Ruby, be careful!" I shouted as I watched Ruby's feet obliterate the outer black dots that represented the unknowable in my papunya.

"Oh, I'm so sorry. I'm having a little trouble seeing this morning," Ruby said, looking very contrite and pushing out her lower lip.

"Ruby, please be nice. I don't feel very well today."

"Well, a little river sand will cure that, I'm sure." Now she was down on her knees sweeping sand with her hands into absurd little mountains.

She stopped her antics and held her flattened palms about two inches above the papunya. After a minute she said, "Ah, ho! So that's why you're so upset. That bad Booru has sent his big bad ally after our little wolf. Woof, woof, woof," Ruby barked, crawling around the floor on all fours as if she were looking for something. Ginevee and Ruby started rolling around in the dust laughing and barking hysterically.

"Thanks for the comic relief, ladies, but I really don't appreciate being made fun of like this. That ally could kill me."

"Yup. May be your last day on earth," Ruby said, wiping the tears from her eyes.

"It's true," Ginevee said, the pink dust floating in a haze around her. "This ally is big and bad. We must prepare for him and maybe even for your death. After all, death is your greatest ally. We will welcome your death, too."

"That reminds me, Ginevee. What did you mean when you said I had been calling this ally?"

"You have been calling him with your fear." Her face was abruptly serious again.

"I have?"

"Yes, you have avoided even thinking about Booru. You have chosen to look away. It's what you choose not to see in life that will eventually rule your life, yea."

"Yes, I guess you're right. But why should I dwell on someone so evil?"

"Dwell, dwell, you don't have to sit on him, Black Wolf, but be aware of all that darkness that he is." Ruby startled me with her sudden serious attitude.

"That's right. If you had been aware and let yourself perceive and even feel the evil that Booru is indeed throwing toward you, he could never have snuck up on you like that. In your avoidance you lost your stance as a stealthy warrioress. Hear my words, my daughter. As I have been trying to show you, the shadows of darkness and evil provide the balance that you so desperately need. You have never journeyed into the underworld. You have felt the monsters of darkness, but never have you truly confronted them."

"But I confronted the evil sorcerer Red Dog."

"You fought him many times, but you've never understood him. You did not look into him. You only saw his outline in the world. That is not enough. Why has the Dreamtime obscured your path with more difficulty in the form of evil sorcerers?" Ginevee asked, the dusty cloud settling around her and leaving a fine pink grit on her arms.

"I don't know."

"Because evil wants to know you. In a way, evil is trying to help you."

"How could evil help me?" I asked.

"You see, in the Dreamtime your image, your spirit, appears to be frayed. You are not clearly defined."

"What does that mean?"

"It means that the light that you are needs a distinct darkness to define it. The darkness that provides your balance and cosmic equilibriums is now only a gray shadow. By witnessing true evil, the opposite of the goodness that you are, your spirit will become more clearly defined. On the other side, the allies of darkness will see that and know your strength and they will leave you alone."

"How do I witness true evil?"

"One way is to confront Dingo Man Dreaming."

"Oh, great. And how do I do that?"

"By confronting his ally tonight."

"But how?"

"His ally will come for you. It is to your advantage that he hunts you on your own ground. When you see him, you must not leave the circle of your papunya. It could mean your death. Ruby, are you going to help us gather some sand?"

"I can't imagine bringing more dirt into this palace. But if you need me, I'll come," Ruby said, taking the coolamon that I handed her.

"It will only be little bit long way, yea." Ginevee slapped Ruby on the back as she smiled at me.

Anxiety was rising inside of me as we followed Ginevee out of the village and down toward the creek. I hadn't seen Willy-D in several days, so I was happy to see him bouncing on a ghost gum branch high above us as we neared the water. He sounded like I felt. I watched him as he lay his head over on his fine feathered shoulder and whimpered and cried like a baby. The crows in Australia sound different than crows do anywhere else I've ever been. They sound like yowling cats as they croon and lament. They seem to bemoan the fate of the earthly laws of which, in the Indian medicine way, they are the lords and keepers. After crying and causing a loud commotion, Willy-D and two other crows, which were as enormous as he, cawed wildly as if it were their morning meditation. Swooping down, Willy-D grazed my head as the three of them flew off toward the village and the smell of cooking fires.

"Here we are." Ginevee indicated a soft bank of pink sand. She squatted down and we did the same. She was whistling and Ruby and I both picked up the tune and joined in as we sifted the sand with our fingers and pressed it into our coolamons.

The rest of the early afternoon was spent spreading a pink layer of the fine sand in a wide radius around the papunya. It took us hours to flatten it perfectly and fit all the edges of the sand painting into it. Finally at dusk, Ginevee was satisfied.

"Well, if you ladies will excuse me, I'm going to retire," Ruby said, extending her hips and dusting her palms with a flourish. "Don't look under your bed for any ghosts," she said, laughing as she disappeared into the shadows.

Ginevee had stoked the fire outside and handed me two nut grass bulbs that had been roasting in the coals. I took a bite. The bulb tasted juicy and good, although I was not very hungry.

Ginevee and I sat together for a half hour or so, alone. But when I turned to reach for another nut grass bulb in the coals, I accidentally elbowed She Who Walks With The Wind in the stomach. She smiled as I jumped and yelled with surprise. She was sitting next to me, calmly eating a lizard that had been roasting in the coals. She smacked her lips as if she had been there all day long.

"My lord, you scared me," I said, watching the dark, remote expression on her face. She appeared even more transparent than usual. The shadows around her seemed to melt into her shape and dissolve her outline into the dry air. I must have been staring, because she and Ginevee started laughing and tickling me.

"Did you bring them?" Ginevee asked She Who Walks With The Wind.

"What?" I asked. They ignored me.

"Good stones, yea, and all of them from around Booru's camp," she said in sign language, as Ginevee translated for me.

"What stones?" I asked.

"She brought stones for our seeing ceremony tonight," Ginevee said, as if she had been talking on a telephone all day to She Who Walks With The Wind.

"But you haven't been around here for days. How could you know?" I was amazed. They looked at each other and shrugged as if I were a complete idiot.

We all looked up as dark thunderclouds blew overhead. Pounding thunder suddenly rolled like giant boulders in the north and sheet lightning rippled on the horizon like a sheer curtain of gold. As so often happened, I could smell rain but none fell. It rarely came down out of the fast-moving clouds.

She Who Walks With The Wind pulled over her dilly bag and set another rolled-up ranga by the red coals of the fire. She crooked her thin angular arms and began handing Ginevee and me medium-sized flat river stones from her bag. I was interested to count twelve as Ginevee and I placed them evenly on the perimeter of the pink sand that encircled the papunya. Then She Who Walks With The Wind pulled me down to sit beside her. She took her rolled-up mat, and placed it like a sacred pipe between us. She touched it with great reverence and studied my eyes and my face. At some point she was satisfied with what she saw and began unrolling the mat and signing with long graceful hands.

"There is a sacred place where the sky beings of the Rainbow Serpent meet with the guardians of their children who still walk the earth. It is a place where no evil can live, yea, and no evil spirit would ever dare to go there. It is a land where there is no sickness and the great ones live free. There is a lake there where the dolphins swim. It is made of silver shadows and in the middle, hmm, grows a native cherry tree. I have brought you leaves and branches from the cherry tree. We burn them, yea, and the smoke will carry you into the Dreamtime. The branches are a gift from Oruncha of Chauritzi."

Ginevee was translating carefully. The wind had come up and I was wiping sand and tears from my eyes. I was mesmerized by the power of her intent as she handed me the branches from the cherry tree. The branches felt different than any I had ever touched. The bark had a subtle green dapple and the limbs had bright pink flowers in clusters on the ends. The petals were falling and I carefully collected each one and placed them in my coolamon. My fingers became slightly sticky from the flowers, so I rubbed them in the sand.

Ginevee had left for a moment and now brought back her red ochre stones and painting sticks. From her waist hung a kangaroo pouch, which she undid and opened carefully. She held it up for me to smell. The women giggled as I turned up my nose. A vivid aroma came from the grease in the pouch; it smelled not unlike skunk. Much to my dismay we rubbed this grease all over our bodies. Through the hours of dusk the three of us painted Ginevee and me with red ochre designs that looped down onto our breasts. She Who Walks With The Wind dipped clumps of vegetable fluff and some feathers into the red ochre and, taking smears of her own blood from a knife prick on her arm, she secured a raised pattern onto our foreheads and cheeks. We looked like beings dropped onto earth from the stars. These designs were very different from those we used for our other ceremonies.

"Why are we painting only with red ochre?" I asked. We usually used other colors also.

"We are being painted to be recognized by certain ghosts of the Dreamtime. If you remember, when you were taught to run and stalk at night, the light of the night runners is always red," Ginevee said as she sat down with a coolamon of water and began singing in Koori. She had taken out her clever bag and took crushed leaves from it. Now she sprinkled them into the water.

I remembered back near the beginning of my training with Agnes and Ruby in Canada, they had once placed a wolverine mask over my head and had taught me about hunting and running surefootedly in darkness. I had been able to develop what Agnes had laughingly called the radar of a warrioress. It was the ability to see in the darkness with the intent of your will. I had had the feeling that my eyes had disconnected and I was seeing with a red illumination that emanated from my belly.

I wanted to ask Ginevee how she knew about that incident, but I didn't want to disturb her. Her eyes were closed and she was in a reverie. She looked fantastically surreal, the black of her body receding into the night so that only a dance of red ochre fluff and design remained, hovering over the coolamon like a mythical creature. In the firelight that was being stoked by She Who Walks With The Wind, Ginevee looked older than anything I had ever imagined. She was examining the herbs floating on the surface of the water in the coolamon as if she were divining tea leaves. She took four small crystals, like nuggets, from her bag and dropped them into the water one by one. She muttered, whistled, and sang as she moved the coolamon around and looked into the water. Then she handed the coolamon to me.

"Those are cherry tree leaves, yea. Just watch them catch the light in the crystals. They represent the four directions. Tonight we need to know in which direction to go. The ghosts of the Dreamtime can speak to us through the crystals." Ginevee pointed out which crystal represented which direction. "You will see something very special from one of the crystals. It will tell you what you need to know, yea. Keep watching them, my daughter."

The rest of the village was very still, again as if it were

deserted. Even the pups were asleep. I sat with the coolamon in my lap, watching the reflection of the flames that Ginevee was now fanning with the cherry tree branches. They leaped into the air and burned orange-yellow and then blue-green. The two women sang for a long time. I hummed along with them, their Koori chant beautiful and as unfamiliar as our faces had become.

I set down the water carefully on the other side of the fire from the papunya, as Ginevee directed. She and I began to dance as She Who Walks With The Wind stepped back from the fire. I saw a glint of brilliance, like lightning falling to the ground. I saw She Who Walks With The Wind, her arm twisting around over her head so that she looked as if she were swinging a Bull Roarer in the air. I heard its unmistakable sound: a fluttering drone spirit-call for the sacred beings of the Dreamtime.

That was the last I saw of She Who Walks With The Wind until much later. But we heard the Bull Roarer. Ginevee put the cherry tree branches onto the fire. The flames began to smolder and eerie billowing clouds of smoke stacked up in a curious fashion in front of us. Instead of trailing off, the cloud grew larger and larger until it was at least twelve feet above us. Ginevee had positioned us with the coolamon, so we sat looking through the fire and the smoke at the sand painting. I held the coolamon and was fascinated by the effect the smoke was having on me. I felt at once screened off from the world and yet the smoke seemed to have the ability to mirror the papunya and make it look magnified. I felt minuscule and huge at the same time.

We sat for what seemed a long while, the cloud moving slightly until it nearly reached us. The pink sand around my papunya glowed like a flat ring in the firelight. I watched it intently through the smoke. Just when I thought nothing more was going to happen, I felt a nudge in my ribs from Ginevee's thumb.

Something was happening to the sand. Little ridges of grease were beginning to form on my body and were catching the light. I had been very hot as the grease we wore was holding the heat from the fire, but suddenly I was ice cold as if I were sitting in a snow bank in Canada. My teeth actually started to chatter and I began to shake uncontrollably.

Ginevee reached over and whacked me on the back, sending me face down into the fire, or what I thought was the fire that we had built. But it didn't burn me. I just felt a comforting warmth and I was aware of the smell of my body grease melting. For some reason I was unconcerned with the fire or the smoke. It was as if I were floating face down in a dream. The Bull Roarer lulled me somehow.

From somewhere in back of me I heard Ginevee command me to watch the papunya. Dingo footprints were beginning to form there and I saw what appeared to be the rear end of a large dingo. It was silvery transparent and had a blue tinge. Slowly, as if walking on clouds, the dingo circled the sand painting, her powerful muscles rippling with iridescent light. She was awesome. Finally, she curled around and lay down, as she must have done the night before. Very deliberately, she turned her magnificent head toward me and looked squarely into my eyes. Her eyes were a brilliant, deep red. I gasped because the impact of the dingo's eyes sent me hurtling backward out of the fire.

Then I realized that I was actually sitting where I had always been. I was holding the coolamon and looking into the water. All of a sudden the east crystal came alive with light. Ginevee saw it too and grabbed me under my arms from behind. The gray smoke was enveloping us like a soft cocoon, and rays of light were emanating from the east crystal and shooting a corridor of illumination up into the smoke.

Before I knew what was happening or how, the luminous dingo was walking up the lit corridor toward the sky and looking back at us from time to time to be sure we were following. We were also walking up the light rays but under a tremendous pressure. It was as if we were trying to walk on the bottom of the ocean under tons of water. I thought my chest would collapse, but slowly we put one foot in front of the other and climbed upward, the cocoon-like cloud still around us like a protective womb. I felt like a woman forced up through the crust of consciousness. For the first time I glimpsed the puzzle in its entirety. I realized I had only a few of the pieces and that I was being wedged up and into still another unknown reality. I was in pain. I felt lacerated and psychically wounded. I had been thrust into a new environment of knowing. I knew that my wounded mind must heal before the actual knowing could take place. But I couldn't see how I was wounded.

Ginevee held my hand. I looked over at her as we continued to move upward, following the dingo that was now trotting eagerly as if she were nearing home. I gasped in horror as I watched what I had interpreted as a psychic wound. The skin was slowly melting off Ginevee's bones. I knew the same thing must be happening to me. My terror grew as I saw her become a skelton of blue-white bones holding my hand.

We continued to walk as I concentrated all of my will not to fly into smithereens of fright as I finally looked down at my own body. Ginevee tightened her grip on my hand as I gaped at my own skeleton. I had a moment of choice. Either I flipped out completely into some kind of mental oblivion or I trusted my warrior spirit and kept on moving toward the light that was now visible at the end of the cloud tunnel. We kept on walking, although for a short distance I felt as if I were being dragged by Ginevee. I focused on the light and soon realized that it was actually emanating from the entrance to a cave. The dingo ran ahead of us and disappeared over a lip of bluishly iridescent rock.

As we entered the cave that was full of an unearthly golden glow, we saw Oruncha of Chauritzi standing tall and powerful in the center of the cave. His attitude was one of welcome. I was past trying to understand or fear or judge what was occurring. I simply looked out through my skull at the ethereal magnificence of my surroundings. Pieces of rainbow light were shimmering in the cave walls as if chips of the sun and the moon or the stars were imbedded there. Then Oruncha spoke in a deep voice that echoed around us.

"Crystal Women, take your strength from the stars in the galaxies. You are as if at the bottom of the sea; you have reached Dhakkan's domain. You are muru muru, you are blessed with life. Pick each a pearl shell and a rore, a sacred crystal, from the walls of the cave. Long ago, the women held sacred rangas for all the people. That tradition was lost and given to the male clans and, slowly, we lost our way in terror and imbalance. But the Koori people will rise again with a new balance. The power of mother nature cannot be ignored or forgotten. We honor your presence here. Be not afraid of hearing the Bull Roarer or taking part in the rites of men. What belongs to men will forever be theirs and what is of woman will always be theirs. There is balance in wisdom and all change is a miracle to behold. You are made from the elements and to the elements you must one day return."

Ginevee went to one side of the cave and I went to the

other. I ran my hands over the dry stone walls that felt like hardened sap from a tree and finally picked out a glistening pearl shell and a crystal that threw prisms of purple light all around me. It just fit into the palm of my bony hand. Walking was even more difficult than it had been before. My skeleton seemed weighted down by an unseen force. It took every bit of my will and strength to move at all.

Oruncha had seated himself on the cave floor. A small fire burned and the dingo sat off at a respectful distance, her shiny paws at the edge of the circle that Ginevee and I were now joining. We sat with great effort, and placed the crystals on a mat in front of us. The mat held the designs of the constellations carved into its bark.

"Hold the pearl shells, Crystal Women, as we journey together." I was surprised that we were allowed to hold the shells. "The karari, or pearl shells, are sacred to men," Oruncha said, looking at me. "They are worn over their pubic hair. You are here at the request of Booru the sandamara. He is a great warrior, but he has lost his way in darkness. He has murdered many women and children. You trusted the message from the dolphins and the spirit of the trees. You have risked your life to help bring balance back to the people. You have much yet to learn, but you have ventured into the mysteries of Oruncha with trust and innocence. You are rewarded for your trials with the eyes of Oruncha. The rore, the sacred crystals, are my eyes. Use them as your own. Look into the rore now and ask Booru to let himself be seen."

Instantly the purple shimmer from the crystals appeared to flatten out. With my eyes I followed a funnel of shadows at the center of the crystal. I had no idea if Ginevee was having the same experience. I tried desperately to hold my concentration. Then I saw him. It was unmistakably Booru, the sorcerer I had seen in my vision. Oruncha had moved over to join me and we were looking together into the crystal. Booru was lying down on a mat in a wurley. I could see the shadows of other people moving around. They were upset. I realized that Booru was actually very ill. I noticed something dark around his body.

"See that bukkur around his neck and chest," Oruncha whispered to me. "That is a sacred cord, but it does not belong to Booru."

"What does that mean and what is it made of?" I asked, my voice sounding like it belonged to someone else.

"It is cord made of hair from the deities of the bugeen. If it were Booru's it would have light, but it is dark, yea. It is a sorcerer's bukkur and it will strangle the life from him within six or seven sleeps."

I noticed something else. Booru's body seemed clear and well defined in every area except around his heart and his solar plexus.

"What else do you see?" Oruncha asked me.

"I see his body looking like it's fraying off or disintegrating in places. What does that mean?" I asked.

"It is good that you see, yea. You see his warrior self is strong, but where the female warrioress should live inside of him there is weakness. That's why a sorcerer was able to attack him. He is vulnerable there. Only the power of woman can save him now. He is a sandamara; he knows that only a clever woman can heal him."

As Oruncha said this, something even more extraordinary happened. It was as if Booru felt our presence. He seemed to look up through the crystal. His right eye was shut, but his left one looked at me. I realized that its dense blackness was unlike an eye. Then he plucked his left eye out, and it turned into a stone of what looked like obsidianite. He handed it up to me. Somehow I was holding it; the stone was hot and seared into my palm as if the birthing fires of creation had given it to me.

"That is a gooma, or spirit stone, but it is really a devil stone for extracting evil spirits. That is Booru's plea for help, yea, and his gift to you. That stone is for your clever bag and is part of your making for a woman of high degree. It is a great honor even if it comes from your enemy." Oruncha smiled and continued, "Sometimes your enemy can be your greatest ally."

I held the circular flat stone in my hand. It was cooling down. It felt smooth, almost like firm skin. Something was happening again inside the crystal.

"Follow the bukkur," Oruncha whispered.

The bukkur that was wound around Booru led off toward the west. We followed it with our eyes but it was obscured by the mist of darkness.

"That darkness is the disguise of a sorcerer," Oruncha warned me.

"Never enter that mist. It would mean your death. Do you know what you must do?" he asked.

"I'm not sure."

"On the other end of that cord is an evil sorcerer who has sung of Booru's death. It is enough to know that the sorcerer is there in the west. Now you must fashion the healing of the sandamara and send the bukkur back to its maker. That will destroy the sorcerer and end this horrible war. In healing Booru you will heal much of what has brought pain and near extinction to our mother earth and to the people." Oruncha looked at me with kindness.

"But, Oruncha, why does he call on me? I don't know enough to heal him. Ginevee or Agnes must do that."

"For some reason, Booru has chosen you. First he wanted to kill you and now, like the true contrary that he is, he begs for your healing," Oruncha said.

I heard a sound behind us. I whirled. Oruncha steadied me.

Two exquisite, primitive creatures stood before us. They looked brown and their bodies were simplistic, almost as if they were carved out of wood. They spoke to me. "Beware of a sorcerer's intent, my sister. Never do a favor for a sorcerer who wishes you evil. Once you do a favor for him, he has you forever. I am Dawn Woman and this is Dolphin Woman Dreaming. We are your sisters of the Dreamtime. We are the reason you are here; you have followed our dreaming well and for a long time and we must appear to you now, though you are very tired. There is little time. Heal Booru, but only from your goodness and not because he wishes it."

I was overwhelmed with all of this sensation. I could no longer sit up, so Oruncha held me and Ginevee propped me up from the other side.

Dawn Woman wore only a necklace of what looked like clouds and Dolphin Woman Dreaming wore the juraveel of the dolphins, pieces of lightning around her neck. Their hips were wide, as if they were goddesses of fertility, and their breasts were pendulous as if they were full of milk. Their faces were round and their foreheads extended well over their eyes. Their noses were chiseled small and straight. Beautiful sky-blue eyes penetrated with the dimension of the vast universe from well beneath their brow. Their heads were oversized for their bodies, giving them, at first, the appearance of strange children. But as they spoke, their strangeness faded and they became familiar to me.

"I live in the split between the worlds, between the

cracks of darkness and light," Dawn Woman said. "I carry the sun in my womb and give birth to it every dawn.

"I dwell in the seas of eternity where the dolphins swim forever. The dolphins live in the seas of the world. They impart their vast knowledge with great subtlety. As a race, you have yet to understand them. But you, as an individual, read their pictures well and we are grateful. If you can heal Booru, you will have healed much. The dolphins, who know the waterways as they know the blood of your bodies, will be with you. They are the keepers of the world's karma as surely as your karma lives in your blood. As I am Dolphin Woman Dreaming, hear me. Swim in Booru's blood, the blood of the sandamara, and cure him. We chose to meet you here in the domain of our brother Oruncha, who imparts the women's mysteries. You stand on the oldest land on earth. We come with such longing. Do you not remember us?"

Before I knew what was happening, we were all crying with our arms reaching across primordial time. We remembered something deep inside of us, something that had separated us over eons of lifetimes exploded, and we were joined together again. Our arms intertwined and formed a bridge of light that flew between us in a shower of stars. It was as if we became the Milky Way and our physical form disappeared. Everything around us went dark like the night universe and I could see the constellation of the Southern Cross floating beneath us. And then everything went black.

The next thing I knew I was sitting naked in the creek bed next to Ginevee, the water up to my chest. She Who Walks With The Wind was dumping cold water over our heads with her coolamon. The river ran red with ochre paint as if the veins of the Dreamtime had bled forth its life-force to revive us. Ginevee was laughing and splashing in the water like a kid, but I could barely stay conscious.

I must have fainted, because I woke up underwater. Ginevee grabbed my hair and pulled my head up. I spluttered red water, choking and gagging. I felt like I had been on a week-long binge. My vision was blurred and my head ached. I could barely move my legs as they picked me up by the arms, dragging and carrying me back to the wurley.

There is a vitality, a life force, an energy, a quickening that is translated through you into action and because there is only one of you in all of time this expression is unique. And if you block it, it will never exist through any other medium and be lost. The world will not have it.

—Martha Graham

❖

CHAPTER TWENTY-FOUR
❖❖❖❖❖❖
THE PRESENCE OF THE UNKNOWABLE

I slept the whole next day. I felt better that night as I discussed with Agnes, Ruby, Ginevee, and She Who Walks With The Wind everything that had happened on our fantastic journey. I ate a little meat and vegetable roots and then erased my papunya with a broom made from spinifex grass.

As I swept it away, it seemed that I was closing a door on the past. The past had existed in a certain cumbersome way for me, because of my limited concept of time. For me everything in life was predicated by time. No more. I realized that things only exist by agreement in this relative world. I let go of many memories of my past as if I no longer wanted to choose to animate them with my thoughts. In a sense, it was like healing a piece of my mind that had lived trapped in years gone by.

The meeting with Dolphin Woman Dreaming and Dawn Woman had affected me deeply. When we had reached out our arms, it was truly as if we had joined hands across the barriers of time and my self-imposed limitations. That act exploded the concept that is born and dies within our human mind that we live in only one dimension of reality, the one that we can see. I realized that when I struggled out of the constructs of time and relativity that other worlds live and that what our deepest imagination can conceive of is ultimately real.

Agnes, Ginevee, and She Who Walks With The Wind sat around my papunya as I erased it. They each held their clapping sticks and played them softly and sang as I swept. I put what pieces of the colored sands I could save into a coolamon and sprinkled them into the creek water. When I was finished Ginevee asked me to sit with them around the fire.

"How are you feeling, my daughter, now that you have erased Wolf Woman Dreaming?" she asked.

"I feel good and a little wobbly."

Ginevee was scrutinizing me. She held her head away from me almost in profile, so that I could only see her left eye. She squinted, making her face furrow with wrinkles.

"What?" I asked.

The three women nudged each other and moved closer. Ruby started kneading the muscles on my arms, Agnes poked my stomach, and Ginevee moved my head back and forth.

"What's the matter?" I asked, becoming alarmed at all this attention.

"Why are you so afraid?" Ginevee finally asked me.

"I'm not afraid," I said as they all stared at me in silence. "Well, maybe, I'm a little nervous."

They still stared at me with no expression on their faces.

"Okay, okay. Of course I'm afraid. What do you expect? I don't think I can heal Booru. And where is he anyway? You're right, yes. I'm afraid he'll kill me, that's all. And furthermore, I don't understand his evilness or the evil in Two Hearts, for that matter. Do you?"

The women were still staring at me. They agreed on something silently by nodding their heads and they laughed uproariously at me.

"The evilness in Two Hearts and Booru has come about through something that is easy to understand, yea, if you just look at it, my daughter," Ginevee said.

"Look at what?" I asked.

"Look at what has happened to the Koori people in the last two hundred years. Many of the tribes have disappeared forever. The aborigines have been driven off their land. They have been infected with disease, television, alcohol, sugar, and all the greedy wonders of the white world. Booru and Two Hearts are great warriors. Their tradition lives in their blood as it has for one hundred thousand years. They are warriors who have lost a whole way of life. They are men who have lost their culture. Their evil came about through the destruction of their culture. It has caused the death of many who know. Now, there are so few to teach. Do you understand?" She looked at me with her piercing eyes, which were cold beneath her heavy, dark brow. I felt stupid.

"I hear you, Ginevee, but I become overwhelmed with sadness. I don't know what to do or where to begin to help."

"This discussion is getting too heavy for me. How about going down to the corner for an ice-cream cone?" Ruby asked as she prepared to leave. She stood above us, her brown skin shining silver in the moonlight.

"Cute," I said, scowling at her.

"If you want my opinion, you all take life much too seriously. But, then, I'm just a blind old Indian woman. Who would listen to me anyway? Come on, Agnes, let's go dig up some evil sorcerers and go dancing." Agnes stood up and put her arm around Ruby's waist. They started to do an Irish jig. For one second Agnes looked into my eyes with an expression I did not understand. They disappeared into the darkness laughing and singing like a couple of drunks.

Ginevee and I looked at each other. We couldn't help but giggle as we listened to Agnes and Ruby fade away into the night singing a war chant.

"You can change the location of evil. You can move it around, but you cannot make it disappear," Ginevee said.

"But there must be some way," I said.

"Understand, my daughter, any solution that you come up with will only give birth to a new problem. It is the way of evolution and the law of life."

"But understand what?"

"First understand that evil is part of the life-force. It is a kind of energy or vitality. It is part of the pulse of life that needs to be transmuted. Evil is energy in need of transformation, yea. What do you think you're doing learning to be a clever woman?"

Ginevee was drawing designs in the sand. The firelight moved through the shadows and animated them. The little mounds made by her fingers began to move like a snake.

"I'm becoming a woman of knowledge." Somehow my voice sounded lame.

"Yes, but why? What for?"

"To heal people," I said.

"That's fine, yea, but understand what healing is, my daughter. You are in a war against the forces of ignorance and darkness, the bugeen. In becoming a shamaness you give your body to Dirrangun, the ancestress of light. You say, 'Here, I dedicate my life to the process of transforming the shadows of existence.' Ignorance, evil, pain, disease, envy, jealousy, greed are all part of the bugeen. With your special abilities you are able to shine light into the darkness. You help reinstate the sacred balance. You might ask, how do I do this, hmm?"

"Yes."

"By the very existence of a great and evolved being, the world and the people who touch that being begin to change. Just by their proximity to that being people are altered and become more. Then if that being actively deals with the forces of the universe, yea, wonders can occur. We call that kind of being a clever woman."

"But, Ginevee, I'm so far from that. How can I heal Booru? You are the one he should have asked for."

"But the truth is he asked for you. Take out the black stone he gave you."

I opened my hand. I had been gripping the stone for hours. I felt its smooth surface. I held it out to Ginevee. It lay in the palm of my hand like a scintillating jewel. It was black, but it had an iridescent depth that held rainbows of blue oxide and gold just beneath the surface. It shimmered with such elegance that we both stared at it for a moment. She plucked it out of my palm very gently and held it to her forehead. She closed her eyes and sighed.

"My daughter, this gooma is a very old grandmother and she holds much power." After running her fingers over it for several minutes, she gave it back to me.

"What does the gooma say to you?" she asked.

I held it to my forehead. The message was unmistakable and urgent.

"I know that I can do nothing else but try to heal Booru. We must not waste time," I said, feeling great trepidation and fear. "What if I fail, Ginevee?"

"You must not fail or even think it. You know more than you are willing to admit even to yourself. We will all be there to help, but in the end it will be all up to you."

"That helps," I said. "And how do we find Booru?"

"I know his camp," She Who Walks With The Wind said with elegant movements of her hands. She had been dozing sitting straight up and now she looked at me through half-open lids.

"You must go to Booru's people and offer him Lynn's wurley. Tell them that Lynn understands what she must do and that she has accepted the gooma. Ordinarily we would go to him but I would rather my daughter work within the safety of this village. Only if he is too ill will we go there. You will know if they speak the truth," Ginevee said.

"How far away is he?" I asked.

"Not even one sleep, they are very near, yea. I will be back tomorrow," She Who Walks With The Wind told Ginevee, who translated. By the time I had turned around from moving the logs on the fire, She Who Walks With The Wind had vanished. A wind had come up from the south and the tree branches swayed and creaked overhead.

"Is she gone already?" I asked.

"Yes, she is gone. Let us talk. We have much to do tonight. We will begin to prepare now."

"Now?"

"Now." Ginevee was very emphatic. She cleared a circle of ground between us and had me place my crystals in the four directions. We cushioned them with sacred sand taken from Oruncha's cave. She spoke with her eyes closed.

"You told me once about diving into a lagoon and seeing a moray eel coming slowly out of its hole in a cliff of coral. It was looking right at you. He was very territorial and would have bitten you, probably fatally, had you not backed away. If he had killed you, would that have been right or wrong?"

"Not great for me," I said.

"It is what is. If you're dead, you're dead. You were in his place and he didn't like that. Many other fish of the deep just swim with you. They don't care, yea. That eel is like a sorcerer. He doesn't like your presence near his domain. He lives in a different world. He gives you a warning, maybe and maybe not, and then he goes for you. That is the beginning, my daughter, of war, of the instinct for possession. That eel may have been male or female. Would it have made a difference?"

"I'm not sure," I said.

"If she were female she might kill you out of fear, fear that you would injure her young. In ancient times women

were known as the most fierce fighters because of this plat-
form of fear. If he were male he would kill you because he
has marked his domain. There is something in a male that
is in the very root of his being; he will go to war for what
he claims as his property. This extends to the domain of
ideas as well. He will destroy even himself for an idea. A
woman will survive to be able to protect a belief structure
that usually houses her family whether it be a family of ideas
or children. So her basis for war usually is born of fear
deep in the primal part of herself. War, like an idea or a
belief system, is man's greatest addiction and his greatest
vulnerability. A warring human likes to live on the sheer
edge of life and death. Such a state can almost be sacred
because it involves living intensely in the now. There's only
one problem."

"What's that?"

"That kind of now, the source of it, is illusion, yea. The
illusion produced by addiction. That's how you can say that
all experience is the same. That kind of experience is all the
same. Because it all is born from addiction and it has one
collective purpose, which is to keep you psychically asleep."

"How is that different from the sacred now?"

"Only the shaman, the sorcerer, or the magician knows
that kind of sacred now. As a shaman you dwell in the almost
fatal crack between light and darkness where the beings of
mystery swim in unknown rivers of energy. As a shaman-
ness you're like a cosmic architect building dams made of
prayer sticks and lightning rods and you alter the shape and
course of those rivers of energy. That is the power of creation.
That too is a world of life and death and great danger. There
are definite laws and formulas. But if you live through the
initiations you have become the ultimate alchemist. Your
own soul has burned through the agonizing fires of transformation and you become the goddess on earth. You can
heal the mind and the heart of your suffering brothers and
sisters because you have also suffered. You can change sand
into gold. You know the ancient formula handed down through
the ages, from one shaman to another, yea. Understand why
you have been born. Not to hurt, but to heal and to teach.
In a sense you have lived your whole life to be here with us
in the Outback of Australia to heal Booru." Ginevee had
picked up one of the West crystals and was rubbing it be-

tween her palms. I weighed her words in my mind for a long time, until she handed me the crystal.

"Look into the crystal, my daughter, and find the black circle."

I held the crystal up to the light of the glowing coals.

"It is said you have the strong eye," Ginevee said, peering at me like an owl.

"Who said such a thing?"

"It doesn't matter. It is true, yea?"

"Well, what exactly do you mean, Ginevee?"

"I mean you can *see* into things. You think it is coincidence or your imagination, yea. But it is not. You have the strong eye. And that is why Booru has laid down his spear and come to you."

"Absolutely not. I do not," I said.

Ginevee was making me uncomfortable. She remained silent as I continued to look into the crystal.

"I don't see any circle, Ginevee, only rainbow colors."

"What do you see in the rainbow colors, hmm?" she asked casually, as she placed her hands on the back of my head and moved it back and forth very slightly. This had the effect of making me struggle to focus and hang on to the images I was seeing.

All at once the colors solidified, or I saw them at a new angle. The rainbow became more definite and I could see that it extended for a long distance, for what looked like infinity. I followed the rainbow back and forth until finally I realized that it was moving on its own or at least looked like it was. The rainbow undulated slowly up and down and began to coil into a circle. My eyes were glued to the crystal. I couldn't have looked away if I had wanted to. What I was seeing was a rainbow serpent moving itself into a circular formation. As it coiled, the inner section of its shimmering skin looked dark, almost black.

"All I see is a rainbow turning into a serpent," I said.

"Oh, is that all, my daughter? There's certainly nothing very special about that, yea. Maybe you don't have the strong eye after all."

"My God, Ginevee, it's making a black circle. You tricked me, I know you tricked me." The image faded as Ginevee sat down next to me. Her face displayed a big toothy grin. She slapped me on the back.

"Some apprentice you are. All you can see in a piece of quartz pulled out of the ground is the Rainbow Serpent, that's all, yea. Just some little old snake, girl. Is that all? Well, and all it did was make a black circle just like I asked for, yea. What's so great about that?"

"My God, I really did see that. What does it mean?"

"If you'd stop distrusting yourself, you'd know. Your problem as a warrioress is that you hear all those voices in your head that taunt your power and strip you of your true abilities."

"But, Ginevee, I don't mean to do that. Why is that happening?"

"It is not happening to you as if something outside of you is making you less powerful. You create your own insecurity. Insecurity is a great addiction, yea. Like any other addiction it robs you of your strength. You use it like a prop, the way many of our brothers and sisters use alcohol, chaos, or anything else. But that prop can kill you. You see it as a defense against the unknowable, yea. When we get too close to something we don't understand, we reach for our props, our addictions. With those addictions we destroy our seeing and the unknowable seems much further away. What is really further away, my daughter, is the realization of your original nature, that part of you that is the All Mother."

I thought for a long time and watched the firelight reflect off the crystals in the circle. I could see, very clearly, that Ginevee was right.

"Ginevee, what is the significance of the black circle?"

"That is something you must learn for yourself, my daughter. It is fine enough that you found it tonight in the crystal. It is good."

"But what does that mean?"

"That means that this old woman is sleepy, and it is time that you took these crystals into your wurley and slept with them. Come, I will show you."

Ginevee gathered the crystals and as I lay down on my back she put them around my body. She positioned them on my heart, at the base of my throat, on my solar plexus and on my lower belly. She placed one above my head and one to the bottom of my feet. She patted my head and was gone. Instantly I fell into a fitful sleep with many dreams, but I lost clear memory of them.

I got up early the next morning. I placed the crystals carefully in my clever bag and had just finished dressing when someone appeared at the entrance to my wurley, throwing a big shadow over the interior.

"Well, I don't think it was very nice of you not to say good-bye to Agnes, after all she's done for you," Ruby said, her hands on her hips.

I whirled around. "What do you mean, say good-bye to Agnes? Where did she go?"

"She left, that's all. She doesn't have to report to me where she's going. How should I know where she's going? She can go anywhere she wants. She probably went home and July went with her to help."

"Agnes and July went home to Canada?" I was in a state of shock. I felt almost wobbly. I sat down. My whole body felt tingly and anxious, but almost immediately I jumped to my feet and ran outside to look for the jeep. It was there. I frantically ran around the village looking for Agnes. Finally I found Ginevee.

"Ginevee, where's Agnes?"

"Oh, Lynn, I thought you knew."

"Knew what?" Something inside of me felt not only abandoned but betrayed.

"Knew that Agnes was leaving, of course."

"How would I know if no one told me?" I was aghast at the thought of Agnes leaving me like this. "How dare she tell everyone and not me." I was truly frightened and confused.

"I just thought you knew, yea."

"No. How did she leave?"

"She left with July and friends of mine from Arnhamland. She said something about them going to the Kakadu Territory and then she would fly home from Darwin. At least I think that's what she said."

Ginevee seemed disinterested in the whole subject and turned back to the women sitting around her wurley, laughing and talking with them in Koori.

I walked back to my wurley. Ruby was sitting outside, her back resting against the bent poles. I sat down next to Ruby and started to cry.

"Ruby, why would Agnes do something like this? Was she mad at me?"

"Why, Lynn, I'm surprised at you. Why are you crying? And, no, Agnes didn't seem mad at you. Did you do something she should be mad about?"

"I don't know. Maybe I offended her. Maybe I haven't been learning fast enough."

"She probably got tired of trying to teach you," Ruby said. "You know how slow you are."

"That's right, I'm slow and stupid. I'll never be a real shaman. It's no wonder she left." By now I was sobbing.

"It's true, it's no use, you'll never be good enough to keep her as a medicine woman. If you had been better and worked harder and been more dedicated she wouldn't have left." Ruby was sitting very close to me, with her face turned in profile.

"Is that true?" I asked, wiping my tears away only to start crying again.

"I don't know. Is it?"

"I guess it is. I'm a lousy apprentice." I felt like a child. I was astonished at how upset I was.

"Lynn, how old do you feel right now?" Ruby asked, sounding like a psychiatrist.

"Honestly, I feel about four."

"That's pretty young."

"I do, I feel like a child." My voice sounded tiny and far away.

"Were you lonely as a child?"

"Yes, I was very alone."

"There's a difference between lonely and alone."

"I was both, I guess."

"You mean you had no parents?"

"I had parents, but I didn't know how to please them."

"What do you mean?"

"Well, my dad, as you know, was very difficult and I was very afraid of him. I thought if I revealed my true feelings he would hurt me. My mother is very normal and she has always wanted me to stop messing around with Indians and spirituality. She always wanted me to stop being so weird. She never liked the way I dressed or wore my hair. I felt I upset her by being who I am. Now I know that wasn't true, but I grew up feeling that and being very lonely."

"I can see what she meant about your hair." Ruby giggled, feeling my dust-matted locks with her fingers. "Did you feel abandoned?"

"Yes, I guess I did. My parents got a divorce and that was really hard."

"Did your dad want you to be famous and successful?"

"Uh-huh, he was always reading me stories about powerful women. He encouraged me to write, and to ride and swim in competition. But often he pushed me too much. He didn't want me to settle down."

"How did your mom feel about that?"

"Oh, she wanted me to be happily married and settled down, I think." I was sniveling and blowing my nose.

"Do you think that when we grow up our parents live on inside of us?"

"Yes."

"It sounds like you have a real problem, then."

"What problem?"

"If you please your father-self and take your power from it, your mother-self will be displeased, and the other way around."

"You're right, but I never thought of it that way."

"Do you feel that somehow you upset Agnes?"

"Yes, I feel that I must have done something terrible. If I'd done better she wouldn't have left. I've disappointed her or hurt her or made her angry or done something wrong."

Ruby had taken out her pocketknife and was whittling on a twig. "Did you actually do something terrible?" she asked.

"Well, no, not that I know of." My feelings of anxiety were enormous. I felt agonizingly numb all over.

"Don't you think it's interesting, little wolf pup, that you assume responsibility for how Agnes might be feeling?"

I was watching Ruby carve a bird more deftly than most people who are not blind. For a long while I didn't answer. I was wrestling with my terrible feelings of rejection. And then I thought of Ruby and how as a young girl she had been blinded and raped by four white men. How extraordinarily difficult it must have been to rise out of the ashes of her broken life, a poor and uneducated girl, to become the incredibly facile old medicine woman that I knew. I wiped my tears and thought with a lessening of anxiety that if she could be happy and at peace after all she had been through then, by God, so could I.

"I feel responsible for Agnes leaving. It must be my fault," I said, trying to smile.

"Why must it be your fault? Maybe she just wanted to see another part of Australia."

"I suppose that's possible, but why would she leave when we have so much work yet to be done?"

"Maybe she thought you could handle it on your own. Maybe it was her way of helping you assume your power as a clever woman. Is that possible?"

Somehow Ruby's words were tearing me apart. I did feel responsible for Agnes' feelings and probably everyone else's, too. The thought of standing in my circle of power without Agnes close by left me feeling nearly paralyzed with fear.

"Ruby, I'll have to go home. I feel terrible. I can't deal with this."

"Can't deal with what, being afraid or playing the part of the Great Spirit?" Ruby was tickled with the bird she had carved and gave it to Skeeter, who ran off to show it to the other children.

"Playing the part of the Great Spirit?" I asked.

"Yes. You seem to feel responsible for everyone's feelings, especially Agnes'. Gee, last time I looked, Agnes was quite capable of feeling her own feelings. In fact, so is everyone else. You must feel very tired from trying to carry all those people. Probably the whole world won't be happy and entertained unless you're there doing your dance of mending and patching everyone's feelings."

"I guess you're right, Ruby. That sounds awful."

"That's a terrible drain for anyone. What are you feeling, now? That you didn't overhaul Agnes in the right way? That if you had been better and more loving she wouldn't have left you?" Ruby was snickering to herself over her use of the word 'overhaul'.

"Yes."

"How does it feel to be God?"

"What do you mean?"

"I mean, if you're responsible for the feelings of the whole world you must be God. A little black wolf certainly wouldn't be responsible for the whole world's reactions, would she?"

"No, you're right. Where are these feelings coming from, Ruby? I didn't even know I had them. I feel like an emotional cripple. I can't believe I'm so frightened and depressed. Why am I so scared?"

Ruby stared at me with her blind eyes and smiled a wicked smile that made me even more scared. The sun had moved behind the ghost gum tree, throwing elongated morning shadows in long, skinny patterns that swayed gently in the easterly wind. A tiny dust-devil twisted through the village carrying a ball of spinifex grass and throwing it up into the air and bouncing it onto the ground in a whirling ghost dance.

"You're scared because you've lost control." She sensed my reaction as my body stiffened.

"I haven't lost control. Control of Agnes? That'll be the day. What do you mean, 'control'? You're right . . . I've lost control . . . but I haven't really lost it, or ever had it. Ruby, damn, you're right." I was furious. Ruby laughed at me and rolled around, making puffs of red dust.

"When a child grows up minding her parents and is always afraid of their reactions to things, she learns to control her environment to survive. Control in those terms means being able to live. Right now, you have lost control. Agnes has done something that has surprised you. She has thrown you a curve. There is an ancient fear in you that grows from your roots, Black Wolf. It's just like with your parents. If your Dad ambushed you in some way or surprised you with a fit of anger, you weren't sure you would survive. Whenever you are taken off guard you feel like you have lost control. That's irrational if you think about it, but for you and what's happened to you as a child your behavior and fears are understandable. The root of all fears is the same. It is fear of death. When you lose control you think you will die. Agnes has also deserted you, so you feel rejected. But, I think, your real terror is loss of control." Ruby reached over and took a sip of water from her coolamon. Several drops overflowed and left shiny rivers down her chest.

"You've nailed me. So now what do I do?" I started fiddling with my crystals in my clever bag.

"Truly realizing all this helps, doesn't it?"

"Yes, it does. But the depression I feel is still terrible. Maybe I don't really realize it yet."

"Black Wolf, remember the sacred spiral. At the center is the formless unknowable. The center represents your shaman death where you finally let go of the lodges of the mind and ego and our relative sense of time. On the perimeter of the spiral is our form and our lodges of earthly endeavor. When I talk to you about enlightenment and merging with the centers of the sacred spiral, your mind becomes frightened. Your mind understands only the concept of enlightenment and loss of form. But we have enthroned the mind as king of our lives and it is really only a tool like your hand. When you speak of a shaman death or formlessness, the mind thinks it's going to die. There is also a keeper of the mind. She would rather see you go crazy and develop many addictions than become a formless shaman. The mind, in its confusion, thinks that's the only way it will survive as a mind. Many times we have spoken of the spiral and many times you've ignored its meaning for you. Now perhaps you will learn. To keep you from the formless unknowable, the mind helps you develop addictions that bleed off your life-force. Do you remember why?" Ruby was scowling at me.

"Yes, to keep you in form," I said.

"Yes, but understand how. We stay in form when we throw away the power of our spirit."

"How is that?"

"Whenever we develop an addiction, whether it is alcohol or depression, it has only one effect and that is the effect of spirit sleep. When your spirit sleeps it means you are losing life-force and you go further and further away from the center of the spiral. You die a little with every addiction. It is the opposite end of the arrow from enlightenment. Fly through the center of the spiral and witness your depression. It is only a trick of the mind to keep you in earthly bondage. Can you see that?"

"Yes, I'm beginning to, Ruby. Oh, Ruby, I'm so frightened." I threw my arms around her for probably the first time ever. She was so startled she jumped.

"Now, now, Black Wolf," she said, pulling my arms off of her like banana peels. "You sound like you're back to being four years old, my wolf pup."

"You're right, I do," I said in a grown-up voice. I straightened up and felt better. "How can I know so much, and know nothing?"

"Because the power of the unknowable is leaning on you. You are beginning to feel her presence in your life. The unknowable is courting you. Be careful. You might even take your power, Black Wolf."

The Soul that rises with us, our life's Star,
   Hath had elsewhere its setting,
      And cometh from afar:
   Not in entire forgetfulness,
   And not in utter nakedness,
But trailing clouds of glory do we come
   From God, who is our home:
Heaven lies about us in our infancy!

—William Wordsworth

CHAPTER TWENTY-FIVE
❖❖❖❖❖❖
BOORU, THE SANDAMARA

T he silence was imposing. An occasional wind came up from the east and whistled around the silver-barked tree trunks. The sky was crystal clear and turquoise blue, but nevertheless the day seemed forlorn. I felt a foreboding of danger and hesitation even in nature around me. I wanted a storm, a hurricane of wind to distract me from the night that loomed ahead. Even the elements seemed to be listening and waiting for the outcome of the healing ceremony. The wind breathed in hushed gusts along the red ground, stirring up tiny twisters that gave up almost as soon as they started.

I wouldn't settle down. I was attempting to create my own emotional storm, to no avail. I walked down by the creek. The water was especially clear. When the sun shone through the swaying trees, it was blistering hot. I sat down in the dirt next to a break in the current where some red river oak branches had fallen across the creek. They created small pools and watery gullies that caught the leaves. They looked like silvery-green lily pads all piled up on one another. I wished I were a frog and could sit on the flat leaves, basking in the coolness of the stream. If I could only hide under those leaves until everyone went away . . . A tiny waterfall rippled over some piled-up stones and other branches. I became mesmerized by the sound of tumbling water, which reminded me of a high wind in the treetops. I thought of Canada and the rivers of the Far North. And Agnes. How could she have deserted me?

On impulse, I took a crystal she had given me out of my clever bag and held it to my heart. I needed her so much at that moment that tears came to my eyes. Then a calmness settled in around me. After a moment I thought I could almost feel her presence. I started complaining to myself about how fearful I was of healing Booru. Then with a jolt of energy, I sat up straighter. Suddenly I felt incredibly disgusted with myself and my own seeming inability to assume my power. As I pressed the crystal to my forehead, it was almost as if Agnes were inside my head. I could almost see her looking at me with her kind eyes. Her whole demeanor gave me encouragement. All I had to do was see those penetrating eyes full of mystery and I knew that she knew I was ready. Somehow this knowledge made it all possible.

I took a deep breath of clear desert air and took a step into my own circle of power. I prayed to the Great Spirit and mother earth and found that shaman place inside of myself where the medicine spirits live. I felt the ancestral spirits clamoring around me. I could almost see them. I understood something which had never been totally clear to me before. As a warrioress, you must first be able to climb onto your own plateau of centeredness before help comes. If you're scattered, the spirits scatter. Once you gather your forces and pray and honor your inward silence, all the life-giving forces of nature become curious and flock into your energy field. I felt secure once again. I was ready. I swung my clever bag over my shoulder and walked back to the village whistling the "go short distance" song.

Ruby, She Who Walks With The Wind, and Ginevee were waiting for me. They were sitting outside my wurley enjoying some red berries. They cleared a place for me to sit between Ruby and Ginevee.

"Well, what happened?" I asked.

There was silence as She Who Walks With The Wind handed me a flat package wrapped in bark and tied with human hair.

"It's for you," she told me through Ginevee's translation. "It is from Booru. Open it, yea." The women leaned toward me, their eyes full of expectation.

I took the package. It was fairly heavy in my hands and about a foot long. I carefully unwrapped it, placing the human hair under a rock so it wouldn't blow away. Inside was a flat red stone with swirls and odd carvings on it. I held it up to Ginevee. She had tears in her eyes as she carefully ran her fingers over the carvings.

"Booru has given you his dreaming. This is his sacred churinga stone," Ginevee said.

"For a warrior to give this to a woman is unheard of for many long time. In ancient times, women held all the sacred rangas and churingas. Then there was a war and the men took the sacred things. We don't know why, but that's what happened. Now the great Booru has given you his dreaming. He is dying and he asks for your healing power. He sent his churinga in the hope that it would calm your fear, yea, and help you to find his pain in the Dreamtime," She Who Walks With The Wind signed. She looked tired from her journey but continued, with Ginevee interpreting. "Booru is very ill. He cannot walk. We will have to go to him."

"Tell us about the camp and who is there," Ginevee said.

"It is very small, four wurleys. There are only his wives, six I think, and six or seven children. There are two young warriors, his apprentices, but all the rest of his people have fled in fear. They all think he will die."

"Why would they desert him when he's hurt? Is it a trick?" I said.

"No, my daughter, remember when a Koori person has been hit by sorcery, most people think there is nothing that can be done and they leave. Usually they even take all the food and water. Then the person dies more quickly," Ginevee said. I looked at her with dismay and thought of Buzzie, but I said nothing.

"It will take until the high moon to get to Booru's village," She Who Walks With The Wind signed, pointing up to the sky and making an expansive gesture with her arms.

"Then let's go." My eagerness made the women turn and stare at me for a moment in surprise. Then smiles slowly lit up their faces like dawn creeps over the desert. They grinned at me and put their arms around my shoulders, giving me luxurious hugs and pats on the back. Ginevee directed us in what to take. We each had our rangas, our rolled-up bark mats, clapping sticks, clever bags full of crystals, churingas, and skins with water. She had me take my coolamon and Ruby carried two digging sticks. Ginevee and I carried our pigments for painting in another dilly bag.

Just before we left, we were ushered into a circle and surrounded by the rest of the women in the village. Mandowa painted each of us in the same way. She placed long white curving lines down our legs and arms for a safe journey. She put white dots on our faces with two red smudges under our eyes. The other women went wild with singing and dancing. As Mandowa had begun to paint us, Alice and the others had taken a spear and tied many rat tails to the end. They thrust the spear into the ground.

"If the rat tails fall to the earth, we will know to move camp, for it will mean that you have passed on to the ancestral villages in the Dreamtime, yea. We will dance and sing until your return or until the rat tails fall, my sister," Mandowa said.

As She Who Walks With The Wind, Ruby, Ginevee, and I reached the top of a spinifex-covered hill, I looked back at the village for one false moment of hesitation. I longingly watched the dancing women below looking like ghost spirits, their bodies adorned with white clay. The tall spinifex grass seemed to be joining them as the rustling spikes swayed back and forth in the gusting north wind. Ginevee placed a hand on my shoulder. I read her silent words and the silver sparkle of her eyes in the moonlight.

I turned my gaze back to the deer track we were following. I knew that when and if we returned to the village, I would not be the same woman who was leaving now.

After several hours of laboring through the red desert sand, She Who Walks With The Wind took us on what she called a short cut. We trekked over a large hill covered with rocky shale that slipped out from under our feet. With each step, pieces of flat stone dislodged and clattered all the way down to the bottom. If Booru wanted to know of our coming he certainly knew now, I thought to myself. She Who Walks With The Wind said that her original path had led around the mountain and took several hours longer.

We reached a rise that was populated with several majestic ghost gum trees. We stopped to rest and for the first time saw the fires of Booru's camp. Adrenaline pumped through my veins. Ginevee knelt down with her ear to the ground, as she often did. She looked up at me.

"They are coming for us, my daughter. We will wait." Ginevee pulled me down onto the ground next to her. She took three objects out of her clever bag.

"These are roots used for healing the bukkur, the cord of death. This root is for you to chew on, Black Wolf, and these two are for Booru if you see that he needs them. It is up to you. These two are sisters from the north and this one lives in the west. Remember that, yea. Their spirits are powerful but kind. They have helped me heal many times, so I give them to you."

She laid the strangely shaped roots in my left palm and briefly touched a place over my heart with her knuckles. The roots felt coarse and knobby to my fingers. I smelled them. Their odor was vaguely similar to that of cucumber or cactus. It was an unusual scent. I thanked Ginevee and placed them carefully in my clever bag, remembering that the darker one was for me.

As I put them away we suddenly heard a twig snap as if someone had stepped on it. I jerked around to my left and gasped. Standing quite still and only a couple of yards away from us were two warriors. Their bodies were painted with white and red ochre dabbed with emu fluff. The meaning of the swirls and dotted designs were unknown to me. They looked at us with a fierce but slightly sad expression. Their eyes were so intense that they glowed red.

She Who Walks With The Wind and Ginevee spoke to them in Pitjanjara with a lot of sign language that I couldn't understand. I held Ruby's hand as we followed the warriors down the hill and into Booru's village. The warriors were at least six feet tall, which was taller than most of the aborigine men whom I had seen. They seemed to be in their late twenties. They each carried a beautifully decorated spear with fur string hanging off one end. Their bodies were strong and lean, their muscles rippling in the scattered light from the moon. Clouds had blown over the desert in large puffy clumps, dotting the village common area with strange moving shadows.

As we entered the village we were met by several dingos and two elder women. Their faces were lined and wrinkled with exhaustion and emotional pain. They welcomed us with respect and offered us some meat and billy tea. Several other younger women were scurrying around a large wurley that had two high poles set into the ground in front of it. A fire burned closer to the inside than usual. I assumed that was Booru's lodge.

Out of the darkness, two very old men joined us and sat by our fire. They paid their respects to everyone and then walked over to me. Their faces were so craggy and dark I could barely see their eyes, which seemed like tiny pinpoints of light under their brows. Each one held my hands gently, their skin rough and weathered. For a long time they felt my hands and looked deeply into my eyes. Ordinarily, this manner of behavior would have made me very shy, but something in their kind and quiet demeanor made all my fear drain away. At last we smiled at each other and a knowing passed between us that at once shocked me and put me completely at ease.

I had brought tubers in my dilly bag. I gave one each to the elder men and the women. The two warriors stood off from the fire and would not accept anything from us. They stood as sentinels, still and waiting. There were a few more people in the village than we had expected. There were about twenty or twenty-five women and children, but no young men except for the two warriors. There were several elder men in an obvious state of grief. I could feel the urgency in the air.

I looked at Ginevee, who stood up and motioned for me to follow her. The two warriors appeared at our sides and the elder men who had held my hands led us toward Booru's wurley. Ruby and She Who Walks With The Wind were close behind me. I took the churinga that Booru had sent me and held it in my hand.

As we entered the opening to the wurley I saw that it was four times as big as mine and much higher and more substantial, as if it had stood for quite a while. One of the elder men made it clear that he wanted only Ginevee and me to enter with him and no one else, not even the warriors. As we stepped forward into the dim enclosure, several women's voices could be heard outside singing a mournful chant.

At first I was hesitant. There was a pungent smell of burning herbs and the air was thick with smoke. My eyes slowly adjusted to the light and haze. There was a small fire burning next to a tall figure lying on a pole structure. All manner of strange things hung from the rounded ceiling.

There were spears, shields, rolled-up pieces of bark, pieces of birds, what I guessed were herbs tied in bundles, kangaroo skins, coolamons, and dozens of other bundles that were indistinguishable in the shadows. I had never seen a wurley with so many things in it. I wondered if his people had given him all these sacred things before leaving.

My heart was pounding as Ginevee and I were led to the pole bed. A young woman was tending the man lying there. The elder whispered something to her and she quickly set down her coolamon of water and left the wurley. The old man knelt down next to this giant of a man, who appeared to be sleeping. I recognized him instantly from the Dreamtime. It was Booru.

Ginevee and the old man spoke in Koori for several minutes. From the movement of their hands I could follow that they were talking about his condition, which appeared to be very poor indeed. The old man touched Booru's forehead. Slowly Booru opened his eyes as if he were coming out of a dream. I watched him with fascination. I could see that he was very old. His hair was white and his face was furrowed with deep wrinkles. But his body was strong and muscular and looked forty years younger than his face. As his eyes opened, his whole face became animated with an expression of wisdom and intensity. Carefully and with obvious pain, he turned his head to look at us. His eyes shone with a brilliance I had never seen in another man. It was as if light were shining through crushed glass or fragments of crystals. I did not see anger or evil in this man, but I did see a true warrior with extraordinary charisma. Fleetingly I remembered what Ginevee had told me about the sandamara, how it was said that he had fought for his people for centuries. Looking at this man I believed every word. I held his churinga to my heart. Booru looked at me and motioned for everyone else to leave. I wondered desperately if he spoke English. As if reading my mind he spoke Koori English to me in a husky whisper.

"We are old friends in the Dreamtime, yea. I haven't much time, woman. Let me hear your name." He spoke at first with great effort, but it seemed to become easier for him as he continued. He reached out his hand and I took it. It felt warm and dry, but more like a heavily padded paw on a panther than a hand. His palms were completely calloused and rough. This was no man of leisure.

"My name is Spirit Woman, but they call me Black Wolf or Lynn," I said.

He thought about that for a moment.

"Lynn," he said with a lilt in his voice. "I have seen you, but I needed to hear you, my sister. You had no name within blood. You write but we do not read. I wanted to hear your spirit tell me if you were true. I sent you my dreaming because I see you from all directions. I know all the people's ways. You know the healing of the drum. You come from the last great healers, from the cottonwoods of the north. But the great trees are falling, my sister. Do you understand?"

"Booru, I am not sure that I do."

"The earthquakes on your homeland were too late after the full moon. The great trees are falling. The sacred trees will be no more."

"What does that mean?" I asked.

"There are prophecies that are common to all sacred cultures. Prophecies about the process of world cleansing, yea. They will come to be, much sooner than expected. Time is being compressed, my sister. All the inbreeding of the plants is not yet completed. Watch closely and have caution. Certain things must not be told too early. The father spirits are happy that you have written. If I die, I want you to hear me now. This is the message for you from the warrior clans. Stay more with the people, and you have written well, my sister. But how many people do you know who can make the sacred sand paintings?"

I looked into his eyes and realized that in some way his warrior clan was connected with all the warrior clans in Australia and on other continents, for I had heard that the great trees were falling from warriors in the Americas. I also saw pain move across his face. I put my finger to his lips to quiet him.

I took my clever bag and found my pouch of sacred sand from Oruncha's cave. Ginevee, Ruby, She Who Walks With The Wind, and everyone from the village began to file into the wurley. Several women were singing with their clapping sticks. I heard the sound of the Bull Roarer and then a didgeridoo droned heavily from somewhere outside near the fire. The shadows of the wurley were filled with expectant faces.

I ignored them all. I don't know exactly how I knew

what to do. It was as if all my allies and guardians propelled me headlong into an ancient healing ritual. I looked up and saw my nari perched above Booru as if protecting me. I placed a six-inch square of sacred sand between Booru and myself. Then I reached for the roots that Ginevee had given me for Booru and myself. Booru was lying to the north. I placed two roots there and my root in the south. I placed his churinga on a little mound in the center with a configuration of crystals around it. I asked for some water, which Ginevee brought me in her coolamon, and I painted more red ochre onto my face. I gave some water to Booru to drink and sprinkled some over his body and over the sand altar. I began to sing the words of my power song and I prayed to the Great Spirit, Oruncha, and the great mothers as they collectively carried my physical body away and made it numb. I felt as if only my spirit body or shaman body were left.

I took the root that I had placed in the south and I broke off a piece and chewed it. It tasted bitter and gave me almost an instantaneous surge of energy. I spit some of the pieces out into my hands and rubbed them over my body. I felt what I can only describe as a sacred heat from the root. I became dimly aware of women crying and singing. Someone was even wailing. There was a crush of human travail and grief surrounding me, but it only served to heighten my concentration.

Moments later I felt my face contort. I jumped up and spun around in the air. My body was shaking violently all over and I rushed over to Booru. I must have been a frightful sight, because he gasped as did everyone else. The wailing and the crying grew louder. I bent over Booru as I motioned for the two warriors to hold down his shoulders. I looked at his body as if from that part of me that had met him in the Dreamtime. Until that moment, I had not realized that I could summon that part of myself that enabled me to see. As I looked at Booru, I could see his flesh melt away, as mine had melted upon entering the Dreamtime.

As his body melted, the bukkur, the sorcerer's cord, was revealed. It was wrapped around his skeleton, mostly around his chest and neck. I started lifting his arms and legs roughly and running my hands over his chest. Booru screamed as he tried to rise, but the warriors held him down. I saw real terror in his eyes as I approached him again and again. I grabbed what I saw as the cord and began to pull it out of

Booru. I can't imagine what this action must have looked like to the others, who could not see the cord. As I pulled it Booru's whole body went into spasms. The cries of the men and women became louder as Booru writhed in pain. But I knew that if I didn't get that cord out of him he would die.

The cord was like a piece of elastic. Everytime I pulled it, it would snap back, causing Booru a great amount of pain. But I was determined to follow my vision. Booru had trusted what I saw and had not questioned it, no matter how strange my actions seemed. I could feel his extreme terror. He must have thought he was dying. I was sure everyone else did from the bedlam rising around me.

Next, I did a surprising thing. I stopped long enough to take a bite off one of the other roots. My body had been violently shaking and instantly my system calmed down and my demeanor changed to one of tranquillity. I knelt by Booru and touched my lips to his and sprinkled his face with water.

I began to concentrate on his heart, rubbing his chest. It was there that I had seen his body fraying off in the Dream-time. It was his place of greatest vulnerability. His weakest point is the only way I can explain it. Somehow with the use of my fingers, I began to draw the cord out through his heart as his body went into convulsions from my hands touching his chest. It was a scene never to be forgotten. I am sure. I pulled the cord into my hands and lay it down on top of the sand altar.

The cord looked almost alive as if it were a luminous coiled snake. The men and women were horrified. I had the warriors support Booru's head as I bit off several pieces of the north root and placed them in his mouth. His eyes were closed as he chewed the root, nearly choking and gasping for air. I focused on his heart as he chewed and I could see the ancient pain and dysfunction in his chest. From my point of view, that of the healing dreamstate, it looked like the interior of his chest was covered with blue snow. By the way the blue snow-like patterns were arranged, I could divine what he had long known but had chosen to forget. I knew that if he lived through the extraction of the bukkur that I could, in fact, heal him.

He kept choking but his wives huddled around him and implored him to swallow the root. I took sand from the altar and precious herbs from my pouches and I offered prayers to Oruncha, the sisters of the Dreamtime, and all the sacred beings I could think of. I sprinkled sand and herbs over the bukkur cord that I had taken from Booru.

Booru rested more easily now and the warriors released him. I asked Ginevee for one of her rolled-up rangas. I took it and unrolled it and placed the cord on it. The bukkur had already gotten stiff and had lost its luminosity. After I put away my crystals and set aside Booru's churinga, I swept all the sand from the altar onto the sacred bark ranga.

I asked for the men to carry Booru and to follow me. They began to argue with me, but I insisted that he would be strong enough. I have no idea how I knew this. They finally lifted Booru off the poles and followed me, as did Ginevee. We walked west of the village to a stand of eucalyptus trees. They lay Booru down as I sang to the spirits of the alcheringa and to Booru's ancestors in the Dreamtime. For one instant I felt the presence of Oruncha and I saw the mist out of which the bukkur had come. I knew the sorcerer that had sung Booru was Two Hearts and I knew what Booru must do. I took the cord in my hands and buried it along with the sand from the altar. I had Booru spit on the grave. I took Booru's churinga, the stone of his dreaming, and stared at the mist that hovered beneath the trees. I knew it disguised the spirit of Two Hearts.

Booru's eyes were watching me. He, too, looked into the mist and nodded his head in unspoken agreement.

"You could say that not only does the mist disguise the spirit of Two Hearts, who is waiting to be sure that his intent of death is successful, but that the mist also disguises the soul of Booru," Ginevee whispered in my ear. "Two Hearts has stolen his soul. The only way for Booru to regain his soul will be for him to make an enormous act of power. Booru will have to renounce his evil, by exposing his source of power. He will also have to throw his dreaming into the fog to regain his life-force. There is no other way for Booru, because even for all the good he has done, he has also committed great crimes."

Booru sat up, pain in his eyes. He took his churinga and with a phenomenally powerful thrust of his arm and snap of his wrist he released it. The stone sang through the air like a Bull Roarer and disappeared into the mist. Moments later we watched as Booru's dreaming stone dispersed the fog. I knew Two Hearts was gone and his evil intent had been returned into himself.

Booru collapsed into the arms of his men. We returned to the wurley, where everyone was chattering and singing and confused. The men lay Booru down, but soon he sat up. The greenish tinge had left his skin and he was slightly stronger. The men and women cheered and cried. Booru was aware that his healing had only just begun. Tears streamed down his face as he lifted a quivering hand for attention.

"The great stone offerings were brought to this world long ago. Some were good and some were bad. My people are an ancient line of sorcerers. All my ancestors were sorcerers, yea. Some were good and some were bad. I lost my way long ago. Now, so that I may live, I must tell you of my blood. I still have the ancient stones of sorcery. They were brought to this world by my ancestors." Booru spoke with great effort.

"Where do you keep these stones?" one of the elder men asked after a stunned silence. Everyone's face had blackened, as all appeared confused by this sudden confession. They obviously had not known about his black sorcery.

"We keep them in the caves by the swirling waters."

"Who are 'we'?" the man demanded.

"At the time of the Green Ants Dreaming, we meet every year. Many sorcerers from all over meet with me and we have done ceremonies every year to prevent the rain and make wars within the tribes of people. We have also disrupted the sacred ceremonies of the women."

Booru was crying now. For some reason, even though Booru had done many evil things, I didn't think he was evil in his heart. I ached for this man or perhaps all men who have thrown away their dreaming. Now Booru was losing face with his elders. As Ginevee had put it, I could still understand how he had fallen away from his path of strength. That didn't make it right, but I could understand.

"You lie, Booru. We would know if strangers came through our land. Why are you saying these things? It is because you have been sung by an evil sorcerer," the elder man said with tears in his eyes. His disillusionment was agonizing to watch. I could see that he really loved Booru.

"No, you are wrong. You never saw the strangers, yea. They came every year."

"It is not true."

"Yes. When the winds change, we would twist the ancient stones into our hair and crossed over our breasts were offerings held to our hearts entwined with fur string, mulga, and prayer sticks. Holding these things we made large rings of spinifex grass and we did ceremonies with the bugeen. We were empowered with a special ability. We could make ourselves into dingos, kangaroos, owls, and crows, depending on the person, and then we could come and go over the land and no one could identify us."

"We would have seen these ceremonies."

"No. They were secret. There is a secret cave, yea. I will take you, if you don't believe me."

"Yes. We will go now and prove that you are suffering from delusions. You are our brother."

The women continued to chant as the men carried Booru and the rest of us followed. We walked east from the village over two hills and down into a dry river gorge. Before long we entered a large rock cavern covered by a huge stone that we found surprisingly easy to roll away from the entrance. The rock had clearly been moved many times. Two torches were lit inside the cave, revealing an interior not unlike the sacred kivas of the Pueblo Indians. There was a shelf around the perimeter, presumably for seating. We saw the remains of a fire in the center and an air hole off to one side. At one end was an altar.

Booru was getting stronger with every hour that passed. With the aid of the warriors, he could walk now. He asked us to sit down. We all sat in a semicircle around him. Booru sat down next to his altar. With tears in his eyes, he picked up the ancient carved stones.

"It is here that we talked and made Nyimbun, the sacred one in the mountains, very angry so that he would not help the people. I can take on the form of a dingo so that I can pass through the villages and the desert unnoticed. Did I not send my dingo ally to rest on your papunya?" Booru asked me.

"Yes, it is true you did. And then I followed the dingo into the Dreamtime. As you know, that is how I came to be here with my teachers," I said. There was a profound silence in the cave.

"I can fill my mouth with spinifex spikes and shoot them out to destroy life. I know the paths of evil. I have killed innocent people; some were women and children. I have killed four babies. I was allied with Two Hearts."

The cave was filled with the sounds of crying and moans

of human shock. The women held their children tight as if Booru would strike them. As I looked at their faces, I could see that Booru was in danger. Fear in the women's faces had turned to anger. They remembered how their ceremonies had failed and how diminished they had become. I was afraid they would rise against Booru and kill him.

"We wear the sacred stones in the knots in our hair. That makes the mountain spirits very angry. If you carry them reversed and drop spinifex resin over the designs, Nyimbun becomes enraged, yea. Then we are able to change forms and become invisible. This also made the keepers of the waterholes so angry that they let them run dry."

Everyone was talking at once about what should happen to Booru, who was desperately in need of help. He looked sad, weak, and tired. Ginevee went to him and, standing beside him, she addressed the people.

"Do not forget that Booru has been your elder for many a long time. There has never been a greater warrior. Many times you turned against him when he needed you. Realize that his bad sorcery power has been destroyed. He has told you the truth and revealed his dreaming. Forgive him, my brothers and sisters, as I have," she said, her eyes fierce with intent.

"I have no more power forever. My allies will leave me. I am now just an old grandfather with his children," Booru said.

"What will you do for the women?" a young woman asked, her voice tight with anger.

"I promise to teach the women everything I know about the plants of healing. I will give away my medicine, which would take many, many long time to learn. It is yours. I know about the breeding of the plants, yea. I know all the ways of the people. I will share them. When I was born, I had all the power of my ancestors. It was grown over generations of my fathers. As I speak to you, you will see that my eyes, that have always been black, are now green."

We all looked and it was true. His eyes were melon green. But as he began to speak again, they changed. I had never seen anything like it.

"Now they will change to brown as the powers of the bugeen leave me forever. I am the last of the line."

Tears rolled down his dark cheeks. He was a proud man

and he was immensely proud of his power over himself and the audience. Even in this state of confession, he enjoyed commanding attention and awe. The longer he spoke to his people, the more strength he found in himself. He was sitting up with more dignity. He was indeed a sandamara, the one who never dies. A few hours before, I had walked in on a dying man who had barely been able to speak. I realized with a kind of shock that I had actually been instrumental in his healing. I had been so taken up with the extraordinary things that I had seen and been able to do in my dreamstate that I had almost felt like someone else was performing such magical feats. I sat up taller as a surge of well-being filled me.

"I shall be part of the bugeen no more. The power has fled." Booru turned and picked up the many inscribed stones off the altar and laid them at my feet.

"They are yours, my sister."

Booru dropped his head down so that his chin almost touched his chest. I placed my hands over his. He took my hands and held them to his forehead.

"It is good. The balance has been restored and the women can go back to their ceremonies in the old way. Again there will be equality between the men's and women's warrior clans," Ginevee said in a husky voice.

Everyone cheered and hugged each other as they left the cave to return to their village. They would prepare for ceremony.

"The sandamara lives, yea," the elder men said in unison to Booru as they walked by him. They had forgiven him.

Ginevee, Booru, Ruby, She Who Walks With The Wind, and I sat in deep silence after everyone left. Booru turned to look at me.

"I must know something, Lynn. You saw something in my chest in the Dreamtime, yea. Tell me, what did you see?" Booru lay down on the shelf to rest as I spoke.

"I could see that the outline of your heart looked shredded." I pulled apart some grass to show him what I meant.

"What does that mean to you?" he asked with his eyes closed.

"It meant that you were weakened there. Your betrayal of your woman-self inside and therefore your betrayal of women in your society had caused it."

He waited a long time before speaking.

"Yes. That is why I called on you for help, hmm. I sensed that weakness in me."

"But why did you not ask Ginevee or someone from your own people?"

"Because my debt to womankind is great. If I lived, I wanted it to be because of a clever woman not of our nations. We have isolated our wisdom too long, yea. To survive, we must step forward and reach out to all the magicians around our mother earth. We must share our dream paintings and our hearts. As I said, the great trees are falling. Our ancestral being Dolphin Woman Dreaming came to me in a vision. She said to me, 'The dolphins swim in the seas of wisdom. Call on your sisters from across the great water for your healing and you will be forgiven.' It was a gift from the great eucalyptus trees. They helped me. Then I waited. I did not know who you were until you arrived. It is good, yea. My heart is full, my sister. It is a beginning."

I thought about what Booru had said. I remembered the cliff in Santa Barbara, the dolphins circling below us, and the vision of Booru and Two Hearts in the eucalyptus tree. I wanted to ask Booru why he had sent me such a violent vision, but Ruby interrupted my thoughts.

"What are you going to do with those stones, Lynn, make a nice gift to Red Dog?"

"Come, we will bury them in such a way, hmm, that their power is gone forever," Ginevee said, putting them in her dilly bag after we had all looked at them and handled them with great interest. As we walked out of the cave Ginevee put her arm around me and held me close.

"I am proud of you, my daughter."

"Oh, by the way, Lynn," Ruby said in a loud voice as she helped support Booru, who was looking at her strangely. "I heard Agnes and July drive into our village as we left."

"What do you mean, you heard them?"

"Well, I couldn't very well see them, now could I," she answered irritably. "I knew they'd be back. When they left I could hear their rear axle grinding. Just thought you might like to know." Ruby elbowed me gently in the ribs.

Ginevee walked ahead of us and led us down through a crevice of rock and into a small clearing. Several red river oaks twisted in the warm wind that was blustering in from the east. The moon shown so brightly that we could see as if it were midday. She Who Walks With The Wind and Ruby sat on the sandy bank of a spring that fed a larger billabong or pond farther on down the gully. They seemed intent on Booru and a conversation they were having with him about a plant that he was holding up to the moon. I could see that his strength was returning and he wouldn't be resting long. I watched Booru exposing a pod of the night-blooming herb. He was already beginning to live out his promise to teach his knowledge. A few hours before he had been near death and now he was carrying on an intense discourse with a woman who had been his mortal enemy. I could see that he recognized her. We watched as he sang softly and dipped his thumb into the nectar of the plant and smudged it on the neck and forehead of She Who Walks With The Wind. Tears were washing down their cheeks.

Ginevee nudged me and led me over to a flat rock on the other side of the spring. We sat down next to each other and stared into the satiny sheen of the pond. It looked like a mirror laying on the sand.

"Your story has been told, my daughter, and it has been laid to rest, yea. This story has been difficult and it has been hard for you many long time. For many people, life is like sitting on the edge of this spring, for they never once enter the water. Your people, they know the words. Because they know the words, they think they have had the experience. The story you have lived with me has been mysterious and you have found your way through much darkness. But you have experienced these things and in the end your experience is all you have. You are a good apprentice. Write this story as you lived it, so that our brothers and sisters in other lands can live the experience with us. Deep in the heart of this story is healing truth for them. It is your purpose, my daughter. You have learned well a good lesson," Ginevee said, touching my hand.

"Which lesson?" I asked. "There were so many."

"You learned to study your own suffering so that the suffering of others could be understood. Teach your apprentices not to distract themselves from their pain. Lead them into the center of pain, to confront it."

Ginevee nodded toward Booru, who was still holding up the night-blooming herb. "Suffering is like the seed of that herb when planted in the earth. That seed remembers itself and endures in the darkness so that it can grow up into the sunlight one day as an entirely transformed flower. When you understand suffering and the forces of darkness you can end suffering and bring light to the people."

Ginevee held both of my hands to her heart. For a moment her wrinkled face looked young and her eyes shown with flecks of silver like the surface of the spring water. I had so many questions I wanted to ask her, but Ruby was helping Booru stand and Ginevee stood up and headed down the gully toward the other pond. I hurried to catch up with her and the others followed close behind. As we rounded a corner between two boulders, I realized with a start that Ginevee had vanished.

"Where's Ginevee?" I asked. We stood at the shore of the small billabong. Its water was placid and it shimmered like a slab of obsidianite in the moonlight. A large black crow cawed in a ghost gum tree overhead. I realized as I watched it hop on the branches that it was Willy-D. He showed us his shiny wings.

A movement near the center of the water caught my eye.

"Look," She Who Walks With The Wind signed to me and she pointed to a white swan swimming in circles in the billabong. Willy-D swooped down from his perch toward the water. The white swan lifted her huge wings and launched into noiseless flight. The two birds flew off together into the night.

I heard Ginevee's voice in my head. She said, "When you see me in the Dreamtime, you see me as a black swan. Swans have great power. They did not mean to but, as it says in the ancient legends, they helped trick woman and the earth lost her balance. When you see Ginevee in the Dreamtime as a white swan, you will know that her work has been completed on earth and that man and woman swim equally in the billabongs, the sacred waters, and balance has been restored among us."

GLOSSARY

aborigine: native; in this book always referring to a native of Australia

alcheringa: a teacher in the Dreamtime or a symbol

Baiame: in the Dreamtime, the sky god

bandicoot grease: a type of pungent-smelling grease made from the bandicoot

billabong: the sacred waters or ponds found in Australia

billy tea: Australian tea made from herbs

bugeen: evil spirit, the darkness

bukkur: the cord of death

Bull Roarer: a flat piece of wood that is twirled on a string. Its whirring sound calls the spirit

bungul: a dance

clever bag: a special bag for carrying sacred objects

churinga: sacred pieces of wood that are carved

coolamon: a hollowed-out burl used for carrying objects

corrsoborees: social dance

didgeridoo: musical instrument made from a three-foot-long or longer hollowed branch; it makes a deep bass sound

dilly bag: a small carrying bag worn over the shoulder, plaited with twisted reeds or rushes or grasses

Dirrangun: in the Dreamtime, a fertility goddess

doowans: shamans, male and female of Australia; clever women or men

the Dreamtime: sacred time

gilarmavell: a fairy woman

good tucker: good food

gooma: a sacred stone, usually carved; spirit stone

goowawa: the little people, or fairies

juraveel: in the Dreamtime, a sacred totemic spirit helper

karari: sacred pearl shells worn by men

kiva: a round Pueblo Indian structure used for sacred ceremonies

Koori: the Australian aborigine language; also refers to all borigines

kudaitja man: a tribal executioner

madagor: fire stick often used for cauterizing a wound

malo: kangeroo totem or clan

marriage basket: sacred basket of the Dreamers, a society of medicine people

maya: state of illusion

medicine wheel: a paradigm or symbol for the process of mind used by various American Indian cultures

medicine woman: a healer, a woman of wisdom

menehunes: little people of Hawaii

miwi: the energy that gives a person psychic power

mulga grass: type of brush grass found in Australia; in the Dreamtime, it is a symbol of the rainclouds that come after the rainmaking ceremony

muni-muni: a child's leaf game, sometimes used for divining

muru muru: to be full of life, to have the spirit

Nagalyod: in the Dreamtime, a sacred being transformed into the Rainbow Serpent

nari: a medicine helper or spirit from the Dreamtime, a familiar

ngaya: in the language of the Pitjantjara tribe, "I" or "me"

nila-nila: a mirage of evil

nyangunanta: in the language of the Pitjantjara tribe, "I saw you"

nyantunya: in the language of the Pitjantjara tribe, "you"

nyimbun: in the Dreamtime, the sacred one in the mountains

Oruncha: in the Dreamtime, a male medicine spirit warrior

pakaria: a sorcerer flying through the air before descending to do evil magic, looks like a shooting star

papunya: sand painting or ground painting

pitcherii: an herb with a mildly intoxicating effect

piti: a large coolamon, usually sits on a hair ring on one's head

Pitjantjara: aboriginal nation of Central Australia

portulaca bird: bird whose feathers and down are used for sacred ceremonies

Rainbow Serpent: ancestral being of the Dreamtime

ranga: sacred symbols

Red Ochre men: the men appointed to uphold the laws; the tribal executioners in Australia

rore: a sacred crystal

sandamara: one who never dies

shamaness: female shaman or healer

Sisterhood of the Shields: a sacred shaman society of 44 women representing the power of woman from different indigenous cultures around the world

spinifex grass: a type of grass found in Australia, it has sharp edges that are capable of ripping flesh and is used for making wurleys and many things in everyday life

wambri: a legendary creature

warrigan: a spirit totem

witchiti: grubs, larva

woman of high degree: shaman woman or woman of knowledge

wurley: shelter or hut made from grass or bark

yunga: octopus, also refers to police